T0128536

THE LAST OF THE LIVE NUDE GIRLS

THE LAST OF THE
LIVE NUDE GIRLS

A MEMOIR

SHEILA McCLEAR

SOFT SKULL PRESS

Library of Congress Cataloging-in-Publication Data

McClear, Sheila.
The last of the live nude girls : a memoir / Sheila McClear.
   p. cm.
ISBN 978-1-59376-400-5
1. Prostitution—New York (N.Y.)—History—21st century. 2. Prostitutes—New York (N.Y.)—Biography. 3. McClear, Sheila. I. Title.
HQ118.M33 2011
306.74'209747—dc22
2011005703

ISBN: 978-1-59376-400-5

Cover design by Aaron Artessa
Interior design by Neuwirth & Associates, Inc.

Printed in the United States of America

Soft Skull Press
New York, NY
www.softskull.com

"When we go it alone, when we deny our interconnectedness, and miss the opportunity to mean something important to each other, we throw away the chance for real satisfaction and real beauty."

–Tom Sheibley, 1955-2004

This is a book of memories. Everything in it happened.
Names have been changed to protect the guilty.

ACT ONE

THE TOKYO BUSINESSMAN

I'm a bit behind in the rent. It is the fifth of the month, and I'm short $175. I've been playing this game with my landlord, tiptoeing around during the day so that she won't hear me and come up to collect the envelope. The envelope is not ready yet.

The men have been coming into the peep show as usual, but they just haven't been picking me. Sometimes they don't. Some girls claim that men are drawn to them when they're ovulating, constantly picking them out of the lineup. Maybe I'm not ovulating.

It's about halfway through a Saturday-night shift when I leave my booth to go upstairs for a break. Suddenly, I see a Japanese man in a gray suit headed my way. I stop and slowly start walking backward, back to my booth. I just have a feeling about him.

Japanese customers are my favorite: They seldom make eye contact, and they rarely speak. They don't ask my name or age or say that I am so beautiful, and that they could make me feel so good, if, you know, I went out with them sometime? They don't plead.

They like white girls, and I am white, which means very often they will like me, and give me money, which makes me like them. They put their faces close to the glass and squint and say nothing. They understand the transactional nature of the experience. It might have something to do with Zen Buddhism. The two are very similar, although many others confuse the peep show with a church, with the two-sided booth as a stand-in for a confessional and me for the priest.

The Japanese man comes up to me, as I knew he would. I explain the cost to him and he doesn't understand: "Type it!" he asks, confused, holding out his palm. This is an Asian custom, I have learned; they trace out numbers or letters onto palms when failing to understand a dialect or language. I move to write the number 35, the price of a show, onto his palm, but stop when I see Ahmed, the security and change man, shaking his head at me: The girls are not allowed to touch the customers. It is the number one rule.

There must never be contact.

It must also be a custom in Japan to tip exotic dancers throughout the course of their performance, even if they are behind glass instead of on a stage. They're the only ones I've ever seen do it in the peep show: dropping dollars or fives through the slot every time I do something different, or smile, or turn around. They nod quickly, as if they understand something, something important I am saying without words.

That's what this man does, except instead of dollars, he uses twenties and fifties. During the five minutes I perform, if you could even call it that, a steady stream of bills drops through the crudely sawed-out money slot and piles up on the floor. The Japanese businessman says nothing and makes no eye contact, focusing his gaze intently on the area above my knees but below my neck. He watches carefully, as if he is trying to figure something out.

He keeps his hands folded in his lap, eyes scanning my body as if he will be tested after the show. I imagine the porters interrogating him behind the booths, leaning on their mops, cigarettes dangling from their mouths: *And did she have any scars or unusual marks?* they would ask.

What about tattoos?

The money is still coming through the slot, piling up on the floor. I had heard about this—nights like this, customers like this—but always dismissed them as legend. "And then he gave me $400," a girl would say in the dressing room. "For no reason!" I never believed them. Now I know these girls are telling the truth.

What impresses me the most about all the money on the floor is its senselessness, its arbitrariness. The Japanese businessman says nothing, studiously avoiding eye contact. When the show is over and the curtain closes, I hear him quietly collecting his briefcase and jacket and leaving. It doesn't make any sense at all.

I take a cab all the way back to Brooklyn that night. I put some of the money in the envelope when I get home at one in the morning. I don't have to tiptoe around anymore.

"I surrendered to the world of Times Square."

—John Rechy, *City of Night*

HOW I GOT HERE

The first time I ever came to New York, I ended up on the front page of *The Times*. I was twenty-one. There I was, above the fold and in color, standing behind a middle-aged woman holding an American flag with the stars replaced by corporate logos. We were protesting, my college friends and I and thousands of others, in front of the Waldorf-Astoria, where the World Economic Forum was being held that year. You couldn't see my face, obscured by my hair, but it was me; I was there.

It was midnight, and I'd been walking with my friends to a party on a boat in Chelsea. I stopped into a bodega to see if that Sunday's early edition was out yet and to see if news of the protest had made the front page.

I pointed frantically at my image to the Indian woman in a sari behind the counter.

"Three dollars," she said.

I clutched the bulky Sunday paper in both hands and skipped out onto the sidewalk, holding it up victoriously for my friends to see. There was Patrick, the nerdy folk musician, who had wrapped himself

in a blanket, and Hope, the spacey sociology grad student. There was
Meredith . . . . Actually, I didn't know any of them that well. They
weren't my friends at all, really, just acquaintances at best. I'd joined
their caravan because I wanted to protest that month's injustice, sure,
but mostly because I wanted to visit New York.

"*What up*, baby girl!" boomed a small black man—an Eighth Avenue
hustler type—who snuck up behind me while I was sitting outside my
closet-size booth at the peep show, startling me so badly that I yelped
and jumped out of my chair.

"Smoke dope?" he hissed.

"What?"

"*Do you get high?*"

"I . . . no. Do you want a live show?"

"Yeah, but I'm tryin' not to spend all my money. You want some
dope? I can give you that. *Weed*," he elaborated.

"I need to get paid in real money," I told him.

All night, men came in off the street and told me things. They were
usually alone. They dropped their pants and masturbated behind
glass windows. They shamelessly bargained and asked us if we "did
sex."

"Two hundred dollars," they'd repeat over and over in foreign
accents, unblinking, until I laughed or sighed or tried not to scream.

A bored Southern salesman chewed a toothpick while watching
me. A sloppily dressed schoolteacher from Westchester passed a note
through the slot reading WEAR THE FLOWERED SCHOOLGIRL PANTIE$!!
They stooped and genuflected to put money through the slot sawed
into the red-painted booth. We told the men the show was five minutes long, but the curtain went down after three and a half.

Sometimes, one of them might enter his side of the booth and
cry. I was not equipped to handle all of this heaviness. It was better
to think of myself as a channel: letting people and their stories flow
through me, releasing them back out into the world.

My survival was based on hustling, convincing the neon-overdosed
tourists and curious college boys and ghetto kids from the Bronx and
Mexican laborers and guilt-ridden street preachers—plus the natives,

the sundry damaged goods of Times Square—to pay $35 to watch me take my clothes off, with the bare minimum of enthusiasm, behind glass.

My fellow live girls were mostly Spanish or black and from the Bronx or the projects. But one girl, named Violet, came from a similar background. She was white, like me, a plain-looking girl with a constant, amused twinkle in her eye. She was around my age and from the Midwest. She had an open relationship with her fiancé, a handsome Asian boy who often visited her at the peep show and took shows with her coworkers. He never picked me—not that I cared, or wanted him to, but sometimes I wondered why he didn't.

"Violet, your man was da *bomb* last night!" said Strawberry, strolling up to Violet's booth. She was an athletic, striking black girl who once threatened another chick by putting razor blades between her own teeth. Her rough edges had since been dulled by classes at the Barbizon School of Modeling. "He was strokin' that thang, ooh, girl, he looked so good, that I came—"

"Oh, yeah?" said Violet, intrigued. "He told me, 'Strawberry said she came, but I don't believe her.'"

"*Naw*, girl, believe me, that shit was for real . . . . "

Like me, Violet had a college degree. Hers was in social work.

"I just wish I were using my degree somehow," she said one day, sitting in the dressing room.

"Oh, you are," I said, thinking of the nightly parade of dysfunctional men. She looked at me askance.

"So, are you, like, an artist or a student or something?" she asked. I shrugged. I wasn't sure either. I was alone in the city, and the peep show provided a place to hide. No one there knew quite what to make of me. Did I just move here? Couldn't I have found anything better? Was I sort of a loser?

Violet was addicted to the peep show. She made at least $400 a shift and worked five nights a week. I couldn't figure out why she made so much money: She wore her hair long and mousy brown, with glasses, no makeup, and a plain cotton bra-and-panty set. She spent her shifts leaning against the door of her booth, one white-platformed heel crossed over the other, flipping through upscale shelter magazines, deciding what to buy next.

It was impossible for me to make money when she was there, and I tried to schedule my shifts around her. It was because she had breasts. "Modelesque" was the term used by men who preferred me, meaning that I was skinny and flat-chested.

"Don't ever change them!" a short businessman once exclaimed while backing out of his booth, holding his hands in front of his chest to indicate balloon-size breasts and rolling his eyes.

But Violet was articulate, and she spoke for everyone in recognizing the dissociative unreality that we all experienced several nights a week in Times Square.

"So last night, I was in a show, right?" she said. "And I was down on the floor, on my knees, you know, pretending to suck this guy's dick through the glass or whatever. And I'm looking up at it, I'm looking this guy's *dick* right in the eye, and it's looking back at me, and suddenly I thought to myself . . . how the *hell* did I end up here?"

Walking into Gotham City Video for the first time in the summer of 2006, I was assaulted by the smell: sharp, pungent, and sickly sweet, a cocktail of Pine-Sol, Windex, and bleach, plus a surface cleaner sprayed liberally around the store as air freshener.

The overall effect of the porn shop at 781 8th Avenue dulled the senses and was profoundly unsexy. Nothing is as numbing as rack after rack of pornographic videos, their covers showcasing clinical, fully splayed genitalia of every variety ("Shemale," "Barely Legal," "Animal"). Mirrored walls were covered with dildos, vibrators, fake-fur-lined handcuffs, and little outfits, the cheap themed kind that came in clear plastic bags. Overhead fluorescent lights were as bright as a Guantanamo prisoner's cell at night, and the stairs were in rainbow colors, each one labeled with the words LIVE! SEXY! FANTASY! GIRLS! A banner at the top advertised LIVE SEXI GIRLS. The carnival environment would lose its effect over time; after a few months, I wouldn't even notice the flashing lights and the dildos.

When I first wandered into the peep show, it was six o'clock, which meant that men were filing home from work, getting distracted by the neon, and slipping furtively inside. It was prime time in live-girl land.

At first, getting regular work was easy. I got my first job in New York by writing a letter. After reading a review of the Classical Theatre of Harlem's version of *Medea* in *The New Yorker*, I sent them my résumé with a note detailing my experience in costuming, which had been my major in college. I was already thinking about leaving Detroit. While I was visiting New York one weekend, the theater called to offer me a job.

I decided right then not to go back to Michigan. I already knew what would happen on Monday, when I was scheduled to return: The tires would be stolen off my car again. I would ride the bus to work, continue typing on a flickering computer running on Windows 95, stirring cheap coffee with a pen, and reporting for a labor publication from an office held together with duct tape and plywood. Our little magazine had been bleeding subscriptions for a decade. Everything in Detroit was ghettoized, shuttered. The city had been dead for years, and it would continue its death rattle whether I stayed or went.

It wasn't just that. There were other things that I wanted to get away from, signs of too many people giving up.

A few months before, a coworker, Tom, a former long-haul truck driver, had shot himself in the head in his truck parked outside his apartment on Hubbard Street. Nicknamed Red Row, it was the street where all the leftists in Detroit lived. He was forty-nine.

I'd only known him for a couple months, but he was a gentle soul whom I was drawn toward. He was quiet and never smoked or drank. He was so tall that whenever he went in the basement office, he had to stoop, but he never complained. He was also a deeply religious man. We went to the same church on the East Side—Tom weekly, me occasionally. We both liked the rowdy, demonstrative service: Black churches gave you a show for your money.

"This is the God I know," he'd said to me once after a service.

No one will ever know if he killed himself on a Sunday on purpose or not, but he did, and I wonder if his faith had finally been shaken to its core, or if it was just a final "Fuck you" to God for not alleviating his psychic pain. He had laid out his identification and the contents of his wallet neatly on the kitchen counter, taped an unused ticket to a Tigers ballgame to the front door, and went out to his new truck with a shotgun. One of my coworkers found him after Tom hadn't shown up to the game.

After his death, more and more things came out about Tom that I hadn't known. I knew of him as a truck driver and union reformer, but did I know he had also been a pastor? A Harvard graduate with a degree in theology? A commentator on NPR? What I still didn't know was how such a gentle person could have inflicted such a violent death upon himself.

I began having a recurring waking dream. In it, I would go down into the basement office after hours, where Tom would be hunched over his computer.

"Oh, hi," he would say, as if nothing had ever happened.

"How are you?" I'd ask, or maybe I'd suggest that he take a break, or go home.

"Oh, pretty good, pretty good. But you'll have to excuse me," he'd say, turning away from me and back to his desk. "There's so much more to get done."

Which was how I was beginning to feel about Detroit. There was so much else to do, so many places to go that were less sad and less broken. There was so much more to get done.

Two hours after the phone call, I found myself backstage in a drafty theater on 145th Street, painting whiteface onto a cast of black actors.

"Oh, honey," said Billie, the eighty-one-year-old dreadlocked director, after seeing my confused face. "You didn't even know what you was walking into, was you? Welcome to Harlem. This is how we do it, baby." The play was called *Funnyhouse of a Negro*.

Later that night, while the production was going on, the actors who weren't onstage were in the dressing room talking. I felt woozy after sewing for six hours and skipping lunch, and the backstage conversations mixed and jumbled in my head with the lines coming from the stage:

"You know those apartments with the old-fashioned sloped tubs?" said Trish, the forty-year-old retired ballet dancer. "I spent two nights in that tub, because I was in so much pain . . . . "

"She hung herself! The poor bitch hung herself! The poor bitch!" floated back from the stage.

"I called the director," Trish continued, "and I'm like, I can't do this anymore. He said, all right, I'll give you one night off, and I was like, no, I mean, I can't dance anymore—"

"*She was a funny little liar!*"

"I trained in dance since I was, shit, eleven, and I only got five professional years out of it—"

"*Her father didn't kill himself in a Harlem hotel room when Patrice Lamumba was murdered! I know the man—he's a doctor, married to a whore! And he eats his dinners on a white glass table.*"

"I mean, yeah, I'd like more TV and film work, but then again, who wouldn't?" Trish continued, patting on her makeup. She paused to survey her work in the mirror, looking satisfied. "I do 'girl' really well," she said. "Goddamn, after forty-some years, I'm really good at this girl thing."

Lincoln, a small, wiry Jamaican man in his late forties whose day job was a masseuse, was playing a post-crucifixion Jesus dressed in yellow face-makeup and rags. He was sitting in the men's dressing room when I went upstairs to hem some pants. His head was in his bloodied hands, going over his most important lines, repeating each word three times: "*I always . . . believed . . . my father . . . to be . . . God . . . but . . . he . . . is . . . a . . . black . . . Negro . . . from . . . Africa . . .*"

Every night, I smeared stage blood on the face and head of the actor playing the ghost of Patrice Lamumba, an affable guy who drove up from Philadelphia every day. Every third night, I took the laundry basket, the costumes inside splattered with bright red stage blood and dirt, to a Laundromat on 147th and St. Nick's. People gave me strange looks, then moved out of the way.

"Tell me about your character," Billie asked the new actress playing the Landlady as I kneeled beside her, sewing sequins onto her house-dress.

"Well, I was thinking, you know, Lower East Side . . . "

"Right," Billie encouraged.

" . . . Jewish . . . "

"Uh-huh," Billie said. "And?"

"And . . . and . . . " she floundered, eager to please but at a loss.

"*And*, she's at home in the middle of the day, *and* she's been drinking, and she's been looking at the TV. Right?"

"Oh, yes, yes. Right!"

Billie came into the dressing room after that night's show to give notes as everyone was changing. She grabbed my hand, clasping it in hers for a long time.

"I think you're doing a great job out there," she said, still gripping my hand tightly. I wasn't sure what she was referring to. I worked backstage. I wore all black, so the audience couldn't see me as I waited in the wings, costumes held at the ready, waiting to perform quick-changes.

"Thank you," I replied. "Absolutely. I was just, you know, changing for the party . . . "

I'd spent the last hour sewing a thrift-store robe into a dress for the opening-night reception.

Later that evening, as I was reaching across the table for another glass of wine, the sleeve of my dress brushed against a candle and briefly caught fire.

Lincoln approached, also fuzzy around the edges. He had crooked features and a crinkly, warm smile. He moved with the assurance of someone acutely aware of his physical self, his wiry body chiseled down to only the essentials: muscle and bone. His demeanor was charmingly childlike.

"I do not know how to handle these things," he slurred. "I am too shy. Everyone, when they meet the real me, is disappointed. Because myself, I am not so free and open, like my character . . . . "

His character was Jesus. How could people not be disappointed—meeting God, only to find him to be a shy Jamaican man with crooked teeth?

At the end of the night, I sat alone in a chair up against the wall, sipping wine out of a plastic cup, surveying the scene. It was one of the moments that I loved about New York: All of a sudden you'd find yourself thrown into a place and wouldn't know exactly how you got there. Here I was, already working in the city when I was supposed to just be visiting, at an opening-night reception in Harlem for an Off-off Broadway play which I was now a part of. A man wearing sunglasses and a rabbit-fur coat sat down beside me. He'd caught on to my newness right away and seemed to be reveling in it, like a predator—*a wolf*, I thought—playing with his prey before going in for the kill. I glanced over at his black, shiny cloak disdainfully: rabbit fur. *The cheapest fur,* I thought.

"You gotta watch out in this city, girl," he was saying to me. "You better watch it. It's full of *wolves,* baby."

With that, he was off. His explanation—that the wolves were at my door, that they would pounce with the slightest provocation—was a boring cliché. I had a feeling that of all the things to be afraid of, *wolves* were the last on the list.

With this, I had a job—$125 a week before taxes, five shows a week, a commitment of about twenty hours. I was also homeless, alternating between various friends' floors and couches. They were labor people, mostly, kids from college whom I had done activism with. About a dozen of us had scattered here and were trying, with mixed success, to find union jobs where we could "continue our activism in the workplace." We had meetings.

I knew I was imposing, but they were philosophically bound to do me a favor, and I was obviously desperate.

Each couch and empty bed I slept in came with a different room in a different neighborhood, with new sounds keeping me awake.

In Park Slope, it was a knocking radiator set at what must have been eighty degrees. In Flatbush, the radiator made a gnawing sound, like a rat. The girl whose bed I occupied was gone for the night, sleeping on a tugboat moored somewhere off the East River. Her mattress, with its mounds of clean white sheets, was the only thing filling her empty, wood-floored room.

Another night, on the foldout couch of my Teamster friend Julian— another Detroit refugee, living in Windsor Terrace, Brooklyn—I was either dreaming or half-awake when I felt a body crawl in and arms wrap around me from behind. I had no idea who it could be, but it felt so comforting that I fell into a deep sleep. When I finally forced myself awake to figure out who was in my bed, there was nobody there; of course, there never had been. Not quite a dream, but a highly palpable figment of my imagination or, perhaps, an equally lonely ghost.

After about three weeks, out of friends to impose on, I discovered the Malibu Hotel, a flophouse on 99th and Broadway that charged $20 a night. It had to be the cheapest bed in town. The Malibu was also terrifying, with rows of creaky metal bunk beds housing men and women in the same room. I'd open the door to the large dormitory at midnight after getting off work and wait for my eyes to adjust to the darkness before stumbling toward an empty bed. I dragged my backpack into the bunk with me and slept with my coat on.

"Shove your wallet down the front of your pants," advised my dad when I checked in with my parents and told them where I was staying. "We used to do that in the army."

After a couple of nights I began to break down. The Malibu scared me: sleeping in a roomful of strangers who could conceivably maim or kill me with impunity, the surly clerk who glared at me like I was dirty just to have ended up there, the seedy mirrored ceiling in the lobby, the labyrinthine hallways. After that, I shelled out $60 a night and got to know the city's various youth hostels.

For several weeks, I stayed in an empty room in a huge, decaying mansion in Jersey City, occupied by my tattooed longshoreman friend Aaron and several of his rarely glimpsed roommates. I slept in a giant room with a fireplace—but no central heat—on the mattress of its former occupant, a schizophrenic who had gone off his meds and disappeared. I lived in hopes that he would not return. During the day, I rattled around the house's four floors with a fur coat thrown over my shoulders, like an estranged heiress on some vast estate.

I'd brought the oversized mink coat that my grandmother had given me on this trip, as well as two pairs of pants, two shirts, and a pair of black boots. At the time, I thought the coat might look glamorous. Now I used it as a blanket to keep warm in various ill-heated apartments, and the fur was becoming matted and worn.

Aaron was rarely home, so I often had the place to myself. I stayed for several weeks, boiling eggs and ramen and tea on the antique stove. "You're still here?" he'd sometimes ask when he saw me, although he didn't really mind. I knew I should leave; I just didn't have anyplace to go. I went into the city to work at the theater or go on wild-goose-chase job interviews, where various pinch-faced women under fluorescent lights would stare at me, then glance down at my résumé, then say they'd call if something came up. On the morning of my twenty-fifth birthday, I woke to a cockroach crawling across my hand and casually brushed it away.

The play's run ended on Valentine's Day under two feet of snow. After that, I found a temporary sublet in Greenpoint, Brooklyn, for $600 a month, rented from a smarmy musician who was going on tour. I'd chosen Greenpoint because it was a Polish neighborhood, which reminded me of Hamtramck, the Russian-Polish neighborhood in Detroit, which in turn reminded me of my Russian grandfather. Also, it was cheap.

I put down my suitcase and sat down on the musician's bed, a million little questions scratching inside my head, like where was I going to work, why had I moved here so cavalierly (had I expected things to magically work out because I was special?), where was the bathroom in this apartment, and what I was going to do with my life. *Wolves.*

I grew up in a small town in Michigan. My parents were lawyers. My mom had been raised Baptist, and my dad's side was Catholic. They never quite resolved that difference, so my younger sister and I went to both churches.

The worst thing I ever did in high school was skip class to stand in line for Pearl Jam tickets, then lie about it. I didn't drink or do drugs in high school—my parents did a good job of scaring me out of most misbehavior. I wasn't cool, but I wasn't quite an outcast, either. Overall, I saw the whole situation as something I would just have to wait out and the second I was set free, I set about exploring. By the time I was nineteen, I was a minor rock star in Flint. I'd joined a band that my boyfriend had, called the Terranauts, playing bass and singing backup. I spent most weekends in dive bars, rocking out for sparse crowds of factory workers and kids from the nearby community college. My boyfriend Ron sang and played guitar, with our friends Rich and Eric "The Boy" backing us up on drums and guitar.

Long before I was old enough to drink, I was most likely to be found sitting on a barstool, talking to a thirty-seven-year-old autoworker about his divorce or entertaining the ramblings of a litany of middle-aged drunks. I was more interested in listening to them, absorbing their cigarette smoke and conversation and listening to the rhythms of the way men talked to each other, than I was in hearing a bored professor lecturing to a roomful of sleepy college kids.

The rush of performing canceled out the noise in my head. I liked having a gig to look forward to all week, to the ritual of picking out what I was going to wear.

The Terranauts played gigs nearly every weekend, in Flint, Detroit, Lansing, Saginaw, Kalamazoo, and Chicago, plus house parties and basements and barns and outdoor festivals. We went on tour, driving down the eastern seaboard in the middle of winter, sleeping in our 1983 Ford Econoline weather-stripped with duct tape.

I attended classes in theater and costume design at the University of Michigan for four—okay, five—years, taking off on weekends to record an EP in Chicago or play a gig in Akron. We toured during my school breaks. Some evenings, in the recording studio located in the back of a water-treatment plant, I fell asleep with my head against an amplifier, screeching feedback into the night. I didn't live fully in either world, the rock-and-roll world or cloistered university life, but always felt suspended in between.

After a girl reaches a certain age, it becomes nearly impossible to lose her virginity. That was the predicament I found myself in at twenty-one. I was terrified of sex because I'd waited too long—convinced that I really was supposed to wait—and now I'd worked myself into a frenzy of shame and terror. In turn, guys were terrified of being entrusted with the responsibility of my first time.

I decided that I had to rid myself of this problem a few weeks after returning from that first trip to New York, the one that ended with the *Times* photo. I was going to be twenty-two in a couple of months, and I was dating a nice grad student who studied piano, and it just had to happen; it had long passed the point of ridiculousness.

It happened when I was supposed to be contributing to the so-called work holiday. I was living with a hippie collective of two dozen students in a ramshackle red house named after the socialist labor organizer Eugene V. Debs, and we were all supposed to be doing chores around the house starting at nine in the morning, a Soviet tradition. The sex was unremarkable: neither good nor bad, just a sticky, slightly painful physical act that left the disconcerting scent that I now recognize to be condom lubricant. Afterward, we climbed out my window and down the fire escape so my housemates wouldn't see me skipping work, walked over to the old Fleetwood diner on the edge of town, and had omelets.

After graduation, I went to work as a labor reporter in Detroit. (The Terranauts, plagued by a marijuana-related arrest that didn't allow our singer to leave the state, disbanded.)

Recent college grads don't move to Detroit. Nobody in their right mind moves to Detroit, save for a few dozen earnest leftists working to revive the labor movement in the shadow of a dying auto industry.

Built to hold three million people, it held about seven hundred thousand, and those left were fleeing fast. It was a vast, post-industrial ghost town that had a raw, apocalyptic beauty. Abandoned mansions lined wide-open boulevards. Empty lots were reverting to fields. Everything was vacated and forgotten—crumbling storefronts, entire factories, even the eighteen-story Michigan Central Depot had been abandoned and loomed over the city like a rotting skeleton.

A Wild West mentality pervaded the city. Vigilantism was not only popular but the only means of protection in a place with no infrastructure, left to its own devices. A vast underclass and a barely perceptible aboveground economy resulted in a kind of controlled anarchy. Burned-out churches sat next to liquor stores, and the men behind their counters openly polished the shotguns on their laps.

I lived in the basement of a crumbling old house in Mexicantown for $195 a month. My housemates owned it as part of a women's collective that was loosely associated with the punk collective over on Trumbull Street. Homes were cheaper than cars in the Motor City; you could get something for a few grand. If you could protect it from the looters stripping the wiring for copper, it was all yours.

I held dinner parties on the rooftops of abandoned houses and drove my ten-year-old Oldsmobile around empty streets at night, smoking a joint. It didn't matter. There was no one around, no cars, no people on the streets.

The labor magazine was located in a run-down, bullet-scarred office on the Southwest Side directly next to a strip club called the Hardbody Café. The club featured an eighteen-foot-tall pink neon sign of a blond naked woman wearing a top hat and heels. The music usually started around 4 PM and pulsed through the walls of the office, where I might be on the phone with my main hotel-union source in San Francisco, a retired hospitality worker who always sang Grateful Dead songs as introduction.

The lefties and socialists I worked with were alternately amused and unsettled by what was going on next door. Of course, no one really *knew* what was going on next door: Not a single one of us had ventured over. Debates occasionally broke out, over lunch or while sitting around stuffing envelopes, about the nature of these mysterious strippers. Everyone had an opinion, from the grizzled Teamsters to the fresh-faced college interns. Some said they were our sisters, working-class folks like ourselves. Others said they were being exploited and exploiting themselves, or doing bad things in the back room. We were all fascinated by the Hardbody Café.

One afternoon, the intern showed up with beer to celebrate making deadline, and everybody stood outside on the sidewalk, drinking and watching as a flatbed truck full of construction workers pulled up and began to dismantle the pink neon lady. Then a crane arrived.

Were they going to take her away? Suddenly I was worried. She had been causing a lot of controversy in the neighborhood since her arrival, mostly among the Catholic Mexicans and Polish. As it turned out, they were just hoisting her up, six feet higher, so she could be seen by more people.

After that, the neon lady seemed to be trying to tell me something, flashing on and off in nightly Morse code, luring passing motorists inside with her long, pink legs.

Another hot summer afternoon soon after, while unloading a vanload of the magazine's most recent issue in the alley, I caught sight of one of the Hardbody's dancers, hanging out the back door of the club, smoking a cigarette. She was white and pale, with long, straight brown hair, wearing a black bikini with tall black boots. She caught me staring, smiled, and waved. I shyly waved back.

Being a stripper was pretty much the last thing I could imagine myself capable of doing. I was terribly shy and awkward. I still felt hopelessly behind when it came to sex, or dating, or even socializing. I was a wallflower and a late bloomer. I spent a lot of time waiting for things to happen to me. I waited for people to talk to me, to call me, to invite me places, to ask me out. It hadn't yet occurred to me that I could take charge of my own life. Even if it had, I figured that any potential rejection just wasn't worth it. So I watched, and waited.

I hoisted a box of magazines and went back to work, just as I was supposed to, just as I had always done. She was still there, leaning in the doorway of the club, sucking on her cigarette and squinting in the sunlight, when I left.

Two years later, alone in New York, I showed up at 30 West 31st Street, after answering an ad for "dancers" on Craigslist.

The club, if you could call it that, was on the fifth floor of a decrepit walk-up. I trudged up the rickety stairs with a red plaid skirt, black halter top, and black high heels in my bag. The costuming aspect wasn't what intimidated me—I wasn't one of those girls who didn't know how to walk in heels or anything. I loved clothes, and I loved costumes. After all, one of the easiest ways for a shy person to express herself is through the armor of clothing. But being comfortable naked, or being naked at all or accepting the idea that someone might find me attractive without cringing in embarrassment or hating them for thinking that—that was completely beyond me. That was what I couldn't get my mind around. That was why I was here.

The man in charge was a guy named Lou, a Lebanese Jew who looked like a sweaty George Costanza. I changed into my outfit in a makeshift dressing room with a bunch of Russian girls. A sign informed me that dancers were prohibited from wearing stiletto heels due to past problems with them being used as weapons.

The club was a low-key setup. Guys found out about the place through its website, then showed up after work to swill bottom-shelf liquor and chat up trashily dressed girls, as if they were at a cocktail party. It was up to us to hustle for lap dances and money. These men were time-sucking energy vampires, passive-aggressive manipulators in their forties and fifties who mostly seemed lost, wondering why they were there, and angry about the fact that they were.

Giving lap dances was shockingly intimate, not the lighthearted one-sided performance I'd imagined. It was also unremarkable and only vaguely uncomfortable, just like the first time I'd had sex. My first dance was with a light-skinned black man, pleasant-enough looking. As I climbed onto him, my senses were overwhelmed by unfamiliarity: the material of his suit, his cologne, the oiliness of his graying hair. Unconsciously, I turned them off.

During the one song I was contracted to dance for, I could only process a string of hard facts: It was cold without my top on. Mary J. Blige was playing. I could feel his hands moving over my shoulders and bare back. I had an unsettling feeling of discomfort, but since I was doing it willingly, I wasn't sure if this feeling was just something I would have to get used to or if it was a warning that I should stop. I just couldn't tell. When the song finished, he handed me $20, unimpressed, and moved on to the next girl. Things like sex and nudity were supposed to be imbued with meaning. But isolated from a relationship, they meant nothing—or rather, I realize now, they became something to be negotiated, and *I* became nothing—little more than a dress-up doll for them to project their narratives onto.

Over the next several weeks, I became a difficult, halfhearted stripper, cold and distant with customers. My barely masked contempt was equaled only by my morbid fascination with this den of iniquity, like poking a dead rat with a stick: I shouldn't do it, I didn't particularly enjoy doing it, I hated how disgusting it was. But some part of me needed to see what its insides looked like.

"The thing about this job," I cracked a week later, straddling my first customer of the night, a cute, ruffly-haired young guy with glasses from a record company, "is that it's not rocket science." Michael was his name. Actually, I forgot his name.

"Right . . . " he laughed. "We both know what we want." But his voice was suddenly husky.

Most men remained silent—either terrified or awed—during lap dances. Half of them seemed just as uncomfortable as I was. But

Michael was different—he was chatty, with witty, well-practiced anec-dotes about Willie Nelson and peyote and the art of nudging record-ing artists: "So how are *we doing?* How's the record coming? Help me help you. How's the *creative process* flowing?"

"What's your favorite movie this year?" he asked. "Remember, I'm a media guy—I have to know."

I rolled my eyes.

"My definition of being professional," he whispered, "is doing what you love with people you hate." He was flirting, playing on the idea that he assumed I hated him on principle but was somehow enjoying my time with him anyway.

I hated all the clients: the businessmen, the younger men, the older men, Lou. I gazed over at the dance floor: There he was, doing what he thought were his slick moves to a Rod Stewart song, in his cheap suit: "*If* you think I'm sexy, *and* you like my body . . . " Lou pointed and grinned at a bleached-blond stripper while attempting to twirl her around with his other hand.

My fantasies involved machine-gunning him down on the dance floor. Multiple bullets would send blood spurting from his chest, splattering all over his white shirt. The other girls would scream at first and then start laughing like hyenas.

But I couldn't hate Michael. He was too young; we had too much in common. His face, his mannerisms, his voice: They were all discon-certingly familiar.

I avoided eye contact, anything resembling intimacy, but I could see him gazing up at me, looking into my eyes, blowing cool air onto my stomach, something that only a lover would do. Before I knew what was happening, he covered my right hand, resting on the side of the couch, with his, and I froze. He had broken the cardinal rule: the rule of my hating him, my professional, psychological boundar-ies. What started as a crude service between strangers became just a moment between two human beings.

THE TURQUOISE DRESS

The mood in the dressing room at the start of the night was always ebullient. We always came in with blind optimism: We were really going to make money tonight—lots of it, more than anyone had ever made before.

The following Friday night, the music was pumping, and Lou was handing out champagne. Yes, we all thought. Yes. Tonight was going to be a good night.

Lou had secured an empty spa on the fourth floor of a building in Little Brazil. 30 West 31st Street had been closed down for building-code violations, and he had been scrambling for spaces.

Ever the hustler, he'd rented the space from a woman who was part of a couple who frequented his swingers parties—an entirely separate line of his business interests that I wanted to keep far away from. From what I'd heard, it involved middle-aged couples from Jersey who were into wife-swapping.

Oversized plush sofas and leopard-print folding chairs were scattered throughout the spa. In the waiting room, heavily made-up and scantily clad dancers sat in wait, lounging on blood-red couches, smoking or sleeping, boredly waiting for the men to arrive.

A girl came out of the dressing room in a skimpy black crochet outfit, sat down, smoked a cigarette, left, and appeared minutes later in an identical white crochet dress.

I decided to change clothes, too. I went back to the makeshift dressing room and changed out of my little black dress into red, ruffly underwear and a red bra. It didn't look quite right. I could never really get it right, no matter how hard I tried. Some element of my outfit, of my hair or makeup, was always wrong. I squinted at myself in the mirror, trying to figure it out.

Simone—one of the oldest dancers at Lou's who worked nearly every one of his parties—had finally had enough. "Honey, no," she said. She was a brunette in her thirties who smoked like a chimney, had a little girl and a husband, and lived in Brighton Beach. She had a super-aggressive Eastern European hustle and made more money than anybody else. Yet, she hardly touched her customers and didn't allow them to touch her— every time I looked over, she was sitting on their lap while whispering into their ear. She could do that for thirty minutes straight.

"What is this, what are you doing? Take this shit off." She tugged my underwear down and handed me a dress.

"I thought it was cute," I meekly defended myself.

"Here," she said, producing a dress from her oversized duffel bag and tossing it at me.

Some older strippers made a side income selling their old costumes to the other girls at the club. The first dress was yellow and green with glitter and made me look like an alien. The second dress, red and silver, wasn't much better. But there was one more.

"This one, yes," Simone said. It was shimmery deep turquoise with swags of black tulle at the hem.

"Wow," I said, staring at myself in the mirror. I looked like a naughty ballerina. "My red shoes will look so good with this."

"Red shoes, what red shoes?" I handed her one, a red patent leather pump. She sighed, as if trying to teach a lesson to a very slow child.

"No," she said. "No, no, no." She threw the shoe at my bag. "Put this shit away." She sighed again.

"Honey," she said slowly. "It's a very beautiful shoe, but to wear with jeans, or out dancing, you know. Not for this. What size do you wear?" She rummaged around in her giant duffel bag.

"Ten." There was no way she'd have a pair of size-ten stripper shoes.

But she did. They had a high platform of clear plastic, and a stiletto heel, also clear plastic. I hated them on sight; they were so tacky.

"I can't," I said, slipping them on, but they actually looked kind of good. They were just part of a uniform, I realized. I didn't have to like them.

"You look good. Tell her she looks good," she commanded one of the Russian girls.

"You look good," the Russian girl said dutifully.

"There," Simone said, reaching over and adjusting my dress again, then gently turning me to face the mirror. "There," she said again, softer now. "Now you look—like woman. Get out there and hustle, honey."

I went back out into the waiting room with the red curtains and the couches.

A tall, dorky-looking guy with glasses came in, the first to arrive. I recognized him as the one who had come to the previous Tuesday's party. He was only interested in getting dances from a gorgeous black girl with a British accent named Bella, an NYU student. He came into our lair and sat down beside her.

"What's up?" he asked awkwardly.

"Um, this is kind of the girls-only hangout room," she replied icily.

He left, more awkward than ever. Lou barged in a minute later.

"Bella, a gentleman has booked an appointment in the Fantasy Booth with you."

The Fantasy Booth was just a closet with a chair in it that customers could rent out for half-hour private dances with a girl of their choice. There wasn't room inside for anything other than that.

"I don't want to go in the Fantasy Booth," she pouted. Lou pulled her up by the hand, sweet-talking while leading her out the door.

"It's just like a regular lap dance, Bella, but in a private booth. Nothing to be worried about, okay? How are we feeling, then? Good? You look great, by the way."

His cell phone rang, and he searched behind him in his back pocket to answer it.

"Hi, Ellis? Yeah, we're having a real nice party, a real nice party. Yeah, everybody's having a good time. So, what should we do about garbage when we're done? The alley? Okay, we'll put it out back. Yeah, okay, Ellis, great. Listen, I gotta go, okay? All right."

At the end of the night, I had to give the dresses and the shoes back. I'd made almost no money, and Simone had given them to me on contingency. The entire evening had been a disaster. I couldn't perform the socializing required for this job, the endless conversations that the club's well-off but socially inept clientele required you to entertain them with before you could actually make a fucking sale, in increments of $20, lap dance by lap dance. They needed their egos to be puffed up and stroked first, and I couldn't do it. My own nervousness made other people nervous.

I owed Simone $30, and the house $60. Nobody was getting paid. I left early, trying to figure out my inability to do this. Failing at stripping was a bad feeling, but it was true—I was bad at it. It had nothing to do with how I looked; the problem was my personality. I left the turquoise dress and shoes behind, folded up in the dressing room.

I took the subway back to Brooklyn, catching the beginning of the morning rush hour, and sat in front of a bodega waiting for the B61 bus to my neighborhood, watching the sky beginning to get light.

Two months later, my last night at Lou's ended with the words, "Cops! Everybody put your clothes on!" Twenty girls huddled in the makeshift dressing room, furiously getting dressed while hiding drugs and panicking about immigration status. I sat down in the shower with two Russian girls, resigned to the fact that everything was beyond my control.

Would we all be arrested, handcuffed, and led down the five flights of rickety wooden stairs to a paddy wagon? Would my photo be splashed across *The Post* under the headline VICE SQUAD BUSTS ILLEGAL STRIP JOINT? Had I made enough money that night to bail myself out? I didn't care either way. I almost looked forward to the change of pace a night in jail might provide from the grind of the club.

"Jesus Christ, try to act normal," said Vixen, the head girl and assistant to Lou, sounding cross. "It's not like we're doing anything illegal, so chill." Vixen, with long, dirty-blond hair and a penchant for black knee-high boots, was pretty in a hard-bitten sort of way. She said she liked her neighborhood in Queens because they let her keep her pit bulls and because it was "all white."

Yet, like a pair of fishnet stockings, Vixen's statement was full of holes. For instance, I doubted that the loft was in full compliance with New York's labyrinthine cabaret and vice laws, especially if one considered that it was most likely serving liquor without a license, allowed under-twenty-one drinking, and hired under-eighteen dancers from Jersey, plus an assortment of foreign girls without work visas or other legal documentation. Those were the sorts of things that might be of interest to the law.

I could hear Lou outside the door, talking to the cops, cajoling them, and they soon left.

This is over, I thought, still crammed inside the shower stall with three other girls. But it had really only just begun.

"'You looked lost,' someone who knew me when I was very young tells me, 'and people just couldn't help themselves by giving you hundred-franc notes.' Not like a woman who was after money, far from it, but like an adolescent who was no good at earning her living and needed help with a little allowance."

—Catherine M.

THE MINNESOTA STRIP

"Come have a drink with me," Stefan had said to me one night around closing time at Lou's. "I'll be at Jimmy's. You can show up and keep me company if you want. Or not. I'll be there either way."

I rolled my eyes—*a customer asking me out?*—but I hadn't had a real conversation with another human being in weeks. I showed up.

Stefan was a handsome semi-regular at Lou's parties. He kept his dark hair short, probably because it was beginning to gray, and had a pleasingly lined face. He looked a bit like Kevin Spacey. He always smelled amazing, like clean laundry and cologne, and gave a $50 tip.

An Armenian who grew up in Beirut, he was forty-one and worked on Wall Street at J.P. Morgan. "I usually think my most basic thoughts—hungry, tired—in Armenian," he told me at the bar, ignoring his beer. "I dream in French, I do business in English, and I swear in Arabic." He had no trace of an accent.

We got into a cab together after the beer.

"Two stops," he told the driver. "Where are you going?" he asked me. I couldn't tell him that I didn't live anywhere at the moment. I was between sublets, waiting for the fifteenth of the month so I could move into another apartment in Greenpoint, and I was staying at a youth hostel in the meantime. I told him to drop me off at the 14th Street subway stop, and I took the 1 train up to the hostel.

Although I knew it was a trap, that I was easy prey—he was one of the wolves—I still found him charming: old-world and old-school, smooth-mannered and tan. In any language, no one else had said, *I would love to have dinner with you*, in the first-date sense of the phrase. The following Friday, I showed up at the upscale Buddakan inappropriately dressed in a hoodie and jeans. He found my faux pas waifishly charming. I was such easy entertainment for him, a novelty, and I was only dimly aware that my charm lay in everything I hated about myself—my wide-eyed, earnest Midwestern naïveté, the fact that I looked and acted as if I'd just stepped off the Greyhound weeks before.

Stefan's apartment at 68th and Broadway was vast and blank, with wide swaths left open and unfurnished. It appeared mostly untouched, the domain of someone who rarely had time to inhabit it fully. The countertops were black and devoid of dishes, and the row of shiny brass pans hanging over the stove appeared to be purely decorative. The living room was long and completely empty, save for a rug. I appreciated its Zenlike qualities but felt intimidated in the grown-up space.

"You want some wine?" he asked.

"No, thanks," I said. I wanted to keep my bearings.

"Sure?"

"Yep."

He went into the kitchen and poured two glasses anyway. While he was out of the room, I looked at the bookshelf: *How to Stop Smoking. The Economist. Foreign Affairs.* I placed *How to Stop Smoking* on the coffee table next to the ashtray.

When he got back, we didn't talk but lay intertwined on the couch. He walked two fingers up the length of my torso, whispering, "*La petite bête qui monte, qui monte, qui monte . . .* " The little creature who goes up, goes up, goes up . . .

Stefan's apartment was also heavily mirrored, affording me many opportunities to look at myself, which I did often, just to check that I was still there. In front of the full-length picture-frame mirror, I ran a hand over my collarbone and noticed the bones below it protruding more than usual; I could feel each one beneath my fingers. My skin appeared bluish in the light, translucent. For a moment, squinting at my reflection, I thought I could almost see through my own skin.

The next morning, I sat on the edge of his bed, staring as he put on his suit with practiced efficiency: pants, dress shirt, belt, tie, Blackberry, cigarettes, jacket. He caught my gaze from behind him in the mirror and turned around.

"It's just another role I play," he said, to reassure me. "Another face I put on." He buttoned his jacket.

I didn't know it yet, but Stefan would sleep with me for approximately three months before disappearing, possibly with another lost girl from the club at 30 West 31st Street. He just wanted to have fun with careless party girls. I wasn't really any of these girls. It was just another face I put on.

The week the fiasco in Lebanon began was the week Stefan appeared to be drifting further and further away. In the heat-induced twilight zone, I started to think a little bit confused and conflate the two events, maybe because he grew up in Beirut during the first occupation. But the real conflict was that sometimes Stefan tried to give me money. Like $200 or $300. It wasn't like he was paying me for sex; it was because he knew I had no money. Still, it was stunningly off, just completely wrong, and I should have known that we were not just on a different page but in two completely different books. I refused the money once and then twice and then he didn't offer after that. He realized that I was going to be stubborn and proud and that there was nothing more he could do for me.

The last time I saw him, we were headed downtown in a cab.

"What cologne do you wear?" I asked.

"It's just cigarettes and sweat, baby," he said with a slight smirk.

We had our usual debate about outsourcing, economics, something he was indulging me in while I tried to show him that I wasn't just a dumb dancer. It ended with him murmuring to himself a long phrase in French ending in *la bourgeosie*. He had a lazy half-smile as he spoke, leaning back comfortably in the seat, gazing outside at something unseen and faraway. He offered me no translation, and I didn't ask for one.

On Sundays, I worked the door at a seedy little dance club on 8th Avenue in the '30s. Four hours, $50, plus maybe an extra $10 I could grift from the cash box, just because. I sat in a chair just inside the propped-open door and watched people stagger by slowly, buckling under the heat. A young girl carried a dirty white cat down the sidewalk, holding it with both hands underneath its armpits, leaving the rest of its body hanging while the cat meowed unhappily. Underground, the smarter women on the train dusted themselves liberally with baby powder, white peeking out from their cleavage or under their arms or below the hairline to absorb sweat.

I had just been fired—twice—for the first time in my life. The first dismissal was from a children's theater, where I worked backstage for $10.01 an hour. I was let go without reason during a meeting with a stern HR representative.

Next, I found a job telemarketing in a windowless room in Battery Park City, for $12 an hour, alongside a dozen stoned Jamaicans. The boss paid us by personal check if and when he felt like it. I was let go after less than a month, halfway through my shift, for failing to meet the quota. He'd been weeding out the weak and inefficient all week, and I had thought I might be spared. But he was right to get rid of me; I was not very good at the job.

"Can I at least finish out the day?" I asked him.

"Nope," he replied cheerfully. Three weeks later, I rode the train an hour each way to pick up my last paycheck, only to find he had stiffed me $75.

I went on at least two dozen interviews to be a waitress or a hostess. I had managed to make it thus far without having to wait tables, and nobody seemed eager to educate me on their dime. All those stories about starving artists getting their start in New York by waitressing or bartending were bullshit, I realized. You had to know people. Half of the restaurants expected a headshot.

My entire plan had rested on the flimsy idea that I would get a $15-an-hour entry-level editorial assistant job at a magazine or publishing house, but I was going to have to lower my standards.

The eight temp agencies I signed up with were less than helpful. Like many college grads, I actually had very few marketable skills. I had never properly learned Excel, or Powerpoint, or, come to think of it, Photoshop.

I applied to make coffee at Starbucks, sell clothes at American Apparel, and bake cupcakes at Magnolia Bakery. I worked the door at the Webster Hall nightclub for one night and one night only before Chief, the enormous Native American manager, told me he'd pay me during my next shift but never called to give me another one.

By any reasonable standard, I was losing it.

"When I was sixteen, I visited Times Square before it got all cleaned up, when you could put in a quarter for a peep show," I remembered Stefan had told me one Sunday afternoon, inadvertently planting a seed of curiosity. "And for a dollar, the partition slid up, and you could touch."

I was fascinated by the honky-tonk idea of an actual peep show, imagining that the girls dressed up in pinup-style showgirl costumes every night. It was the same curiosity I felt about Detroit, in all its damaged beauty, and in stripping, in all its ugliness. Was it even possible that they still existed?

Walking north on 8th Avenue one afternoon, I found my live girls in a porn store sandwiched between a trendy bar and the headquarters for the Grey Line Bus Tours: Gotham City Video. Under the gaze of winking, plasticized genitalia, I asked the men behind the counter, wearing uniform bright yellow vests, if they were hiring *girls*. It was July, and I was sweating, my hair stuck to the sides of my face.

"You want to work cashier?" shouted the Chinese one, as if he were deaf.

"Nooo," I said, trying to imbue the word with hidden meaning.

He glanced me up and down. "You have ID?"

I handed him my passport.

"Fine, fill out paperwork and put your name on the schedule," he barked.

I signed up for the ominous-sounding graveyard shift and told myself I probably wouldn't show up.

"Oh, yes, she will make money here," encouraged the other man, a handsome West African. "Is beautiful, no?" I looked up at the video monitor on the wall and saw three tough-looking girls sitting in front of booths, located on the second floor. "Live girls," a large black girl boomed into the mike, startling me. "Live girls!" She saw me on the monitor and started to cackle. Her laughter ricocheted through the store.

Flustered, I quickly left after signing the schedule, so distracted that I forgot my ID, something I only remembered two weeks later, when, bleeding money, I finally limped in for a shift.

The same men were at the front of the store, in the same yellow vests, but they had forgotten they hired me. I was barred from the dressing room, eyed with suspicion, and had to repeat the process. Soon enough, however, I had a black bobbed wig, a pair of cheap plastic stilettos, and a booth of my own. I was twenty-five and had been living in New York for three months.

Nude entertainment is the female version of the same-day-pay shape-up job, and my experience was not unique. In my time at the labor magazine, I would have described the peep show's setup as the "alternative labor market": an off-the-books job where nothing was guaranteed. My journey towards the peep shows was the same Broadway boogie-woogie that girls looking to make quick cash in New York had done for decades. A girl might first make the rounds of classier joints, like Scores or the Hustler Club, and, if they weren't hiring, move on to the slightly seedier ones on Broadway or 8th—Flashdancers, Lace, Privilege. Then there were the peep shows, in the backs of porn stores: Gotham Video, or Empire Erotica on 33rd, or the Playpen, down the street near the Port Authority. They were the last three peep shows in a city that used to have them lining Times Square by the dozen. Once a famous shorthand for vice in a dirty city, they were now the last of their kind.

In the '70s and '80s, this same stretch of 8th Avenue was called the Minnesota Strip, after the hundreds of Midwestern girls who debarked the Greyhound bus at the Port Authority and followed the blinking lights into various aspects of the flesh trade. It was nice to know that I was following some sort of tradition.

The following week at 10 PM, I walked up the rainbow stairs of Gotham for my first shift. The second floor was home to the live fantasy girls. A girl who called herself Heidi was there, packing up to leave once she saw the next shift coming in.

She was pretty, with blond hair and pale, nearly translucent skin. I eventually learned that she was twenty-six, from Colorado, and lived with her boyfriend in the Bronx, where she was the only white person on her block. She showed me a picture of him on her cell phone, a caramel-skinned guy with braids and sleepy brown eyes. Heidi was a workaholic; she was also a colorist at a salon and worked seven days a week.

"By the way," she said from behind her long, fluttering false eyelashes, "there's a bird that got in here. So don't be afraid if you see something flying." On cue, a sparrow flew from his perch on top of the peep-show booths to the railing leading to the third floor, where gay men cruised for anonymous blowjobs in the "buddy booths" that played movies and had small openings at waist level—the Male Box, they called it. It was a glory-hole setup that was somehow legal: Each guy put money in his own booth to activate porn videos, with the money going to the store. If they were so inclined, the partition between booths slid up.

I knocked on the dressing-room door, which I later learned the girls kept locked, not to keep people from walking in on them while they were changing but so nobody unexpectedly busted in on them smoking weed. A minute went by.

"Who is it?" somebody shouted in a Spanish-and-Bronx-accented voice.

"Sheila."

"Who the fuck is Sheila?"

"I mean Chelsea!" My stage name, not that she knew that one either. It was Stefan's idea to use the name of the neighborhood where I had first started dancing.

A tired-looking Puerto Rican woman opened the door. "Heeeey, mami," she said, dazed, smoke swirling around her face. "I was like, Sheila, who the fuck is that, you know? Sorry. I'm Cheshire."

Stepping inside, I saw a wig and a bouquet of roses in the trashcan. There were two long gray counters, in front of mirrors surrounded by bare light bulbs, and gray lockers above and below. It smelled of cigarettes, weed, Lysol, and microwaved food. I sat down in one of the chairs and began unpacking my makeup. I applied red lipstick, gave myself raccoon eyes, and put on a sparkly see-through black dress over my bra and underwear, purchased downstairs with my employee discount.

I put my hair into a short ponytail and pulled on a nylon wig cap, which I was used to putting on actors when I had worked backstage, but never myself. I brushed out a black bobbed wig that I'd purchased from a nearby wig store for $35 and fastened it behind my ears with bobby pins. All my theatrical training was coming in handy.

A striking girl with long, dark hair and dark eyes was the only person to speak to me in the dressing room that first day.

"So have you worked at these sorts of places before?" she asked, looking up from putting on black fishnet stockings.

"No."

"Where're you from?"

"Michigan."

"Do they have places like this in Michigan?"

"No, I don't think so."

"I've worked in a few of these places," she said, sounding grateful for the chance to reflect. "Here, Portland, Minneapolis . . . " Her lack of a hard New York accent reassured me.

"I'm Ruby," she said, then turned around and abruptly went back to the business of getting dressed.

In front of the line of six peep-show booths, I put down my bag and sat down in one of the chairs alongside Ruby and a short, tough-looking woman named Lourdes, who had transformed from a butch lesbian wearing baggy boys' clothes into a Latina exotic with red lingerie and shiny black knee-high boots.

"These shoes stink, yo," she said, waving her foot around. "I don't know why my shoes always stink." Cheshire emerged from the dressing room, wearing a faded flowered bra-and-panty set and the requisite see-through plastic platforms, and flopped herself down in a chair. Ruby sat quietly with a book, a little red sweater demurely covering up her bra and booty shorts. She wore shiny white heels and began rubbing baby oil onto her legs until they were dewy and sleek.

I looked around. The store was sterile and well lit, as clean as an establishment of this type could get. Our area, sequestered in the back behind a curtain of plastic chains, resembled a hospital waiting room with mirrored walls. The radio station wasn't piped in, and it was eerily silent, so quiet that I could hear the whir of the motor operating the mirror ball spinning above our heads. It scattered light over the room, keeping everyone disoriented.

The booths were a clinical shade of gray. They were closet-sized—standing inside, you couldn't hold your arms all the way out. There was your door, and then there was your customer's. They were identical, except the girl's side had a stool in it, and the guy's side had a chair. Mikes in the ceiling picked up sound, presumably so you could talk to them. There was a tiny, eighth-of-an-inch slit of an opening on the left-hand side of the glass, exactly the size for slipping a bill through. The two sides were separated by a viewing window the size of a full-length mirror. Once a bill was inserted, the fogged glass immediately cleared with a click and flick of the lights and—*poof!*—a girl appeared. Lourdes, the four-foot-eleven, thirty-six-year-old Puerto Rican–Dominican lesbian—in the business for a dozen years—explained what it was we did in the booth during a peep show:

"Okay," she barked, casually holding a floppy, flesh-colored dildo, her long, fake ponytail brushing the middle of her back like a horse's tail. "Want me to show you? Guy comes in, picks the girl he wants to see, whatever whatever, he picks you, you go in the booth, you take off your clothes, spread, show him your pussy, whatever"—she slapped her crotch with her hand for emphasis—"he can do whatever he wants, usually jerks off while he watches." She accompanied this description with a jerking-off motion, then slapped the dildo against her leg. "When he comes, you're done. You don't have to do shit after that, I don't care if the window is still open. You wanna use toys like this, it's extra."

She stared me down. I stared back dumbly. *We saw people jerking off?* I'd never even thought about that.

"That's cool," I finally said, with forced casualness.

My first customer, incredibly, turned out to be Lou. It somehow made sense when I saw him huffing his way up the stairs.

"Lou?" I asked, dumbfounded. "What are you doing here?" It was 2 AM on a Tuesday.

"Oh, hey, Chelsea," he said, hardly surprised to see me. "Nothin' much, nothin' much, just buying a dildo. What are you doing? You working here now? You know, you're lucky. This place is real clean."

"Um . . . " I looked around. It was pretty clean. "Would you like a live fantasy show?"

I went into my side of the booth and awkwardly began taking off my clothes. I felt the same way I did at the gynecologist: uncomfortable, cold, just trying to keep still and get it over with.

Lou began to masturbate—trying to, anyway, sweating and straining. Disgusted, I avoided eye contact and silently panicked for the next three minutes until the light snapped off and the window abruptly went dark.

Putting my clothes back on, I felt guilty and stupid, as if I had somehow been cajoled by a guy into doing something I didn't want to do, like a high-school girl pressured into letting a boy feel her up. But I hadn't been cajoled; I had done it willingly. I had already made my choice. I didn't have to do this, but I had chosen to. It wasn't something I was forced into out of poverty or circumstance; I certainly could have found something eventually, or moved back to Michigan temporarily. But I didn't want to. I wanted to be here, in New York, right now, and I was tired of waiting. This, for now, was what I was going to do.

After the show, Lou paused outside his side of the booth, mopping his brow.

"You know, Chelsea," he said. "If you're going to be doing these kinds of shows, you might want to think about getting rid of the rest of your, ahh . . . " He made a hand motion, gesturing towards the area between my legs, suggesting that I shave off my pubic hair like a Playboy centerfold.

I motioned to the porters on duty, and they loomed in: "Hey, man, no talking to the ladies," boomed Jerry, a recent immigrant from Ghana.

Lou put his hands up in the air, as if he were under arrest.

"All right, all right!" he said. "I just paid for a show! I'm leaving!" I watched with satisfaction as he was escorted down the stairs.

Months later, Lou wrote a message on a website for strippers about me, confirming my worst fears:

> [Chelsea] had worked for [my club]. She was awkward and just not that hot. She did not do that well as she could not compete with the other dancers. A few months later, I saw her working at a pathetic peep show in Times Square.

He was mad because I'd been talking shit about him on the same online forum, warning dancers away from his club with anecdotes about his penchant for getting touchy-feely with the dancers, especially the underage ones he could easily manipulate. "Lou is a scumbag," I had posted. "Don't bother working at his 'club.'"

A year after that, my biggest nightmare—being dragged out of the semi-legal club, my picture splashed across *The Daily News*—actually happened, only I was long gone. Lou Posner—not Lou Post, as his business card said—had expanded into prostitution and was laundering the money through a Democratic front organization. The raid ended up on the cover of *The Daily News*, which ran with the story for a couple days. "Big Daddy Lou" and his "lap-dance bordello" were in big trouble. The ensuing headlines were just as delicious: "Cops Say Lawyer Ran Midtown Brothel." "Strip Club Owner 'Shocked' At Allegations." He sat in jail for a week before finally making bail, set at $150,000.

"One dancer called him a 'sleazy, disgusting, and very unloyal' boss who often cajoled the girls into giving him freebies," wrote *The Post*. "His wife, Betty, 56, was charged with helping him launder the proceeds, which the sources said totaled more than $1 million a year."

Lou responded in *The News*: "I'm sure if you asked the girls, they would say that 'Lou is one of the best bosses we ever had.'" I imagined the creepy glint in his eyes while talking to the reporter and felt immensely satisfied. Lou was one of the wolves, but at least he had been trapped.

When I started at the peep show, I thought there would be some sort of training period on how to execute a live show, or at least a few words of advice on standard operating procedures. There wasn't. That I should take off my clothes was obvious—now, what to do with the remaining three minutes? It was easy to be clumsy in such tight confines. When new girls began, I often heard the familiar thump of a head or shoe banging against the glass as they learned how to maneuver in the small space.

Eventually I developed my routine. Soon I could do it without forming a single thought: off with the bra, pose, then the underwear, slouch against the back wall of the booth, running my fingers over my hips and my breasts. Then I'd turn around and bend over, running my hands up the backs of my legs. Finally, I'd sit on my chair and open my legs.

That was the $40 show, what we called the "masturbation" show. If you wanted to just see nudity, but nothing else, it was $30. It was so arbitrary. It was 2006, the same year a Nielsen study found that one quarter of all Internet searches were porn-related. Free porn was everywhere, yet men still came in for us.

I didn't think much about the price. I wasn't offended by it. The seemingly arbitrary number was just another depressing reality, like the $4 latte. I didn't take it as a reflection of what I was worth. It was a hard number, unsentimental, and it was simply the highest amount that the market was willing to bear to see a girl behind glass in Times Square.

Management got the first $10, which went into the machine that made the glass unfog, and the rest went to us, so we made either $20 or $30 per show. Guys usually went with the "better show," as we called it.

I took a vacation from my mind every time. I didn't watch the beady-eyed voyeurs; I didn't even look at them. I watched my reflection in the glass partition instead. Being fully present was too personal, and soon I found myself able to completely dissociate. It was the only way to do the job: not to look too closely at the man on the other side of the glass.

The other girls did the same: "I don't look at them," I heard Heidi telling a new girl one day. "I look at myself, in the glass. A guy might say, 'Look at me,' and I will, but if you look at my eyes, you can tell—I'm not there." She waved a hand in front of her blank-eyed face to demonstrate. None of us were all there. The live girls were numb.

I didn't remember anyone's faces. By the end of the night, I couldn't tell you a single customer's description, pick him out of a police lineup, or even remember what he was wearing—unless he was a regular, someone I'd seen at least four or five times.

The lineup of girls was a brutal setup that bred competition and jealousy. The customer chose the girl he wanted. "You're all cute," they would say. "How can I choose?" We stared back in stony-faced silence.

Somebody might get on the mike to encourage customers to come upstairs:

"Hey, fellas! Remember, we have three floors for y'alls' enjoyment . . . movies, video booths, and toys on the first, buddy booths on the third floor, and live fantasy girls on the second! We have chocolate, we have vanilla, we have . . . caramel!" This was repeated in Spanish: "*En vivo!*" Live, live, live.

A man came upstairs, stood before us, and stared. They were all the same: nameless, faceless, shuffling, nervous, their eyes darting for the nearest exit. This one was white and blue-collar, maybe Italian, with a sparse mustache and a baseball cap. He spoke in short, reluctant mumbles, as if trying to conserve energy, full sentences complete with enunciation being too much work. He shifted his weight from foot to foot, glancing at an invisible point somewhere over his right shoulder.

"Pick a lady for a show!" we chirped, smiling. "It's thirty or forty for a show. Pick a girl!" He turned away and stared at our TV, temporarily entranced by a commercial for *Everybody Hates Chris*.

"How long?" he finally asked.

"Oh, 'bout five minutes."

"That's all?" We lost so many this way, but it was risky to lie: Some cheap obsessives were known to time their shows, angrily pointing at their watches when a girl emerged from an "eight-minute" show after only three minutes and thirty seconds had elapsed.

"You don't need any longer. C'mon, pick a girl, it's fun. You're not going to find anything else like it." Some girls got more graphic here: "What's wrong, babe, you don't want to bust a nut?"

Next came the second most popular question: "You the only ones here?"

Almost every man asked this, whether there were one, four, or six girls. It was impossible not to be insulted. The hyperreality of Times Square had seeped into their brains, making them demand endless variety, which they now needed in order to make one simple choice.

"Are *you* the only one here?" one of the girls retaliated.

The mood when a man was standing before a lineup of girls was tense. If he took too long to decide, it disintegrated into open aggression: "What's wrong, you don't like pussy?" "You look like you don't got no money to spend."

Sometimes, negotiations veered toward the metaphysical: "You want a show?" I asked a friendly-looking professional in his forties one night.

"No, honey, I'm all right."

"*Are* you all right?"

He threw up his hands, flashing a lopsided grin. "Who knows!"

As each evening wore on, men skulked their way up the stairs, some slinking straight to the third floor where the gay porn was, some popping in simply to harass us, peppering the girls with questions and rhetorical comments: "Where the black girls at?" "Man, you ladies look *bored* as *hell*." "Where Mocha at? Mocha is the bomb!" Some took shows; most didn't.

"Mama, what are you?" they asked, bending down to peer into our faces to discern whether a girl was a light-skinned black girl, or Dominican, or Russian like them, or just white. Some girls were more mercenary about affiliating:

"You Puerto Rican?"

"I'm whatever you want me to be, honey."

For my first few days, the girls blended together. They were mostly tough-talking Latinas from the Bronx who dropped their r's and refused to speak to me, a hazing ritual meant to bully the weak into quitting. As a white girl—and all non-white girls in the stripping industry mistakenly believed that white girls always did better—I was seen as a threat to their money.

They didn't realize that if I couldn't cut it here, I was going back to Michigan. So I didn't budge, not even after Lourdes threatened to punch me in the face after I gave a show to a shifty-looking dude who turned out to be the boyfriend of a coworker named Baby.

I locked myself in the bathroom and cried, but came back out and finished my shift. Fuck it, fuck them all.

I'd also picked the worst time to start. Summer was mysteriously the slowest time in the nude-girl business.

"These days, niggas be trying to hustle you while you hustling them," said Latte, a cute, light-skinned Puerto Rican from Queens. Her curly hair was pulled back, and she was wearing her glasses, short cutoff jeans, a bikini top, and large white furry boots. "I tell them a show's $40, and they all, 'Well, I got $25.' What's that leave—$15 for me? The fuck outta here."

We weren't guaranteed to make anything. I could make over $300 in a six-hour shift if I was lucky, $30 if I wasn't. Going to work was a gamble: Nobody ever thought they were going to be the loser. The nights I drew the bad-money hand were crushing. I felt like the worst of failures, which was normal. Everyone felt like that after a bad shift.

My second week, a well-dressed man in a suit came in for a show with Ruby. Then he turned to me:

"Can I see you, too?" he asked. "And will you, um, fight? You know, call each other a bitch and stuff."

"Um . . . " I glanced at Ruby. Her face was blank. "Sure."

"Your booth or mine?" she asked. We squeezed into hers, waiting for the machine to eat up the $10 bill that made the fogged-glass partition clear.

"What the fuck are you doing in my booth?" she demanded when the lights went on.

"Fuck you!" I said. "You think you're better than everyone else."

"I hear you're a slut. That's what they're all saying about you up in, ah . . . "—she fumbled to remember my neighborhood—"Greenpoint."

"Not as big a slut as you." Both of us were trying not to laugh. At the same time, I was a little scared of her; she was so convincing. The man in the suit had unbuckled his belt and was masturbating diligently, as if this were also in the script.

"Can you guys, like, kiss?" he piped up.

"Yeah, right," I snapped. "With her?"

"Yeah, *right*," Ruby added. "Like I even want that nasty ho in my booth in the first place."

Ruby rallied toward the end. Taking out the bandana used to cover her chair for hygiene, she twisted it and raised it threateningly. "I'm going to whip you with this if you don't step away from me!" She lifted a foot. "I'll ram you with my fucking stiletto!" She turned around and leaned over, hands on the chair, heel still pointed toward me, stabbing the air. "I'm going to take a dildo and shove it up your ass!"

With that, the window went dark, the show—and the exhausting, awkward improvising—finally over.

Ruby became the only real friend I ever made in the peeps.

Gotham had a sign outside the video booths boasting THE LARGEST SELECTION OF VIDEOS IN A PEEPSHOW EVER, and I once overheard a porter telling a customer that one could technically watch for years without seeing the same thing twice.

Certain men appeared to be testing this theory: Some clearly unmedicated obsessives stayed in the video booths for close to twenty-four hours, pausing only to urinate into a cup—or onto the floor, which would leak out under the door toward the live-girl area. We'd point and scream for a porter, who would appear with a mop, sighing and shaking his head. The video-booth addicts also brought food in there, or beer, or cocaine. They chain-smoked, tipping off the underpaid porters for the privilege.

One evening, I heard the following conversation drifting over from the video-booth area while I was giving a show.

"Is you serious, son—they got animal porn here?"

"They got *animal* porn, yo!"

It wasn't that I didn't find bestiality repulsive; I did. But if you started taking offense to one thing in the peep show, you'd soon find it was impossible to figure out where to draw the line.

It wasn't one big decision but a series of small ones. They all involved my allowing myself to look away. It was little things, like buying a better pair of heels, getting a push-up bra—the sort of things that hinted at some sort of long-term commitment. I stayed in the peep show because in there, I no longer had to think, and that sense of nihilism was perversely satisfying.

Another night, working by myself at three AM, I noticed that a customer had not left his booth after a show. I peered into the narrow money slot to see what was going on over on his side. An eye blinked back. The man's forehead was pressed against the partition. In lieu of paying for another show, he was trying to watch me get dressed through the slot. I drew my hand back and slammed it into the wall, banging it against his face.

The porter on duty shook his head incredulously. Most of Gotham's mop-up guys were either tough young men from the Bronx or Queens, or immigrants from West Africa, Sri Lanka, or Trinidad. "Man, you gotta be *raw* with these motherfuckers!" he said.

This attitude—this rawness—was fine for survival at work, but I had to be careful not to take it home. Not everyone in the world was trying to cheat me out of a couple dollars. Not everyone hung around porn stores at three AM.

There was a moment, after every show, after the light abruptly snapped off and the glass fogged to opacity, when I could suddenly see my reflection: naked and alone, untouchable, on display like a zoo animal, suspended behind glass.

> "Upon walking down the street, it would appear that many people are
> standing around. Some appear to be waiting, for someone or something,
> and to some extent, everyone is waiting in one way or the other."
>
> —Robert P. McNamara,
> *Sex, Scams, and Street Life: The Sociology of*
> *NYC's Times Square*

ZEN

"You never know when one of these niggas gonna turn out crazy and be waitin' after your shift with a baseball bat," Mimi announced one night in the middle of the graveyard shift. "That's why when I come to work, I come *protected.*"

Despite being as broke as the rest of us, Mimi sauntered in with a new weave every couple weeks. Today, it was wild caramel-colored curls. She wanted to be a model, and her work costumes were carefully styled, accented with oversized jewelry and professional-looking makeup.

Many of the other live girls appeared tired and old, in drooping lingerie and cheap, worn teddies. Mimi wore fishnets, studded black fetish heels, a lavender see-through slip with a matching butterfly thong, body glitter, half a dozen jeweled rings, and three shades of glittery eye shadow—mauve, deep purple, and gold—up to her eyebrows.

"Fuck Mace," she continued, popping her gum and scrolling through texts on her phone. "I make my own Mace. I got my own special potion. Wanna fuck with me? Nigga gonna be blind when I'm done with him."

Her "Mace" contained bleach, cayenne pepper, and Drano. She kept it in her backpack.

After only five or six days at Gotham, I learned that she was right to be paranoid. For example, a short time after I started, an elderly man died of a heart attack in a porn-viewing booth. Before his corpse was discovered by the store management, someone had already stolen his wallet. (I was out of town visiting my parents at the time and missed the excitement.)

I also worked with a girl who had been followed home by a disgruntled customer several years earlier. He had sliced her across the face in the vestibule of her building, leaving a long, jagged scar.

Her name was Sunshine. These days, her famous scar generated awe but not a lot of sympathy—not anymore. Management had paid for plastic surgery, so it was barely noticeable when covered by makeup. And with her long, blond hair and corn-fed looks, she made all the money, and it was pissing the rest of us off. Her costumes looked like the underdressings of a virgin bride: white thigh-high stockings and garter belt, white platform heels, white lacy lingerie, a white headband in her hair. She came up every few months from North Carolina, where she lived with her young son, and worked a straight week of double shifts.

To add to our annoyance, Sunshine stood up every time a customer came in, which violated the collective laziness we so carefully maintained. Everybody lolled in chairs, watching TV and bootlegged DVDs from the Port Authority. We were all on a level playing field without exerting ourselves unnecessarily for every drooling gawker.

But Sunshine jumped out of her chair every time a guy wandered into our area, composing herself by primly folding her hands in front of her and batting her eyelids. We all resented having to haul ourselves up out of a chair just to be given the once-over by some yahoo. I refused to stand, and eventually everyone else did, too.

In the fall of 2005, Gotham City Video 4 opened bright and clean as a whistle, touting itself as a modern porn superstore. The live girls had been destroying it from within ever since.

Even if daily life in the cleaned-up, post-Giuliani Times Square wasn't as dangerous as the live girls—deep into drug- and poverty-induced paranoia—thought, it still seemed like we were under constant threat of violence, either from ourselves or each other.

The sink in our bathroom was held up with a two-by-four. This was Juicy's fault; she had broken it on her first day of work by sitting on the sink while smoking a joint. Her second day, she announced that she was going to fuck Will. Fucking Will was a high priority among the live girls—a tall, handsome Puerto Rican floor-mopper with a gold chain, he was a total player, and everybody went giggly and flustered in his presence. It was thought that he was messing around with Kylie, however. A tough little redhead, she ran Juicy out with threats of physical violence; by the third day Juicy was gone.

Ruby broke the mirror in the bathroom soon after, on the phone angrily discussing man problems. "Fuck Rashid," she said, smacking the mirror with her hand for emphasis. "Fuck Abdul," she added, smacking it again. The mirror shattered, blood running down her hand.

The dressing-room door didn't close properly because of Lourdes. Hopped up on cocaine one night, she had had a fight with her girlfriend over the phone and ran out into the street in her underwear. She dented the dressing-room door on her way out, and woke up at her apartment in Queens the next afternoon, not sure how she'd gotten there. Everybody else had been on Ecstasy and booze that night. Mimi added muscle relaxers to the mix, leaving her drooling and staring at her cell phone in the dressing room, trying to figure out how to dial.

There were multiple alliances and grudges between the live girls, some dating back years, to incidents from various defunct peep shows—the Playground, Show Word, et cetera. Some of Gotham's girls had either been fired or banned from the Playpen peep show down the street, or couldn't get along with someone working there, so that place was simply not an option.

All of this, however—the bursts of self-immolation, or the customers and their vacillations between annoying, stupid, and dangerous—was simply exclamation points. Real life in the peep show consisted of waiting, sitting around for customers while slowly losing your mind.

Here's what mostly happened at Gotham: nothing. It was as quiet as a funeral home. The live girls and our live, nude shows were an added value to the store, but most days we were just a sideshow attraction, a magnet for a parade of slack-jawed yokels who had neither the means nor inclination to spend money—guys on public assistance or disability wandering Times Square with nowhere to be, or tourists, or professional pervs who made the peeps part of their daily rounds. Hours could go by between paying customers.

The experience was a meta-exercise in Zen. Patience was key but next to impossible for all but the career peep-show girls, the thoroughbreds. After the obligatory freezing-out period, a few of them started talking to me. Zima, a thirty-five-year-old career peep-show girl who had stage-named herself after a clear malt liquor, saw me grinding my teeth and crossing and uncrossing my legs and shaking my foot and said:

"Girl, you can't think about the money. Even though that's why we all here, you can't sit here stressing about money, because it'll drive you crazy, and nobody wants a show with a girl who looks all tweaked out. You'll get yours eventually. Don't worry about what everyone else make, don't worry about what Heidi make—you just do you. I'll tell you what, I'm gonna sit my ass up in here 'til I make the $400 I need by Friday."

With that, she sat back in her chair and rearranged her cleavage, looking determined.

The best way of thinking about work was not to think at all.

Our boredom was punctuated by a fortysomething black man in a baseball cap. He looked back and forth between us with the wide eyes of a sugared-up little boy in a candy store, his oversized striped T-shirt adding to his childlike look.

"Aw, you ladies look so lovely," he said. "Make my heart go pitter-patter. I ain't got no money for y'all, though."

I sighed. Zima crossed her arms and slouched in the other direction, staring at the wall. He turned to leave, then changed his mind and ran halfway back up the stairs.

"One more thing. My mama used to tell me to look for five things when lookin' at a woman: skin, hair, teeth, nails, and feet. And if she got busted-up feet, she certainly not gonna take care of you."

A pause. We waited for the kicker.

"Y'all look like you got some pretty nice feet." He flashed us a grin. "Bye!"

Around four, three young guys with crew cuts came in, pleasantly drunk and full of energy. They all took shows with me and Mimi. I asked them what they were up to that evening.

"Oh, man, we're partying," one of them said. "We're all being shipped off to Iraq next week." Suddenly, I snapped out of the idea of them as the enemy. They were kids, younger than us, and they were about to be shipped off to war. I didn't ask any more questions after that.

The Jeffersons came on TV at three every morning. Mimi and I slapped our hands against our legs, singing along with the theme song: "Mooo-oovin' on up!" We were rooting for the Jeffersons. We were slightly delirious.

The song ended, and I looked around at the empty store: the mirror ball, the mirrored walls, the booths, the video monitors, the endless, exhausting hustle.

Nora Ephron was right: My life would have been completely different if I had breasts. I had no problem with having A-cups, but I was convinced that the girls who had boobs made all the real money.

The Spanish girls and the black girls, on the other hand, complained that if a white girl was on a shift, *she* automatically got the majority of the shows. Dark-skinned black girls felt passed over for the light-skinned ones. I saw myself passed over more often by white guys wanting to look at someone more exotic, somebody unlike themselves, and also by Hispanic and black guys who preferred women with curves and an ass. To some men, being pale and skinny meant I was attractive. To others—especially the brothers—I just looked unhealthy.

Everybody was convinced everybody else made more money than they did.

My demographic—mostly because of my pale skin and dark hair—was Indian guys, Asians, weirdo older white men with strange interests, and Africans. Not black guys, but men *from* Africa, where whiteness was exotic and rare. And Mexicans, the many delivery boys of Times Square—they were all short and shy and they loved white girls, too. It got so that I could instantly racially profile a man's preferences within seconds of him wandering upstairs to the lineup.

If no one liked how we looked, we trudged back the next day, smoking and cursing in the dressing room, vowing to quit. But where would we go?

Somebody always had a getting-the-hell-out-of-this-business story; she was always back within a month or so. Massage school, professional domination, figure modeling, working security, waitressing, being a court typist—everybody tried something, and they always seemed to end up back at Gotham. So we sat up in the peep show, staring at the ceiling, buzzed off beer or weed, and waited for customers. There was a certain laziness that kept us there; it was a passive way to make a lot of money in a short amount of time. Usually.

Shit-talking and smart remarks were an art form honed during downtime. Girls wove personal narratives with a combination of ghetto fatalism and dizzying hope. I sat and listened to Green Eyes talk about how her husband learned to sharpen his nails to a point in prison so he could stab an opponent in the face with them, barely hurting the victim but leaving a lot of blood, and how he recently used this method to defend himself against a thug in front of everybody at their homeless shelter.

"Now they all have our back, and these mothafuckas is trying to sharpen they nails like his!" she said.

Green Eyes was thirty-two but looked younger. She was half Jewish and half Puerto Rican, "although I don't speak a word of Spanish."

She started out in the 33rd Street peep show called Empire. Her skin was clear and glowing, a side effect of being pregnant with her sixth child. Nobody was sure what happened to the other five kids, though we heard that she sometimes went to visit them; I think they were scattered among relatives.

She often sat with a well-thumbed Bible next to her. "Okay, you take care now, okay?" she called after customers whether they'd taken a show or not. "Godspeed, God bless you, okay?"

Every Saturday night, Vito, the de facto weekend manager, walked the 8th Avenue gauntlet, keeping his eye on Gotham and the Playpen, both managed by Vito's brother, Big John. Vito got into a lot of fights in the four short blocks between Gotham and the Playpen, anyone from "that redheaded homeless prostitute" to "faggots" he occasionally had to punch.

He strolled back and gave us all the once-over. Big John and Vito were both large and Italian, with flash-flood tempers aggravated by cocaine. Rumors of their mob connections were always at a low boil.

Vito was talking about his sixteen-year-old daughter again. "She was all dressed up to go to the prom the other night," he said. "I swear to God, if she wasn't my daughter—I'd fuck her." We all hated Vito.

Seeing an empty chair interrupted his monologue. "Where the hell is she?" he asked, pointing to Green Eye's chair.

"She had to leave; her curfew's at eleven," Ruby told him.

"Curfew? She in fuckin' high school?"

"She lives in a shelter," Ruby said pointedly.

"Oh," he said, uncharacteristically subdued. "I didn't know that." He put his hands in his jeans pockets and rocked back and forth on his heels, trying to think of something else to say before finally strolling away.

No matter how slow a night started out, I never knew what was going to happen. I could, for example, sit for five hours and forty-five minutes and make nothing until the last fifteen minutes, when, say, a cocaine-addled john might drop a few hundred dollars in my slot in a matter of minutes.

Around two forty-five one morning, a large, fortyish gentleman came in with his companion, a middle-aged Hispanic woman dressed conservatively and elaborately made up. He asked Ruby for a show and then asked me if I'd give a show to his lady friend.

Sure, we said. Whatever. Maybe that was what older couples did to spice things up, I thought. But when I saw him giving the woman two $50 bills—to pay me and also to pay her to watch me—I realized she was an escort and that they barely knew each other.

Once we were in the booths, the woman watched me dance patiently. She kept her hands clasped formally in front of her, as if she was in school and trying to pay attention to an important lesson even though she had no idea what was being said. She looked like a grandmother.

In the booth next to mine, where Ruby was, I could hear him talking: "Okay, hon, thanks a lot. Why don't you get your friend over here?"

Ruby knocked on my door, and I unlocked it.

"He wants us to switch," she said breathlessly. We knew to move quickly—we didn't want to lose that precious window of time where he thought giving us money was a good idea.

I quickly slipped into her booth, and she disappeared into mine. The man knocked on my window when I came in, putting $40 through my slot.

"Thanks," I said. He'd given a $10 tip.

He smiled slightly but was concentrating more on shaking cocaine out of a plastic bag and onto his clenched first, snorting one, two, three, four, five bumps in the span of a minute.

I began removing my bra, and he knocked on the window again, this time offering $50, no, $100, shoving the bills through the slot frantically.

"Thank you very much," I stammered.

A minute later, he knocked on the window again: "I have to go!" he said, jittery now. "My friend, she needs to leave! I have to respect her time, okay!" He exited my booth, and I could hear them both rushing out. The frenzy was over as quickly as it had begun.

After getting dressed, Ruby and I emerged from our adjoining booths at the same time, both holding a handful of bills. Even the security guard got tipped; he seemed a little shell-shocked.

We looked at each other.

"Okay," she said. "What the hell was that?"

But we knew what it was. Here was another situation similar to ours—a transaction playing itself between two people in yet another convoluted, unknowable way.

The E train was the sleep express weeknights after midnight. It came to the 50th Street station at twenty, forty, and on the hour. I had it timed.

I was usually the only female on the train. The rest of the after-midnight crowd was laborers and Latino men slumped over in their seats. There was also a track-worker contingent in orange MTA vests;

the train often stopped between stations in order to let the other crewmen on, burrowing up from whatever tunnels they were working in. Being the only woman on the train at this hour, I felt vulnerable. They were often deep into their sleep cycles, these men, but I was always wide awake.

THE BROOKLYN SLOVAK-AMERICAN
SOCIAL CLUB

I had a new apartment, a share steps away from the Nassau Avenue G stop, above a private social club for Brooklyn Slovak-Americans.

My room, for which I paid $725 a month, was eight feet by seven and accessed only from the hall. It was mostly taken up by my bed, which was pushed up against the third-floor window. Every night, I put the cash I'd made in my sock drawer and sat cross-legged on my bed, drinking a beer and watching the street below. For that moment, everything was quiet, the brief respite after the bars closed and before the buses started up again.

I was starting to worry that I didn't know anyone outside of the peep show. One night, I came home to find my roommate Jesse's bearded friend sitting at the kitchen table with a six-pack.

"I got this for you," he said, gesturing toward the beers and leaning back in the kitchen chair with a grin, one cowboy boot crossed over the other. His name was Scott; he'd just moved here from Texas and was sleeping on our couch while looking for an apartment. He was a writer, too. Of course, I wasn't really writing anything anymore; I was working the graveyard shifts in Times Square. But nobody knew that.

I was still recovering from work and wasn't sure what to do about this guy in my kitchen. I stared at him blankly, accepted the beer, then took it to my room and shut the door, drinking it on my bed while keeping an eye on the street.

Every day around ten or eleven, I woke to the sound of Jesse banging a glass pipe against a desk, shaking loose the resin so he could pack another bowl.

Usually I went back to sleep until twelve or one. I couldn't see the point of getting up, since there wasn't really much to do. I'd given up looking for real work.

It wasn't always like this. I'd never been a slacker before. But at least I had money—not a lot, but enough—folded up in my sock drawer, enough to keep me solvent as long as I watched every single dollar I spent and didn't eat too much.

Most of the time this seemed okay, except for when it didn't. Then, ennui mixed with despair washed over my brain, until I tilted toward the void, paralyzed by a feeling I couldn't name. It didn't occur to me to put a name to it. I just thought of it as *the void*.

In the afternoons, after I finally got up, I went to Peter Pan, an old-fashioned doughnut shop run by Greeks and staffed by stoic young Polish girls wearing short pink-and-green dresses, lined up in front of the colorful pastry display. The regulars were old men, neighborhood workingmen on their breaks, and a few shiftless hipsters like me, hunched over the white Formica countertops. I sat at the counter reading the paper while listening to the old-timers banter. Peter Pan was the bright spot in my day.

There was plenty of time to read. I figured out that *New York* and *The New Yorker* came out on Mondays and *The Observer* on Wednesdays, and then, of course, there was *The Post*, the paper of record for those who wanted their news presented in the most headline-screaming fashion. The girls at work favored *The Daily News*. As Jay McInerney wrote, "*The Daily News* is for working stiffs, *Newsday* is for bored housewives on Long Island, and *The Post* is for crazies."

I took my shower around four, bringing my boom box into the bathroom and listening to the same mix tape every day while standing under the streaming water. It had Marvin Gaye's "Inner City Blues" on it, and James Brown. By five-thirty I was on the train, headed back to Times Square, working against the rush-hour crowds.

For the first seven months of my career, I worked only at Gotham, where earnings were spread so thin I often had to work five nights a week just to scrape by. During the lucrative fall months, I was able to cut back to three shifts. No one knew why fall was good for money and summer wasn't, but there was a marked difference; my income almost doubled.

I'm still not sure what I did with all my free time. I must have done something. I worked on my 'zine, a little chapbook full of stories about living in Detroit that I called "Old Weird America." I spent a lot of time xeroxing, collating, stapling it together by hand, then recording the name of each bookstore, distro, or person who purchased copies in a notebook. Eventually I sold more than six hundred copies. For the second issue, I paid $250 in stripper money to a local illustrator, herself a former nude model, to design the cover. It was nominally about the peep show, but everything was too new to have any room for reflection.

In one week, two different customers asked me, as I was stripping behind glass, what my "future plan" was. They seemed more concerned about my career path than I was. "I'm working on it," I wanted to say. I just needed some time. I had to figure a few things out first.

Jesse, my roommate, was six foot four, blond, and striking, a photographer specializing in death metal bands and codeine-guzzling Texas rappers. A print of tattooed hands caressing a pit bull's face against a chain-link fence graced the hallway. In another photo, a black stripper spread on a stage in a hot-pink shirt and denim cutoffs, a dozen disembodied hands reaching toward her crotch, cell-phone cameras flashing.

He returned every afternoon from Bikram yoga soaked with sweat and usually shirtless. As a roommate I was too quiet for his taste, but he warmed to my company considerably after we smoked a joint together one night, and I confessed how I really spent my evenings.

"Whoa," he said, without exhaling, keeping the smoke in his lungs as long as possible.

"Do you ever think," he asked after exhaling loudly, "about documenting that? You should set up a secret camera in your booth. That could be—" he inhaled again, "—amazing." I hadn't, in fact, thought about documenting it. I didn't even write in my journal anymore. Documentation meant some sort of permanence, and I preferred to stay floating above it all.

Sunday nights, he came home from working at the coffee shop around twenty minutes after midnight. Frequently he'd bring a girl home, and I'd respectfully go down the street to the bar while they hooked up. It never took long; he usually called her a car the minute she came. I wondered where he found them; I usually didn't see the same one twice.

The Sunday nights he didn't have a date, he'd come home, shut the door to his room, and watch porn. For a creative soul, Jesse was a creature of habit, obsessive-compulsive and orderly. His days and nights followed a strict pattern. Bed by two, up by ten, smoke a bowl, do some work, yoga.

He never bothered to turn the sound down on his videos, and I could hear everything through the wall.

I listened to his breathing get faster and faster, sharp and high and ragged, until it broke and released, and he exhaled, and the TV went silent. I listened to his breaths become slow and relaxed, and it lulled me into drowsiness, until we both drifted into sleep.

One month passed like this, then another, then several.

DRINKING IN AMERICA

About forty miles outside Flint, there is a bar called Hoover's Corners, named after the intersection of four different counties, surrounded by fields and dirt roads. That Friday night, they'd set up a beer tent in the parking lot. A live band was playing Van Morrison, cover charge $2.

I was back in Michigan.

New York's boom-era bars had been trying to create this very atmosphere with faux-slumming-it dive themes, but they always failed. It was mostly a space issue. You needed lots of room for a beer tent, plus parking space for a couple Harleys with dogs panting in the sidecars.

I was visiting my parents for the first time since I moved. I felt weird and uncomfortable, because I couldn't tell them anything. I didn't have much of an explanation for how I spent most of my time in New York, or how I made a living. I assumed they were wondering why I hadn't been remotely successful. I told them I was working as a cocktail waitress. They were distracted by problems of their own.

My mom had had a heart attack when I was fifteen. I remember when it happened; she was coming up the back steps through the garage, telling me to hurry up so she could drive me to my piano lesson, and then she was suddenly telling me to call 911. I didn't know what was happening, and she didn't either—she was only forty-six. My father happened to walk in the door at that moment, and he drove her to the hospital, the same one my sister and I had been born at, half a block from our house.

My dad didn't tell me what had happened at first. "Your mother's having a little health problem," he said that night, and I had to eavesdrop over the phone to figure out what was going on. We were reserved people. We didn't talk about sex or medical catastrophes.

My mother sunk into a deep depression that summer and mostly stayed in her room reading her Bible. We'd always gone to church, but her brush with death gave her a new solace in religion. She recovered and went back to her law practice, but now, years later, it was my dad who wasn't doing so well. He had just retired from his job as a lawyer with the state Attorney General's office due to diabetes.

Still, Dad and I did what we usually did: loaded Mike, our red Irish terrier, into the truck and drove out to visit the farm. Dad was a gentleman farmer; it had been his hobby for years. I remembered how much everyone had made fun of him when he first purchased the land and the tractor and started reading agriculture magazines, but he'd ignored them. He loved everything that had to do with farming. When his health was good he planted feed corn and soybeans.

My friend Adam, who still lived at home with his mom, picked me up at my parents' house. Within minutes we were careening down a pitch-black dirt road and setting off industrial-grade fireworks.

He'd gotten them in Indiana at $1.80 a shell—a good price for this class of explosives, which were illegal in Michigan. We put the shells in the Rocket Launcher, lit the match, and backed up quickly. It sailed straight up with a bang before exploding into the night sky.

We were going to the country bar at Hoover's Corners. Adam didn't seem to feel my need to escape Michigan. He knew everyone's gossip and wanted to get into local politics.

Farmers in muddy boots and work jackets sat at the bar, entertaining themselves by calling the bar phone from their cell phones hidden under the counter, then hanging up amid peals of laughter every time the barmaid answered. She was in her late fifties, with a leathery face lined from smoking, bleached-blond hair, and heavy mascara. She was probably a stunner back in the day, but now her fingers were nicotine-stained and beginning to gnarl.

"Very funny, guys," she shouted. "I know what you're doing!"

"I think that's Tim Schwartz's mom," Adam whispered. "I can't believe she's still working here. Tim was always so embarrassed that she worked here.

I bought us two whiskey colas for eight bucks. We punched in three AC/DC songs on the jukebox, then sat down at a table and gazed at the wood-paneled walls, waiting for the drinks to work.

"I love being drunk," he said dreamily, the buzz setting in. "All the aches and pains in my body just go away . . . . Yeah, that's definitely Tim's mom.

"Betcha can't drink at a place like this in New York," he added.

"Hell, no," I said. "They've got some bar called Motor City and it's supposed to be like Detroit." I searched for a way to explain. "It's like a dive-bar-themed dive bar."

It was Adam's idea to leave Hoover's Corners with a bang. To pull the stunt off, we were going to have to abandon the Rocket Launcher. I pulled out of the parking lot and onto the road's shoulder, and Adam ran around in back of the car to set everything up.

He lit the fuse and jumped back in the car: "Go, go, go!" I made a hard left and drove off, looking over my shoulder to see the fireworks exploding in front of the beer tent, lighting up the sky. The drunks cheered and clapped as we drove away.

When I returned to New York a week later, a shift had occurred. The oppressiveness of the summer had fallen away, and everything was a little crisper, cooler; it was finally pleasant to be on the sidewalks again. Something also seemed to have changed with the people—on the streets now, they were no longer laconic but energized.

I went to a warehouse party in Bushwick with my friend Sharon, whom I knew from Lou's club. She was a librarian who danced for extra money. She had long, blond hair and introduced herself to men at the club by flinging herself into their laps and giggling.

A flimsy, silver, geodesic dome dubbed "The Moon" had been constructed on the roof of the warehouse. Partygoers crawled through a tunnel into a dark open space, full of people sitting closely, talking and smoking weed. It was impossible to sit without coming into contact with at least three other people.

"This," said Sharon, "is, like, so Burning Man."

A boy with a rockabilly haircut crawled toward us and smiled. He ran a hand up my leg and lay down with his head in Sharon's lap.

"Can I touch you?" he asked me, reaching for my hand. I let him. "Wow," he said, taking a drink from a can of beer. "Here I am, in New York City, and I'm on a roof, on the Moon, with two beautiful women."

"And we're both going to make out with you," said Sharon. Before I realized what was happening, we were taking turns kissing him, and then each other. I'd never kissed a girl before, but it wasn't strange. When I closed my eyes, it felt like kissing anybody else, but softer. It was almost, like, *political*, I thought. I was stoned. The boy who said he was from Kansas City watched us in a trance.

After a while, I extricated myself, removed my tongue from both of their mouths, and crawled outside the Moon tent onto the roof and back into the warehouse, feeling calmer somehow.

The next day, I figured out what felt so different: The light had changed. It was coming down in angles now, more fragile, filtering gently through the buildings and the trees.

A THOUSAND DOLLARS
IN A PAPER BAG

I ran into Ruby outside the drugstore in Greenpoint as I was leaving the Peter Pan Donut Shop. She was standing just outside the door, looking at me almost as if she'd been waiting there the entire time.

She looked even prettier in natural light, wearing clothes instead of just underwear and heels, the only things I ever saw her in. She was half Mexican, but the bane of Ruby's existence was that everybody thought she was Chinese.

I burst out laughing when I saw her, only because it was so strange to see somebody in the neighborhood from my double-life in Times Square.

"Just gettin' some groceries," she said, not laughing, swinging a plastic bag. There was an organic supermarket up the street. I smiled at her, and we both stood awkwardly for a moment.

"Yeah, well," she said a little too brusquely, not sure what else to say. "Bye now." I was eager to talk more with her, to become friends, but it wasn't going to happen at that moment. It was just too strange and uncomfortable for us to see each other in broad daylight, outside of the video store.

Ruby was nineteen when she first went to work in a porn store. It was on a dare. Back in Oregon, she had been into punk rock, yoga, and veganism. Although she performed in a local punk band, she was shy, and her friends thought it would be funny if she applied for a job at the local smut parlor. So she did and was soon working as a clerk.

Eventually, she joined the girls behind the glass. "I don't know where all the discipline came from," she told me, "but I used to get up at four o'clock every morning and just meditate and stuff, drink herbal tea, do yoga, and get on my bike and ride for an hour out to the peep show. I worked from eight in the morning 'til two in the afternoon."

"I was so healthy; I wasn't drinking like I do now, I was eating all raw food, all organic . . . and people could see it! They were just drawn to me. I . . . *glowed*. And I was super, super skinny then. I'd get back on my bike, ride all the way home, do some more yoga. I was living with somebody then, we were in a relationship . . . "

She moved to Seattle, although she didn't work in the two peep shows there because they took too much of a cut. She worked as a cocktail waitress instead.

She later moved to Minneapolis and got a job at Sex World, a huge, carnival-themed sex emporium that displayed their live-girl attractions in a terrarium-like setup called the Dollhouse. She started out as a clerk, a pony-tailed punk girl walking around jangling huge sets of keys and making popcorn, responsible for rousting the men masturbating in the aisles. "I was like, all right, Spanky, get out of here!" she recalled, laughing. "I don't know why they always sent me."

She came to New York around 2000, living on the Lower East Side at Avenue D before moving into a big house in South Williamsburg dubbed "the Seattle house," since most of its inhabitants were friends from the Pacific Northwest.

"The days of touching had just ended," she said, referring to the windowless peep-show experience that came and went throughout the years, ending for good around 2000. "And I'm glad, because I never would have worked here if things were still like that." A lot of girls said that, but they were full of shit, because they had worked there anyway. Ruby really wouldn't have. Like me, she had a Puritanical streak at odds with her vocation.

She worked at the now-defunct Playground, across the street from the Port Authority, and then the Playpen, and then Gotham, where I met her.

I sensed a certain heaviness about Ruby, a painful awareness of the world, which was what drew me to her. But Ruby's melancholy came from an entirely different place than mine: Her mother was murdered when she was ten. She was raised by her maternal grandmother. She never offered any further details, and I never asked. Times Square was not a place to constantly be asking *how?* Or *why?*

"Okay, what you wearin'?" Mimi asked me the following Monday night. I was working with her, Ruby, and a new girl. "A blond wig now, all right. But . . . makeup?" she eyed me suspiciously. She wanted to make sure everyone put as much time into looking good as she did.

"I'm wearing makeup!" I told her.

I looked at Ruby and we both started laughing. The new girl, sitting in the corner, looked confused.

"They crazy," Mimi told the new girl. "They be tippin' the bottle up in they booths. They think I don't know."

Ruby and I only laughed harder, tears running down our cheeks. We were drunk. We *had* been tipping the bottle up in our booths.

"Now, I can drink," Mimi continued. "Runs in my family. My grandfather, he named all his kids liquor names. They were all named after different liquors."

A middle-aged man with a beard walked in.

"I'm back!" he announced with great fanfare, looking at us expectantly. Ruby and I looked at each other blankly. Apparently we had hustled him earlier in the evening, but the alcohol, plus the fact that all the men looked the same to us, made us unable to remember him or his request.

"Remember, I was going to get a two-girl show?"

"Oh, right," Ruby replied, unenthusiastically. The man looked like he'd had the wind taken out of his sails, confused that we clearly didn't remember a conversation that took place less than two hours ago. We went into my booth—hers was too full of empty bottles—and when the light went on, stripped while being careful not to touch each other. I licked my fingertips and ran them over my nipples. She rubbed baby oil all over her body. He left four minutes later, looking vaguely dissatisfied.

Ruby had no idea what attracted me to her in the peeps: "I think maybe it's because I look a little like a bad girl, stoner, something." She had long, dark hair and dramatic half-Mexican, half-Caucasian features, with dark, almond-shaped eyes. She was thirty, but looked younger.

A full sleeve of tattoos—red and black flowers, and ornate Japanese designs—decorated each arm. She hid them under a long-sleeved button-down shirt that she kept on at all times, even during shows.

"Can you take off the shirt?" I sometimes heard men pleading from inside her booth. She only unbuttoned it.

"Mmm, no, can't do it."

She told me that she didn't want to show customers her tattoos because all the ink would turn them off, but I think it was because she wanted to keep some part of her body to herself, private.

Ruby was just as snotty, angry, and smart-alecky as me. The other girls didn't really drink like we did; they were stoners or cokeheads or took pills.

We ordered beers from the deli all night long, until one of us inevitably went on a short-lived pledge to "stop drinking" or at least to "stop drinking at work." I imbibed just enough for a buzz to make the hours pass quicker; Ruby could easily work her way through a six-pack during a shift.

She could be a volatile, maudlin, earnest, or angry drunk, depending on the night, and she recounted her latest episodes with bewildered amusement, as if they had happened to someone else.

She referred to them in shorthand: There was the Bagel Night, the Underwear Night, the Throwing of the Water Bottle, the Deli-Meat Night. Most of her acting out was reserved for her boyfriend Abdul, a Yemeni immigrant who owned a deli near Port Authority.

"He's the reason I quit the Playpen and came up here," she confessed one night when it was just the two of us working. "Because the Playpen is right across from his deli. I used to go in there every day and buy beer because I was so in love with him, until I found out he was Muslim, so I stopped buying beer. I told him that I quit the peep show. He thought it was dirty and terrible. Then I got so paranoid that he would see me, so tired of sneaking around. This one night I worked graveyard, and I was walking out of the Playpen at six in the morning, when I saw him coming up the street because he was on his way to the deli."

So that was why she kept so covered up outside of work, I thought. I always saw her walking in wearing long skirts, long-sleeved tops, hats covering her hair, sometimes even pants under her skirt.

"I actually took a pay cut to be here. But over there, it's like, doors opening and banging shut every five minutes, all these customers, and you have to really be aware or you just get the scraps, but the scraps are still way more than you make here."

When she was on a bender, Ruby terrorized Abdul—a kindly-looking bear of a man whom she affectionately described as a chubby Bin Laden—his deli, and its workers. The police had been summoned more than once. One night ended with her chucking a water bottle at his head ("It was only the small size of Poland Spring"), allegedly damaging the lotto machine in the process.

Maybe, just maybe, her anger had to do with the fact that he had a wife and six children back in Yemen. It had been an arranged marriage, when he was eighteen and his wife was fourteen. His wife was also his first cousin, so it wasn't exactly a love match. But still. Ruby tortured him by telling him that his wife was a lesbian, that she was fat, that all she did was sit around watching TV all day.

Abdul learned to ignore the outbursts, which infuriated her more and led to an escalation of tactics, like going to his Hell's Kitchen apartment in the middle of the night and leaning on the buzzer for half an hour, then going back to the deli to stick meat and cheese to the windows.

The first night Abdul called the police on Ruby was dubbed "the Underwear Night." Drunk and ready to fight, she rang his doorbell around 1 AM, which he answered to avoid further disturbance to his cousins, asleep after working the early shift at the store. He came to the door in his underwear and wordlessly walked outside, down the steps, and down 9th Avenue in his slippers. She followed him. He ignored her and kept walking, determinedly, all the way to his deli, where he called the police.

"What seems to be the problem here?" asked the cops, looking back and forth between Abdul, in his underwear, and Ruby, wild-haired and drunk.

"This one night at Playpen," she said in the middle of a long night of drinking in an empty store, "Raven convinced me to go out to a bar after work. I think we worked 'til midnight. Anyway, you know how I am at work—I party while I'm there, and by the time I leave I'm lit up like a Christmas tree.

"So we go down 8th Avenue to this bar, this dive bar, because we want to score some coke, and there are these old ladies, these Spanish *mamas* standing in the bathroom, selling coke. So we bought coke from them. And did you know that they also hustle? Yeah, I can't believe it, but they also make money, like, fucking younger men—I don't know how, but they do. Anyway, we met this guy, this black guy. He seemed gay. He sold us some weed. So, you know, I've been drinking, I'm smoking pot, we've done a little coke, and he wants us to go back to his place. I'm all, no way, but Raven is pulling me aside, and she's telling me—well, anyway, all I hear is, '$300 for the each of us, and all you have to do is watch.'

"At the time, I was planning a visit to the West Coast and taking some time off from work, so I needed money more than usual. So we go back to his place in Chelsea—I still think he's gay—and we're, like, picking out porn to watch, and doing more drugs. And I am so high, and Raven, well—she did it! She sucked his dick, and I was off to the side, watching or whatever . . . oh, shit."

A customer came back and poked his head through the plastic chain-curtains, peering at us.

"What?" I snapped. He disappeared.

"So then I leave and grab a cab," she continued. "The cabdriver—you know how I like foreign guys—he's kind of cute, and I get in the front seat. I'm riding *shotgun*. Oh, God, and I'm asking him stuff like, 'Heyyyyy—where are you from? How old are you? What's up?' I think I was scaring him.

"I woke up at home the next day and I was still wearing my boots, and my coat was still on, my contacts were dried up and stuck to my eyeballs. I'm remembering bits and pieces of the last night and trying to figure out if it was all a dream.

"So I stuck my hand in my right pocket and . . . oh, no! I pulled out a bag of coke. Then I stuck my hand in my left pocket and, oh, no, I pulled out $300. Not even in my wallet, in my coat pocket.

"I didn't go into work for a long time after that. I really needed to think about things."

"Damn!" Ruby said one night in December, crouched next to the TV, flipping through the schedule book. "I wanted somebody to go to Karaoke Killed the Cat with me, but I see you're booked for Monday night."

"No, I'll just cross my name off," I said, excited by the idea of doing something outside of work. "I want to go."

The following Monday I waited for her to call, idly wondering if she'd ask for Chelsea or for Sheila. What were the rules?

She asked for me, not Chelsea, and I was glad. Ruby's real name was Rubi. She always made sure to write her name with a "y" in the schedule book to differentiate. Ruby was a stripper who worked in Times Square; Rubi was not.

I headed over to her house, the first time I'd spent with anyone from Times Square outside of work. She lived just down the street from me, behind a door covered with punk band stickers, with an assortment much like my friends from back home in Michigan: a motley but lovable collection of slacker guys, smart and creative but with an undercurrent of white-trash roots and general shiftlessness.

"Dude," muttered a tall, skinny guy with messy brown hair, wandering into the living room at 10 PM, having just woken up from a nap. "What day is it? Shit, is Rob bartending tonight?"

I sat on the couch and looked at the decor: a giant Britney Spears tapestry hung above the TV, underneath a decorative string of empty Pabst cans.

We were going to visit a karaoke night at a Lower East Side bar, where a boy she had been pining over presided every Monday eve. Cheating on Abdul wasn't the goal; she only wanted to drink and flirt a bit.

"Have a beer," she said, offering me a Corona.

As we headed toward the train, I noticed she didn't know the route of the B61 bus, which stopped half a block from her house. Except for work and visiting Abdul, it didn't seem like she left her room or her neighborhood very often.

"I don't go out much," she confessed. "This is a big thing for me."

She often walked home from work: down 8th Avenue to 14th Street, and then all the way over to 1st Avenue, where she conceded to the L train, only because it was too dangerous to walk over the Williamsburg Bridge at night.

We bought bottles of beer to drink out of paper bags for the subway ride, and spent the walk to Piano's continuing to drink, ducking into another deli to buy more beers.

At the bar, we hung back on a couch on the second floor. Snow was falling past the windows. It was Christmastime, dark and cold outside, and it felt like we were lost in New York together. An inebriated Mexican man plopped between us and kissed us on the cheeks.

"Two beautiful women," he slurred. "I want to sit with two beautiful women." We pushed him away, and security gently dragged his limp body down the stairs.

Around 3 AM, the karaoke really got going. Ruby found the boy, a husky Jewish hip-hop head whose gold tooth flashed under the lights. We took to the dance floor. She jumped up on a coffee table, six beers having shaken loose all self-consciousness. The last thing I saw as I spun around was Ruby falling sideways, like a felled tree, off the coffee table and onto a couch full of people, her body still straight. They caught her and propped her back up. Unruffled, she resumed dancing on the floor.

The next evening at 6:30, Ruby rushed in, late for her shift. "Oh, good!" she exclaimed upon seeing me. "Thank God you're here. I wanted to apologize. I'm so sorry about last night."

"About what last night?"

"About what I . . . *did*. What I *said*."

I mentally flipped through the postcards of the previous evening: our stumbling walk through the Lower East Side to the J train, a subway ride I didn't remember, walking back to her house in Williamsburg before continuing twenty minutes to my place in Greenpoint, waking up around two in the afternoon . . .

"But you didn't do anything, I don't think. We just got drunk and took the J back to Brooklyn."

"Really? Oh, good! Okay! Man, I was with you up until, say, midnight, but after that, I'm not sure what I did. I found a bunch of angry texts to Abdul that I sent while I was in the bathroom and then I was like, oh, no, I wonder what I did. I wonder what I *said* . . . "

A few months later she broke up with Abdul.

Due to interest on some investments—I could never figure out what the "investments" were, Ruby was vague about it—Abdul had about $4,000 that he needed to give away. Something about Muslims not being allowed to charge interest. He earmarked some for his family, some to a respected Muslim teacher back in Yemen. He promised $1,000 of the money to her when they were together, saying she could use it to go to Minneapolis to visit her younger brother, or for whatever she wanted. She refused it, but post-breakup, reconsidered and decided to extort it through a series of phone calls, threatening texts, and deli appearances.

Finally, he told her she could pick up the money from Manuel, one of his night-shift workers. She met Manuel inside the bodega around midnight, and he told her to meet him around back. She went outside, around the corner, and down the alley. The $1,000 was in cash, and Manuel had stuffed it into a small, brown paper sack, which he hurriedly thrust into her hands.

"Not even hundreds," she recounted in disbelief over the phone. "Like, twenties and tens."

"Here it is! Be careful! Go straight home!" he urged. He liked her, despite the havoc she'd wreaked on the deli. She got back on the subway with her $1,000 and rode back to Brooklyn.

"Loneliness has followed me my whole life, everywhere. In bars, in cars, sidewalks, stores, everywhere . . . "

—Travis Bickle

PROOF I EXIST

I'd responded to yet another job ad, this one for a photographer's model. "Must be comfortable with nudity," it read. No problem.

I wanted to be photographed because I needed proof that I was here, even though nobody knew it. I seemed to exist only at night, in Times Square, alongside girls who didn't know my real name, or use their own, and came to work disguised in scarves and sunglasses.

Having an alias wasn't new to me. I'd been obsessed with name-changing since I was a little girl. When I was in third grade I wanted to be called "Claudia." When I went to camp one year when I was twelve, I told everyone my name was Cecelia. Everyone called me by that name all summer, and I was amazed that they didn't know I was just pretending.

It was a childish way of thinking that if my name changed, my per-sonality—and its defects—would magically change along with it. They never did, but I kept on doing it. I was doing it now.

At least having a different name made it easier to dissociate and separate the areas of my life. Girls had their stage names and their real names. Customers always wanted to know what your "real" name was.

They wanted to own that part of you, too. So girls also had fake real names, or they'd pretend that their stage name *was* their real name, which was what I did.

"I don't have a stage name," I'd say. "This is my real name."

"Then what's your last name?" they'd ask.

There were so many layers, like a Russian nesting doll. It drove the men crazy that they'd never get to the bottom of it.

Sometimes I worried that between this name-changing and moonlighting, whatever was at the center of my personality might disappear, and there'd be nothing left.

Ivan the photographer lived in a tenement building on Essex Street. His photos were moody nightlife portraits of drag queens and pin-eyed waifs in compromising positions, his Manhattan an endless party, decadent and sexually tense, the city I envisioned before moving here. They maintained the fantasy, at least.

I rang buzzer six while balancing a suitcase full of men's clothes, heels, stockings, and underwear. The winter light was hard and bright. Ice crunched as I shifted my feet back and forth. After a moment a very tall, boyishly handsome Russian with ruffled dark hair and a goofy smile came to the door. He carried the suitcase up the staircase. Dim, yellowed fluorescent light buzzed over the blue tile in the hallway. Ivan's apartment was cluttered yet mostly empty. A flyer reading CHINATOWN YMCA POOL SCHEDULE was stuck to the fridge.

Ivan stood about six foot five. He'd been in New York for seven years, he said. It seemed like he knew everybody, or at least he dropped names like he did. He took a long moment to assess me, looking over what he had to work with today.

Ivan took out a thick envelope stuffed full of money: $3,000 in $50 bills to use as props. "It's payday, and they pay me under the table, so . . . " He shrugged. The last several months conditioned in me a Pavlovian excitement in the presence of large amounts of cash, and I stared at it.

"I want to do a story that kind of takes off on your job. You know, stripper comes home, counts out her money, rolls around in it."

"I come home and count my money and put it in my sock drawer," I told him. He laughed.

The bedroom-studio was empty save for a platform bed. He stripped off the sheets and blankets until it was just bare walls and a naked mattress. Handing over a chunk of fifties, we scattered them over the bed, money fluttering onto the floor.

I undressed matter-of-factly and sat down on the edge of the bed, unsure of what to do. He positioned me by reaching over with his foot and slowly pushing my right foot across the floor, then started shooting, bending and crouching and contorting himself. He stopped a few times to sit down on the edge of the bed, holding his head in his hands. "Low blood pressure," he said.

He clicked away, each shutter release sounding like a mini explosion with the pop of the lighting umbrellas. He'd broken a sweat and was panting slightly, making breathy little noises. He paused every so often to look through the images on the camera, smiling to himself. His voice sounded very far away.

"I mean, I'll admit it," I heard him saying. "I've done the whole thing where, you know, I'll seduce a model. You know? But I'm over that. I'm a professional now."

I had already floated away inside my head, detaching my mind from my body. Nearly three hours passed before we were done.

"Stay where you are, though," he said suddenly. "Get down on your hands and knees." His tone of voice had changed.

The tension in the air was palpable, as real as the soot on the windowsills and the biting cold outside. I did what he said. I wanted to be seduced by Ivan, even though he said he didn't do that anymore, that he was a professional.

I sensed him behind me and felt his breath on my back. Half a second later, there was a rush of air and a hand coming down on my backside, startling me into submission. He smacked me again, then checked in: "You want more?"

"Yes." He did it again, and again.

No one had ever done anything like this to me before, but at that moment, it made sense. It was almost like I'd been waiting for it. The pain wasn't pain, it was warmth. It didn't hurt. It didn't feel like it hurt. It made me feel like I was fully present, after shutting down and checking out so often for the past few months. I was like a broken light switch: After being flipped on and off too many times, I could no longer turn back on without a massive jolt.

"More?" he asked. I said yes until I couldn't take any more.

I collapsed on the bed. Lying facedown, panting, I felt euphoric and woozy. I could hear him packing up his lenses and lighting equipment. I wordlessly gathered up my clothes and put them back into the suitcase.

We stood and faced each other. Ivan was wound up now, talking fast.

"I've been shooting this one girl?" he said. "And every time I shoot her, it never really works between us. She just gives me all these cheesy poses. It's bad. I was going to quit shooting her. Then one night, she puts her hand in her mouth. Not just in her mouth, I mean she puts her hand all the way down her throat. I mean, this girl could deep-throat a—well, you know. She put it so far into her mouth that I swear to God I could see her fingers wiggling around on the outside of her neck.

"So when she took it out, I put my fingers in her mouth, too. My hand—practically half my arm—slid down her throat, like, so easily. I wiggled my fingers around and they were so far down her throat I could feel phlegm. I was like, *fuck you*. Is this how far I have to go to make you give me something? I mean, is this what it takes?"

He took my suitcase, carrying it back down the stairs and walking me to Delancey Street. He kissed me on the cheek. I headed for the subway but took a wrong turn. I knew where I was, but high on endorphins, I couldn't seem to locate the subway entrance no matter how many turns I made. I spent the rest of the evening in a daze, wandering lost around the Lower East Side.

HOW TO LAUNDER MONEY

We were all so sick of Vicki. Sitting up on her stool in her fake blond wig, her pointy nose making her look like a witch, her pasty skin powdered white like a prostitute in a Toulouse-Lautrec painting, her lips painted in bright-red lipstick, she made all the money. Cellulite winked out from her cheap black-lace ensembles, which looked like they were scavenged from a Salvation Army underwear bin.

No one could figure out why she was so popular, until we found the tooth.

Vicki was quiet and mysterious. She never chatted or shared any personal information, thoughts, or feelings. I knew that she was thirty-five, had a one-bedroom apartment on the outskirts of Greenpoint for which she paid $1,000 a month, and had maybe lived in Philadelphia before because she mentioned it a few times. She mostly read a lot—occult-type books, paperbacks, sometimes books I couldn't identify because she'd taken the jacket cover off.

The only time she wasn't quiet was when a guy came in. Then she'd sit up straighter in her chair, arrange her cleavage, and perk up with a nauseating, "Hi, sweetie!"

And they picked her again and again, despite—or maybe because of—the tranny makeup, the wig, or the polyester-blend satin.

Ruby and I sat across from her, looking short and insignificant because Vicki was perched on the high stool she had dragged out of her booth.

A short Mexican man in jeans and a ball cap wandered in tentatively and gaped at Vicki's blond wig. Ruby cut her eyes toward me.

"Hi, sweetie!" Vicki chirped. "Want a show?"

"Can I touch?" he asked. It was always the Mexicans who would ask about touching. Mexicans and foreigners.

With a grunt of disgust Ruby got up, stomped inside her booth, and slammed the door. She knew what Vicki was going to say and couldn't take it anymore.

"I can't, sweetie!" Vicki sang out cheerfully, smiling and batting her false eyelashes at him. "It's not me, it's the law! Otherwise I'd love to, I really would!"

We, of course, would *not* love to and hated it when she told them this. These guys seemed to think that, if only for the pesky rules, we would be all too willing to crowd into a tiny booth with them and let them paw us with their dirty hands. Vicki had made it her mission to perpetuate this myth.

The thing about touching was that these men were not completely crazy to ask. Right up until 2000, in most of the New York City peep shows the windows actually went up and touching was permitted.

The Mexican man just stood there, blinking. "But I want to touch," he whined.

"*What about what I want?*" I wanted to scream. I got so worked up every time. These guys wanted everything they could take from us, and they didn't care how we felt about it.

"It's a good show, sweetie," said Vicki. "Come on." She stood up and ushered him into her booth. She never told customers to "pick a girl," which was the unspoken rule. You had to give them a choice; you couldn't scoop up a customer just because you talked to him first. Saying "pick a girl" was playing fair.

She and I both worked the six-to-twelve shift. Some nights I just sat there burning holes in the crown of her head with my eyes as she bent over a book. Many shifts it was just the two of us. We sat in silence—Vicki never spoke to me; it was as if she was above the pleasantries and shit-talking that made the night go by faster. Guys came in, one after the other, and chose her for shows with nary a glance in my direction. One night, she'd done about ten shows in five hours, while I hadn't done anything at all. After that, I changed my schedule so it didn't overlap with hers.

Not only did Vicki ruin the weekday six-to-midnight shift for me, but she was single-handedly destroying the earnings of the rest of the night shift. Guys were even choosing her over Ruby, who stormed out of work in a huff one night after one too many rejections.

"I think it's a degradation thing," said Ruby when she returned the next day. Vicki rarely worked Fridays. "For some kind of guys, if they have the choice between someone young and healthy-looking, or someone old who looks like trailer trash, well. . . . It must make them feel better about themselves or something."

Vicki was actually beautiful when she wasn't under full Halloween makeup and that cursed wig. She had long, lovely red hair and a Rubenesque figure. But even in her natural state, there was something off about her that I was never able to place.

In her mid-thirties, she seemed to be all alone in the city, living day-to-day like the rest of us and scratching out a living in cash at the peep show. That wasn't how it was supposed to go. This was all supposed to be temporary. Wasn't it?

Ruby found the tooth above her locker, a large human molar with a filling still in it. While there were Haitians and Dominicans at Gotham who were into santeria, this stunt had Vicki written all over it. We'd both seen the books she'd been reading.

At home, I looked up hexes-by-tooth online. Human teeth were used in voodoo rituals for "justified revenge," or to get back at an enemy.

"I don't want to scare you, but I think we should get rid of it," I reported back.

Whether or not we really believed in hexes, the tooth served a purpose in spooking the hell out of us. Vicki had the place cursed in her favor.

But maybe there was something to it. Once we got rid of the tooth, the men suddenly lost interest in her. Outraged, she sat in her chair and banged her head against the wall as they passed her over. She lost her cool: snapping at customers, glowering if they chose another girl, storming into her booth and slamming the door. Sometimes—to my delight—men would ask her for a show and then change their minds after she stood up.

After about two months like this, she stopped showing up. She moved over to the Playpen but couldn't hack it there either—the bad luck followed her. Eventually, she disappeared from the avenue altogether.

"That's what happens when you use magic to help yourself at the expense of someone else," said Ruby with satisfaction, sitting in her chair, rubbing baby oil up and down her legs.

Even without amateur voodoo, Gotham operated under a low fluorescent hum of hysteria. In close quarters, our moods affected each other and spread like a virus.

I was paranoid about a host of things. Every day there was something new to worry about. Germs was one of them. I became convinced it was possible to pick up an STD from the place, even though I came in contact with no one. We all covered the chairs we sat on with our own bandana or towel for hygienic purposes. But was that enough? And didn't I kind of . . . *deserve* to catch something working here?

Zima had an elaborate routine of cleaning and wiping down her booth, the seat, the walls, and the window before starting her shift. I never felt compelled to obsessively clean my booth. The dirt and psychic residue could never be completely scrubbed off.

My anxiety first manifested itself with the physical handling of money. Who knew where the customers had been before they wandered into this porn store? And if they bought a second or third show from us, it meant they would take a pause from masturbating to put our extra money through the slot, which meant they touched themselves, touched their money, gave *us* the money, and then we touched ourselves as part of the show. Think about it. I did. I let the money fall through the slot and onto the floor.

I rushed to the bathroom and scrubbed my hands after every show. Every time somebody handed me a bill I cleaned my hands with two baby wipes. You could get a communicable disease from bills, right? Couldn't you?

So I began cleaning my money. I'd spread out all of the bills on the floor of my booth, spray them with disinfectant, and do my shows in another booth while they dried. Then I flipped them over and sprayed them again. After they dried, slightly yellowed and brittle from the chemicals, they were sterile enough to put in my wallet. I didn't see this behavior as unusual at the time. In the context of the environment, it made perfect sense.

If I was this crazy after six months, no wonder the girls who had drifted in and out for years were unhinged.

Like Kylie, whose strawberry-blond bangs and freckles made her look eighteen, which was the age she was when she first started working in the peep shows. She was thirty now.

Kylie was white, but she talked like a black 8th Avenue hustler. She also spoke Spanish, a skill left over from a Puerto Rican ex-boyfriend. I loved to listen to her talk; the profanities and bravado and pain just flowed right out of her.

She had danced pregnant when she and Ruby worked at the Playground. The show went on until she was so big she could barely wobble around on her heels. Later she suffered a miscarriage. Of course it probably wasn't from the dancing, but when Ruby mentioned it in a hushed whisper, I could tell we were both thinking the same thing: Maybe it *was* from the dancing. Maybe what we were doing here really was that wrong.

She reappeared in the peeps years later, when I was there, after an abusive ex-boyfriend started stalking her. She'd been working as a diner waitress, but he knew all the places she worked and had taken to showing up during her shifts. Another time, he had followed her home from work and attacked her, but she fought him off. There was a certain amount of protection in coming back to the peep show; he wouldn't know to look for her here.

She pimp-rolled into Gotham one day as if no time had passed.

"I tried going back to Lace," she said of the strip club three blocks down. "But they said I had to lose some weight first." Kylie was petite with healthy thighs, a nice ass, and a tiny waist. Guys loved her kind of body, but the strip club managers didn't. To them, it was all about the scrawny 110-pound Russians with implants.

Tonight, however, she was sitting in the dressing room, mid-panic attack, counting out her life's savings on the counter. It came to about $300—about $300 more than I had saved up, I noted.

"Shit," she said, frantically rifling through the bills. "I'm thirty years old, my mama is dying of cancer, *and I only have $300 if something happens to me.*"

Standing over her and her money, I tried to say something comforting, but she just continued talking to herself in the mirror, as if no one else was there. I headed out to the floor before another one of my itching fits started in sympathetic reaction to her distress. I glanced at myself in the mirror on the door; the circles under my eyes were getting darker.

The itching: It only happened at work. I'd suddenly start scratching myself frantically, hives climbing up my arms or stomach. Occasionally it got so bad that I actually left, and it always subsided soon after I got home. I never knew if the episodes were a psychosomatic reaction to the claustrophobic space, or an actual allergic reaction from the bleach, or the cleaning agents, or just . . . everything.

We all felt penned up in the back room, which only added to our angst. The setup was dangerous—our little area was in the rear of the store, so there was no way to escape if something happened.

"They could come back here shooting," Midnight said in her gravelly voice. "You've never thought about that? I *always* think about that."

Midnight was bizarre even by peep-show standards. A black woman around forty-five years old, she had been a model and occasional actress in her prime, plus she'd worked at the high-end strip club Scores. Her history in the peeps went back to the Show World days. Now, she worked at Gotham and occasionally appeared as the freak-show entertainment on talk shows. She'd been on a "Man or Woman?" segment of *Maury Povich* once. Ruby had texted me while watching a rerun. ("Seventy-five percent of the audience just screamed 'Man!'" she wrote.)

She did sort of look like she could have been a man, but it didn't seem to bother Midnight in the slightest. She was just focused on making money, and the only way she'd ever made it had been off herself—her looks, her body, her willingness to take her clothes off, or be ridiculed on *Maury Povich*. She had the same quality of so many long-term peep-show thoroughbreds that scared me: gutted, only the flesh remaining.

Midnight was fucking nuts, but she had a point. Everybody worried when they were working alone at night about some guy shoving them into their own booth and raping them. It had never happened, but it *could* happen. Anything could happen. Sometimes large groups of men would come in drunk and stand so close to us that I would instinctively start backing into my booth. The porters, who doubled as security, were never really around when we needed them. I shoved a guy backward more than once. They always seemed so surprised that I reacted that way, that their advances were unwanted.

The store had to be cleaned constantly. The scent of bleach permeated everything.

They cleaned up cum and sometimes urine out of every peepshow and video booth with the same mop and then plunged it back into a yellow industrial bucket, a gray soup of bleach and Pine-Sol. After a show, the porters would mop the guy's side of our booth and then spray it liberally with a surface cleaner.

And the booth windows. Sometimes they would have to clean the windows. There was no getting around it: Guys would cum on the glass. It was disgusting. It was like working in a hospital.

The fumes filled our small space until we choked on it. "I can't breathe!" said Ruby.

"Could you please not spray the booths?" I asked Basil, the night porter, my eyes stinging. He shook his head. This was part of the porters' job, and since half of them were working illegally, they couldn't afford to lose it.

"This place is *bad* for me!" Ruby said, as she always did whenever we got worked up over the chemical fumes. Her eyes flashed and she swiveled her head back and forth. "We're breathing in these chemicals, these . . . *toxins!*"

As if on cue, Angel, another porter, ambled back to clean the floor, mindlessly swishing the mop back and forth. He flung the mop against a wall with particular vigor, and a droplet of filthy water flew through the air. We picked our feet up off the ground, practically jumping on top of our chairs.

"Angel!" Ruby snapped.

"Yo," Angel said, pointing toward the filthy bucket of mop-water. "Don't worry. There's so much bleach in this motherfucker, it kills everything it touches. There's no way anything could survive."

This fear of the mop went back decades. With lots of free time to read during my shifts, I'd become a scholar on the history of Times Square. One of the best books about its sleaze heyday of the '70s and '80s was Joshua Alan Friedman's *Tales of Times Square*. He'd interviewed a peep girl working in 1986 who had the same problem:

> Oxuzana Brown, four-year veteran of Show World, always claims she's going to leave her post at Times Square's biggest sex circus and head for Europe. She plans to live there a long while, but can't seem to get going. This big-bosomed Harlem child, of "French and Nigerian background," who still possesses a soft glow in her face, is ready to retire.

> "My biggest fear about Show World are the mops. You got AIDS, herpes, gonorrhea, and syph out there—and guys come and come and come. There's not enough detergent in the world for me. I'm terrified to get touched by a floor mop. They skeeve me out. You can't rinse them enough."

Her words made me feel less alone. I wasn't crazy. The *peep show* made me crazy.

MENTAL HYGIENE

I'd been drinking more and more: at work, after work, to fall asleep . . . . I just needed to take the edge off, but the problem was, the edge kept getting sharper and sharper. I imagined filling out an AA questionnaire: "Do you drink alcohol at work?" *"How the hell am I supposed to get through work without it"* would have been my response. Ruby relied on it, too. The rest of the live girls smoked pot incessantly; weed is the coffee of the stripping industry. This crude all-purpose remedy usually worked well enough. Sometimes, however, not even alcohol could dull the overwhelming feelings of dread. One evening in the fall, they had snowballed to the point where I felt like I was suffocating. Everything appeared to be in a fog, and the ground felt as if it was rolling under my feet. My throat was tight, and I felt myself dissociating, floating above my body, watching scenes from my tiny, invisible life from above.

This was worse than the void: I could see reality bending, opening itself to interpretation. I had been like this for the last three days now. I hadn't slept, and booze had long since stopped working. I needed a Xanax—I needed a couple dozen Xanax, or heavy-duty tranquilizers. I showed up to the Bellevue emergency room around 11 PM, shivering.

Filling out the paperwork with shaking hands—Bellevue had its own program for the uninsured—I realized that having no verifiable income made me look even poorer than I actually was. It wasn't just me, of course. I was now part of the underclass, the invisible sub-economy of people working off the books: the busboys, the waiters, the bicycle deliverymen, the illegals, the Chinese storefront masseuses, the hustlers, the bouncers, the bottle girls and coat-check girls in nightclubs, the nannies—and yes, the strippers. I wrote "unemployed" on the intake form when it asked for my occupation.

The waiting room was in the middle of a nonstop production of theater of the absurd. It was crawling with police because so many of the patients were in custody. Two cops escorted an emaciated black man to the bathroom, uncuffed him, and waited outside the door.

People screamed at each other in a medley of languages. A guy started a shoving match with a male nurse and was subdued by force. A huge Dominican woman stood up and announced that someone had stolen her cell phone. Children shrieked. Scared-looking Mexican men sat quietly, staring down at their hands.

Although it could easily induce a total break in reality for paranoid schizophrenics, something about the place's hellishness provided cold comfort. It was so bad here that at least people couldn't fake cheerfulness or pretend that everything was okay.

Bellevue's loony bin was named the Mental Hygiene Clinic, as if patients were just coming here to get clean, to hose down their brains. It made sense, given my current obsession with hygiene.

I thought back to my childhood home and its proximity to the local locked mental facility, which was connected to the hospital. Patients escaped from it on a regular basis, and since they were on foot, our street was often the first place they went. One day when I was playing next door with my cousins, a man in a hospital gown and a colostomy bag still taped to his leg burst into the garage.

"I need to use the phone!" he said, a piercing yet faraway look in his eyes. "*I just need to use the phone!*" That was a good one. We loved the drama and talked about that episode for weeks.

Then there was the time a patient threw a chair through a window and jumped out. He was eventually found wandering the neighborhood covered in blood. Unfortunately none of us kids were there to witness the spectacle, but the story became neighborhood lore.

Mental illness ran in my family, and I'd inherited the depression/anxiety/obsessive-compulsive trifecta that my mother and grandmother had struggled with.

After two hours, they called my name. The doctor was a young man probably not that much older than I was. I was suddenly embarrassed to be there.

"I'm having a lot of anxiety," I mumbled. "Like, kinda freaking out."

"Okaaaaay," he said, letting silence hang in the air, trying to draw me out so he could figure out just what type of crazy I was—a garden-variety unmedicated neurotic or "the tinfoil on my radio keeps the government from spying on me" type.

"I haven't been able to sleep in a few days. At all. Also, I'm kind of a hypochondriac. I don't know what it is, but there's something seriously wrong with me. I think maybe I have cancer."

"Can you tell me what this is?" he asked, holding up a pen.

"A pen?" Was this a trick?

"Good. What's the similarity between a tiger and a mosquito?"

"Uh, they're both animals?"

"Good!" he said with a beaming smile, scribbling something on my chart.

The reality tests over, a nurse handed me two Xanax and a paper Dixie cup of water. The doctor handed me a prescription for antidepressants. The scrip sat on my bookshelf for months until the next episode occurred and I started to think that filling it might be a good idea. I never bothered.

I couldn't imagine that they would help any more than my previous rounds with mood stabilizers had. I'd had more than my share, starting in my senior year of high school—first, there was Effexor; then Pamelor, which made my heart race; and then the two-week hell that was Zoloft during my freshman year of college. Then Luvox—that was a pretty good one, actually, why had I stopped taking it?—Lexapro, desipramine (for anxiety), Trazadone (for insomnia), and finally Paxil, back in Detroit, during the halcyon days of health insurance. Their effects had all been minimal.

I'd always been morbidly entranced by the idea of an old-fashioned sanitarium, a place where people went when things just got to be too much for them. A time-out period, a break. I was beginning to suspect that the peep show was my own self-prescribed version of the rubber cell and that Times Square was serving as a waiting room between me and the rest of the world, when and if I was ready to deal with it.

SURVEILLANCE

Somewhere in New Jersey, a thin, gray-haired man sat in his house before several TV screens, watching surveillance video, in real time, of nearly all the peep shows left in Manhattan.

Big Sammy owned everything—porn stores up and down the avenue and around the country. He also supposedly owned the company that manufactured peep-show booths, ShoTech, so any store with that kind of setup had to go through him. The peeping business had made him a good deal of money.

The rumor was that he kept a former live girl named Sofia as a mistress. Camry, a lesbian Dominican girl whom I worked days with on Saturdays, told me all about it. Camry was easy to work with. She said it was because we were both Aquariuses; I thought it was because we both enjoyed just sitting quietly, drinking beer.

Big John, Sammy's number-two guy, also surveilled us from his New Jersey home. The two of them regularly screened footage from cameras at the other stores, including those placed throughout the Playpen and Gotham.

John and Sammy were mysterious figures. Nobody was certain of either one's last name. "I'm not sure he has a last name," Ruby said once when I asked about Big John.

There were a million angles for the staff to work, so constant vigilance was required. They had to keep an eye on the cashiers to make sure they weren't pocketing change—or porn—and they had to keep an eye on us girls to make sure we weren't selling or doing drugs (outside the dressing room, at least), or turning tricks by bringing a guy in the same side of our booth, or stealing lingerie. The cameras couldn't see us inside the booths, doing our shows; they just captured us sitting in front of them. That was what they told us, anyway. We took that at face value because we had to.

There was a rumor that all the cameras that showed the Playpen were in black-and-white, except the one in front of the live girls, which was in color.

Although it was the middle of winter, management was standing by its policy of leaving at least one door open at all times. Cold air gusted to the back, where we were sitting in our underwear. Management's theory was that men didn't want to be seen entering a porn store. If the door was open, they could just slip in, unnoticed.

The doors were plate-glass with a handle attached, so the entire front of the store was a window. It was open twenty-four hours a day, so there was never a reason to lock the place up securely. Even if we did convince a porter to please, please, for the love of God, close the door, he'd soon receive a call from either Sammy or Big John ordering him to open it. They were sitting at home, with central heat, watching it all on tape.

We had to dress for the cold: argyle knee-high socks, or knee-high stiletto boots, or little fuzzy sweaters over our bras. Soon, it wasn't enough. It got colder, and I took to wearing a long cashmere sweater wrapped around myself.

Finally, we gave up and started wearing our actual winter jackets. It couldn't get any more depressing to walk into a peep show looking for a hot nude show and seeing three or four women sitting on chairs, trembling in full winter coats.

"No one wants to see a bunch of shivering girls all covered up," grumbled Ruby. "That's not sexy."

Even worse, some of the customers were starting to complain that it was too cold for them to get it up.

"Basil, *pleeeeease*," Lourdes wheedled. "You don't know how it's like. You guys are all wearing clothes. We're half naked back here. Come on, man."

Basil shut the door. An hour later, the phone rang. It was Big John this time. He demanded that the door be propped back open, no matter how much the girls bitched about it.

"Those bastards," I sputtered.

"Fucking *pimps!*" said Lourdes, her voice getting louder and louder. "Motherfucking Big John, he's not the one sitting up here in his underwear. *We* the ones making *him* money, mother*fucker!*"

Big John didn't let us forget that he could see us when he wasn't there.

"I saw you dancin' in your chair the other night!" he boomed to Mimi, fake-jovially. "I was wondering who it was wearing that new red wig," he said to me.

"When I sit at home and watch you girls in the monitor, it looks like you're huddling around a campfire." He laughed. He was referring to the ancient space heater he had dragged in for us.

And so it went all winter long: hunched over in our chairs, shivering, clad in parkas and cute sweaters and kneesocks and leg warmers, around the kicking space heater. The one that, viewed on CCTV, looked like the glow of a fire.

N TO ASTORIA

It wasn't like I didn't try to do something else.

The summer before, I worked as an assistant to a costume designer where, for $12 an hour, I spent the daytime hours running around the Garment District with her sketches, swatching material from fabric stores. Which would be the best for the Bird-Girl costumes in *Seussical*, the blue leopard print or the purple leopard print? Better to take a swatch of both. After getting approval from the designer, I'd go back and buy the chosen fabric by the yard, hauling the heavy rolls by bus to the studio on 7th Avenue, where they would be made into costumes.

The Garment District was a foreign bazaar in the middle of Manhattan with stores named Spandex House and New York Elegant Fabrics run by bearded men and women in saris, sitting in the back of hot, cramped spaces with bolts of fabric stacked to the ceiling.

You had to get permission to cut swatches, and every store was a negotiation. "I need ten," I'd say. "Okay, you can cut five." I'd swatch until they cut me off, then return the next day for the rest. I understood why they didn't want their yardage snipped to bits, but it had to be done.

I met other assistants like me in the dusty fabric shops, their hands full of sketches, balancing the costumes for three or four different shows in their heads. Most of them assisted more than one designer at a time in order to make ends meet—pay seemed to top out at $15 an hour.

The designer herself wasn't particularly fond of me, probably because I was completely out to lunch. I did the job competently but had a hard time mustering enthusiasm because of my schedule, which had me sleeping in four-hour shifts, twice a day. I worked from 9 AM to 2 PM in the Garment District, then 9 PM to 3 AM in Times Square. On any given day I went from Greenpoint, Brooklyn, to the Garment District, back to Brooklyn for four hours of sleep, then back to Times Square, where I worked until 3 AM. Then back to Brooklyn for another four hours, and then it was time to wake up and start the cycle all over again.

When the job ended and fall crept into winter, I thought maybe I could try bartending. I just needed to find a dive that would train me. I showed up one winter night at Club 123, a bar off the last stop on the N train in Astoria, Queens. "No experience needed," the Craigslist ad had said. "Will train."

Christmas lights blinked in the window of the little bar. I opened the door and walked directly into the Mos Eisley bar scene from *Star Wars*.

A gaggle of Latina girls, their boobs spilling out of their bras, sat next to lumpy, odd-looking male customers. They all stopped what they were doing and stared at me as I walked in. I got the idea immediately: It was like a lower-end Coyote Ugly–type place, where the bartenders were also the entertainment. *No one here is pretty enough to be a real stripper*, I thought, then felt bad about it. "*Sorry, but it's true*," I heard Mimi's voice in my head. Not even a peep-show girl would be caught in a place like this.

I fumbled through the bar, ignoring the stares, until I found the person in charge. The barmaid was an officious midget—about four feet tall—in her fifties, with yellow, peroxided hair.

"I hope you brought something better than that," she said, looking me up and down and frowning at my jeans. "Go back to the kitchen and get changed." Shivering next to the industrial sink, I pulled my clothes out of a plastic bag. I had a black Dickies dress that zipped up the front and could be strategically unzipped enough to be sexy, and silver go-go boots.

A hard-looking white woman in her late twenties was changing in the corner. She had dishwater-blond hair pulled up in a ponytail and was wearing plain white cotton underwear.

"I'm Drew," she said, pulling herself up straighter, as if I were going to challenge her on that point.

"Hey."

"What's your name?"

"Chelsea."

"Listen, Chelsea. I'm a fucking lesbian," she snapped, while squishing her cleavage into place. "Do you have a problem with that?"

It was shaping up to be one hell of a night.

"Um, nope."

"This job is easy," she said, relaxed now that she'd gotten the lesbian thing over with. "These guys are so stupid. I just get drunk and let them suck whipped cream off my titties."

Oh, God. All I wanted was to make some easy cash that didn't involve whipped cream or talking to people. That same laziness was the reason why I ended up at places like this.

I wondered how long I'd last before bolting. Hopefully, long enough to pick up some basic bartending skills, but already that seemed like too much to ask for.

Stationed behind the bar, Drew showed me the difference between highball glasses, rocks glasses, and beer glasses. I wouldn't be in charge of ringing up the drinks, however. That task went to a dark-eyed Haitian girl, who stood in front of the cash register, refusing to move as the rest of us maneuvered around her.

"One more thing," Drew said, glancing nervously in the Haitian girl's direction. "Don't touch that shrine under the bar. Okay? It has, like, special herbs in it. It's Tabitha's. *Don't touch it.*"

I looked over at Tabitha, who stared back at me silently, her deep brown eyes flashing angrily. A brass bowl full of what appeared to be grass and leaves sat on the floor under the cash register.

"She does stuff before the bar opens," Drew continued. "With sage. To bless the place." Silently, Tabitha walked around to the other side of the bar and began tossing what looked like oregano on the floor.

"Just don't knock it over," Drew repeated. "Seriously."

A working Joe lumbered in and sat down at the bar in front of me, grinning expectantly.

"How ya doing?" I asked him, hoping it sounded light-hearted and casual. "I'm Chelsea. I'm new here."

He ordered a beer and handed me a bill. I grabbed the bottle out of the cooler and told Tabitha to ring up one Corona, $6. She stared at me wordlessly, taking a good three minutes to perform the transaction.

I stood around awkwardly for the next half hour. Clearly, every girl here had her regulars who ordered from her in exchange for flirty conversation and suggestive leaning over the bar. Some of them went to the other side and sat on their laps. I wasn't going to be able to do this. I tried to look busy or at least deep in thought and slipped into a near-catatonic state.

Around eleven, I snapped back to reality when two short Hispanic barbacks hauled an irregularly cut piece of plywood covered in graffiti out of the back room and set it on the pool table. It fit over the top like a jigsaw puzzle piece, creating a makeshift stage. Someone hit "play" on the jukebox.

That could mean only one thing: A show was about to begin. I didn't want to see it. I could already tell it was going to be humiliating. I could not be there when it began.

Two of the Spanish bartenders hauled themselves onto the table, breasts spilling out of their button-down schoolgirl shirts.

"I'm going to smoke," I told Drew.

When I got to the kitchen I threw my long winter coat over my dress and grabbed my bag. There was yet another girl back there changing, and she stared at me with suspicion.

"Hi," I said. When she turned around, I slipped out the back door and booked it down the alley.

"Hey!" the bouncer yelled after me, as if I didn't have the right to leave on my own. The talent was escaping.

"*Hey!*" he shouted again. "Shorty, get back here!" I reached the alley, made a turn, and didn't stop running until I was back on the sidewalk, a good block away from Club 123. People on the train stared at my silver go-go boots and bare legs, but I didn't care. I had made it out with the remaining scraps of my dignity.

"Today they decorated the porn store for Christmas."

—from author's journal, Dec. 8, 2006

XXX-MAS

Lights and tinsel were everywhere—all over the racks of shemale and hermaphrodite porn, and on the staircase leading to the gay cruising area on the third floor. A big paper cutout Santa decorated our dressing-room door. Someone had taped two round ornaments to his hand, so it looked like Santa was holding his balls.

The guys who worked in the store had thoughtfully hung sparkly candy-cane ornaments from the top of each of our booths. I wasn't sure whether to be touched or deeply disturbed.

Big John handed out a Legs Avenue catalog and told us to circle the Christmas costume we wanted him to order for us, which we would be required to wear during the holiday season.

"You only get an outfit if you plan on working the week of Christmas, *Chelsea!*" he growled at me.

"*Fine,*" I said, exasperated. "I signed up for my shifts already."

Flipping through the stripper-wear catalog, I noticed that everyone had chosen some type of sexy Ms. Claus outfit, complete with Santa hat. As if Christmas themes in a sex store weren't creepy enough, the thought of working in the peep show on December 25 was the most depressing thought of all. I wasn't working on the holidays, just around them. I picked an inoffensive red babydoll dress. Valentine's Day was coming up, I thought, so I could wear it then too. Actually, Valentine's Day in a peep show was even worse.

Jesse, a quiet, plump Mexican girl with straight black hair that fell to her waist, told me she had signed up to work Christmas Day. "I dunno, maybe someone'll come in," she said with a shrug.

I'd worked on a Christmas before, back when I was living in Detroit and working backstage on a play. I remembered a feeling of stoic solidarity among the cast and crew. At the very least, we were providing Christmas Day entertainment to the area's Jews.

Christmas in a peep show, however, was just sick.

I did wonder how New Year's Eve would play out in the Square from in front of the peep-show booths, with thousands of people gathered in the porn store's immediate vicinity, waiting to see the ball drop.

I imagined it was sheer hell, ten times worse than the annual aftermath of the Puerto Rican Day Parade, the second most unpopular day to work in the peeps. I could predict the scene: teenagers yelling and staring, tourists grinning, smirking and chewing gum, nobody spending money. Events like the parade brought an onslaught of curiosity-seekers marching through, gawking, commenting on our bodies, and talking about us like we couldn't hear them.

Asking around, though, I learned that neither the Playpen nor Gotham was open during the height of the New Year's festivities. The doors were closed for about four hours, due to safety and crowd-control concerns. It was the only four hours of the year they ever shut.

I saw in the newspaper that the Classical Theatre of Harlem, where I'd worked less than a year ago, was doing an adaptation of *Black Nativity*, set on 42nd Street in 1973.

Walking into the theater, I was struck by the re-creation of Times Square up on the stage: the Amusement Center, hand-painted signs for LIVE NUDE SHOWS and XXX movies. In the middle of the stage was a large neon sign reading PLAYPEN.

I sat, stunned. The Playpen didn't even exist in 1973, but that wasn't the point. I felt as if it was a message aimed exclusively at me.

In the musical, Mary and Joseph were a penniless Dominican

couple who had to have their baby in the Port Authority after being turned away by all of the area's fleabag hotels.

As I left, it was dark and snowing heavily. I walked down a deserted street off 9th Avenue to avoid the post-theater crowds.

A crippled man was lurching and struggling through the deep snow. Another man was walking beside him, gripping his arm to keep him upright.

From behind me, a well-dressed blond woman in a long wool coat clicked by in high-heeled boots. Seeing the man, she looked down and crossed herself. I could hear her thoughts: *There but for the grace of God go I.*

One week before the commemoration of the birth of Jesus Christ, I was working alone at 3 AM. The store was completely empty, "Your Cheatin' Heart" was playing on the radio, and I could hear a dog barking faintly.

The barking sound was coming from one of the video booths, which meant a customer was watching animal porn again. I put my head in my hands. *No one is redeemable,* I thought. *Everybody is beyond hope.*

There was a rustle in the plastic chains. I looked up: An 8th Avenue street hustler was leading a toothless, drunken geezer into the peepshow area. The hustler pointed at me and whispered to the oldster, then collected money from the man and peaced out.

I had just spotted my first Murphy Man, one of the bit players in the Times Square's sub-economy. In the '60s and '70s, Murphy Men snared their victims with the promise to lead them to prostitutes, but often mugged the john instead. Today, men not associated with our store roamed the crowds looking for a tourist or a drunk, telling him that they knew where to find some girls.

It was usually a small-scale game, $5 or $10 just to lead them to the peep show, where they could then buy a show with one of us. Sometimes, however, like tonight, they tricked the man into believing that we were prostitutes and he was our pimp.

Now, the duped drunk was lurching over me, reeking of booze, gray hair sticking up wildly.

"I already paid for a BJ," he growled, a Southern twang seeping through his alcohol-slurred voice, "and I'm not gonna leave until I get one!"

I looked up at him and calmly called for security. My indifference infuriated him even more, and he pounded on the wall in frustration. Two porters appeared and grabbed him by each elbow, hauling him backward out the door. After they'd taken care of him, Basil came back and grabbed a mop so he could go clean cum out of one of the video booths. We exchanged glances, acknowledging the absurdity of it all.

"You know," Basil said, wringing the mop out into a bucket of filthy water, "there's gotta be a better way to make a living."

ACT TWO

ACT TWO

THE PLAYPEN

One night after our midnight shift, Ruby took me and a friend of hers, a visiting Finnish journalist, down to the Playpen, wanting to illustrate the difference between the joints, after having spent an hour failing to explain it through words.

Housed in a former vaudeville theater, the Playpen was a study of layers. The marquee featured a neon skyline that included the Twin Towers, which the owners hadn't bothered to remove after 9/11, presumably to show the terrorists that while they might be able to destroy our buildings, they could never crush our reluctance to spend money on cosmetic changes. After 9/11 the lights on the Twin Towers buildings were simply disabled, although you could see their outline. In the windows, more neon advertised LIVE FANTASY BOOTHS.

The theater, a faded beauty at 693 8th Avenue, opened in 1916 as a vaudeville house. When the 1970s rolled around, it enjoyed several iterations as a porn movie house, including the Adonis, a notable gay theater rumored to have sold small tubs of Crisco at its concessions stand. When the Adonis was shut down in 1994 by what the Health Department called "rampant sexual activity," the Playpen took its place—a two-story palace of sex toys, video booths, movies, gay buddy booths, and "live-girl private one-on-one fantasy shows."

In stark contrast to the funereal, eerie silence of Gotham, the Playpen had a carnival atmosphere. At the entrance, you were greeted by a large, faded sign of a cartoon woman on a swing in a green bikini. Past the door, it unfolded into an odd space, cavernous and garage-like and painted black, the walls covered with a glitter finish. It was visibly dirtier than Gotham.

I was frightened upon walking in: The place felt like an autobody shop—all loud, disconcerting echoes—and it smelled. Girls—all kinds of girls, in all kinds of colors and shapes and sizes, flesh spilling out of the tops of ill-fitting bras, bellies and asses and big thighs hanging out—were lined up in front of seven booths underneath a neon sign flashing HOT, WET N' WILD. They looked aggressive and crazed, their makeup painted on garishly, teeth missing, blurry tattoos and scars on display. One or two looked old, forty or more. Everybody looked hard. When I started working with them months later, I came to see how most of them were individually, quirkily beautiful, but right then they were frightening.

Ruby greeted them heartily, smiling and hugging a few, chatting and catching up with everyone. The Finnish girl and I stood back warily, staring at a large neon sign by the entrance leading to the video-booth aisleway, glowing PEEP SHOW in sickly red. The world I had just entered—and it was a world unto itself, an island with its own rules—felt dangerous. Of course, the draw and allure of the Playpen was that there was money here—a lot more money.

"My name's Strawberry," said a muscular black girl with a smudgy red tattoo on her ass, recognizing me as a friend of Ruby's. "*Straw. Berry.* 'Cause my *pussy* smells like *strawberries!*"

"See how different it is?" Ruby asked as we were leaving. I was a little shaken, actually. We walked down to 14th, where there was an all-night deli with seating that sold beer after four. The three of us sat drinking and talking until 7 AM.

A table of young Mexican guys, also drinking after a long night at work, sent over three beers. Embarrassed, we drank the beers but studiously ignored the men. Back in Brooklyn, I walked home down Bedford Avenue in the glaring sun with the beginnings of a hangover.

I passed my friend Sharon, who was jogging cheerfully before work. She waved, looking at me pityingly, because she wasn't really a stripper; she just danced because she needed a little extra money. She was the librarian and was training for a marathon. I, on the other hand, was still awake at eight in the morning, eating cereal out of the box I'd bought from the bodega. I fought the urge to lie down on the sidewalk and moan.

A couple months later, I went back to the Playpen because I had no money. The $150 to $200 a night I made through the fall and winter had trickled down to $80, $60, even $40. Around December, I started asking around about working over there, boosted by the other girls' overzealous prediction of how much I might earn: "Four, five bills . . ." they speculated. "You're white."

When I asked why they didn't just work there, the ones who didn't do Playpen shifts already cited either drama with the girls there or a previous firing.

It was not so easy to defect. Big John told me no without explanation. Finally I just went down there in my wig and full makeup and asked for the night manager. He looked at me suspiciously and told me to come back during the day.

The next afternoon, the Sri Lankan on duty acted as if he didn't know what I was talking about: "Why you wanna work here? Same company, same thing!" It was true—Gotham and the Playpen had the same owner, the mysterious Big Sammy.

I just stood there blinking until the Sri Lankan man realized I wasn't going to go away. He instructed me to go sit on a chair next to the wall of dildos while he started making phone calls.

And so it was approved by whoever was on the other end of the line, although management did not take my emigration lightly. It was stipulated that I had to split my time between both stores; Gotham had a hard enough time finding girls to work. "We need girls Saturdays and Sundays," he said.

"Okay," I said. I had been working in the peeps for seven months.

The Playpen's dressing room was right above the marquee, its windows blacked out. We had to ascend a steep, winding metal staircase to get to it. Several low-end marijuana deals were in progress when I came in for my first day. A skinny, worn-looking Spanish girl named Summer with large plastic breasts was demanding $6 for a small bag of weed, while the girl she was selling to protested that her bags were always short. Candy, whom I'd worked with at Gotham, was trying to sell somebody else a single joint for $2.50.

A porter named Renee, a short Puerto Rican man with a goatee and baseball cap, walked in and shouted, "*Does anybody have any drugs?!*" Everybody shook their heads. "*Fuck!*" he yelled, and left.

No one would look at or talk to me in the dressing room for weeks, as was the custom.

"I walked into the locker room, and I couldn't find an empty locker," Ruby told me of her first day there four years earlier. "And then all these girls came in, screaming in Spanish, talking about . . . *asses*, and I just sat there, I didn't know what to do, nobody talked to me and I couldn't find a locker. Raven was the first one to talk to me, and she started opening all the lockers and was like, 'There's *got* to be one that's empty.'"

I began my own search for an empty locker, settling on a broken one that didn't completely close. There were two thick books in the bottom of it—prep books for the GRE and the GMAT. I sat down on a wooden bench and began to dress, avoiding eye contact. The other girls had caught on that there was a newcomer and were giving me the side-eye. It was the junior-high locker room all over again.

At exactly six o'clock, the door at the bottom of the stairs creaked open, and a Southeast Asian–accented voice called up, "Live girls, come down!" There were several variations of this call ("You girls come down now!" and "Okay, everybody come down!"), which I eventually learned to mimic for the entertainment of my coworkers.

Six of us clanked loudly down the metal stairs, precarious in our heels, carrying bags stuffed with makeup, baby wipes, and dildos. Only one person could fit on the narrow staircase at a time. The day-shift girls were waiting at the bottom of the stairs for their turn to come up.

As a fresh batch of live girls dramatically descended the staircase in full view of the store, men stopped and stared, some licking their lips appreciatively, some looking distinctly uncomfortable. They were greeted with either a coy smile or a snarl.

Ahmed, the change man, sat in a chair near the booths, assigning booth numbers in order to prevent fights: "You, number six. You, number two." He tried to separate the girls who looked alike or were of the same race. I learned to glare at him if he put me next to another white girl. For the most part, however, I was the only white girl there.

Since the side booths were more lucrative, nearer the store's foot traffic, we rotated every half hour. They were papered with yellowing, handwritten signs disintegrating with age, written carefully by those for whom English was a new skill: "No touching girls," "*No tocar las mujeras*" "No cameras or cell phones," or, my favorite, "'Chairs' only for girls," "chairs" being inexplicably graced by quotation marks.

Working in the 8th Avenue peeps was surreal enough, but the Playpen elevated it to performance art. Instead of slouching in a dark back room reading magazines and watching TV, here we stood all night long on constant display, winking and smiling and chirping, "Come over here, guy," hustling the constant flow of humanity. Lose focus for one second, and the show would go to the girl next to you.

I looked around at my new domain. The Playpen's ceiling soared high, creating echoes. Two large vending machines sold soda and snacks with 1980s prices—50¢—and were beaten and pounded on daily when they failed to spit out the goods. Many of the building's structural details from its theater days were still in place, and architects occasionally came in to take a look around. Tilting my head back, I saw beautifully carved, high-relief cameos of Greek female nudes holding laurel wreaths lining the edge of the ceilings. I imagined that they were angels, watching over all of us.

The neon sign with the words HOT, WET N' WILD that glowed over the line of booths was pure honky-tonk. Nothing was too over the top. The booths were painted a womblike red. A phone was inside each one, which men either ignored, or, when using it, all had the same reaction: "*Hello . . . can you hear me? Can you see me? Oh, you can. I . . . oh.*" They got flustered and hung up after realizing they could hear us without it.

To start a show, a man slid a $10 bill into the bill reader, and a black plastic curtain ascended. It moved slowly, presenting the girl on the other side little by little, its motor wheezing and whirring as it struggled to raise itself yet again. When the show was over, the curtain went down just as slowly. At Gotham, the glass simply fogged itself up after a show: poof, goodbye. At the Playpen, I could wave farewell as the man on the other side of me disappeared from view. Sometimes the men panicked, reaching toward the glass, bending or kneeling to catch every last glimpse before I was gone. I took pleasure in their desperation.

Then there was the noise, the Playpen's default ambient state being a dull roar, a combination of street noise, shouting peep-show girls ("*Mire, papi, mire, ven aca!*"), the radio station, and the combined effect of dozens of porn movies playing at once. Soon, I began conflating the moaning voices of all the porn movies with the Greek nudes near the ceiling. Guttural cries escalated into a chorus of female voices, crescendoing and bouncing off the rafters: a chorus of X-rated angels.

The blaring radio station contributed to the lost-in-time effect. For some reason, it broadcasted only dance and disco hits from the '70s and '80s, matching exactly the look and feel of the place. "Hot Stuff," the title song to *Fame*, "On the Radio," "Heaven Must Be Missing an Angel," and, my favorite, Donna Summer's "Bad Girls." Listening to the lyrics ("Bad girls . . . talkin' 'bout the sad girls"), I thought the song seemed to have been written exclusively for the Playpen girls. I wondered if this station actually existed outside the peep show, or if the Playpen was able to pick up special radio signals from the past.

Even the girls' choice of costume seemed eerily outdated and shopworn. Raven, a post-op transsexual—although no one was supposed to acknowledge that—looked like a 1980s Meatpacking District hooker. Every night without fail she wore the same pair of black underwear hugging her chiseled physique, a belly-baring black T-shirt, and falling-apart white stilettos—the right heel looked as if it were about to snap off. Joyce and her two sisters wore cheap black spandex chaps—full-length leg coverings that hooked on to the straps of their g-strings. I was so tired of flesh, so sick of looking at other women's half-nude bodies and all their flaws, including my own.

Midnight, who also did shifts over here, enhanced her bosom by stuffing it with toilet paper, which was always sticking out the sides of her bra, smudged with body makeup.

Katrina, a six-foot blond from Georgia with a tummy tuck and recent double-D implants, wore lingerie that was faded and yellowed. She used a clamp in the back, an old modeling trick, to make her flimsy negligees appear more form-fitting.

The Playpen required the most outlandish, artificial look possible. I started my career at the Playpen wearing a black bobbed wig. Then I went for a raver-girl look, with rainbow outfits, white kneesocks, and a lavender wig. Then I bought a long, wavy, light-brown fall. My income upticked with every change. But gentlemen truly did prefer blonds, even unnatural-looking ones whose skin tone didn't match their hair color. Once I became a blond, I had to wear even more makeup to keep my complexion from washing out.

I tried out several looks before settling on the most popular one. It involved the blond wig, a red-and-white gingham corset top, ruffled red underwear, and white fishnets. I looked like I was backstage at a Broadway show from hell, some twisted version of *Oklahoma!*

The overall effect of the place was downright eerie, shot through with caffeine, drugs, and anxiety over money. A river of 8th Avenue hustlers and ghetto kids from the Bronx streamed through the place at all times. It was like living in a John Waters movie.

Three months into my Playpen stint, I began to get dizzy at the same time every night. Of course this happened only at work. I usually went in two nights a week, plus two at Gotham—I just couldn't deal with the place any more often. The rhythm of constant hustle was exhausting. I got nauseated when the other girls called the men by making exaggerated, juicy kissing noises.

If I went any more often, I would get used to all of this. It would all become normal. And if the Playpen became normal, I would be in trouble. I would fall through the cracks.

The Playpen created many Times Square casualties. It afforded girls a modest but healthy amount of cash on a regular basis—more than enough to keep us from seeking other work. Working the six-to-midnight shift, I got out of work at prime time for going out. I got into going to clubs after work, making out with some randomly-chosen guy, and leaving by myself. I just needed to feel something after being trapped behind glass all night.

I didn't know it yet, but I was lucky that the Playpen would close almost six months after I began working there. My resolve not to get deep into its lifestyle would have broken down over time. The Playpen was a blinding neon headache, but it was also an escape. Here, nothing was asked of the misfits in front of the booths. I was generally needed to be on time, not to get too drunk or visibly wasted, and to refrain from physical fights. Some nights it was a struggle just to accomplish two out of three. Everyone went a little bit crazy after spending enough time in the Playpen. I could have easily slipped further into a nocturnal life and incurred damage there, somewhere between 8th Avenue at midnight and the corner of Delancey and the twilight zone at 3 AM, the drunken cab rides home, the drama-filled phone calls from various girls, waking up at two every day.

But for the moment, I didn't care. The peep show, Times Square, it had all snowballed into a big enough part of my life that it seemed ridiculous to hide it, and I resented those who expressed concern or found my choices questionable. It was part of my life now. I lied to the friends who I knew would disapprove, and I avoided the rest in order to avoid lying to them. After-dark Times Square had seeped into my blood, like it or not. I kind of liked it.

"Rent and clothes and school-bills are an unending nightmare, and every luxury, even a glass of beer, is an unwarrantable extravagance."

—George Orwell, *The Road to Wigan Pier*

THE PAIR OF STOCKINGS

On New Year's Day, my roommate called me while I was at home in Michigan visiting my parents for the holidays.

"Hey," he said, sounding nervous.

"Hi," I said suspiciously.

"Hey, when does that article you were writing come out?" he asked.

"I have no idea," I said, letting the silence hang in the air. "I don't know if they're actually going to run it." The article of mine that the *Village Voice* had killed was a sore subject.

"You know my friend Chris, the one who was living in Egypt? He decided to come back to New York, and I always told him he could stay with me. So I guess, could you be out in four weeks?"

"I need more than four weeks." It was going to take longer to find something in my budget that didn't ask for more than one month's rent up front.

"Well, actually, he's going to be here in four weeks, so you really need to be out . . ." he trailed off. I realized he didn't really care about tossing me out. Suddenly I hated him.

"I need six weeks, and if we're lucky, I'll be out in four. Okay?" There was nothing I could do about it. I wasn't on the lease.

Back in New York, I began a frantic search on Craigslist. I called the number from an ad about an apartment for rent in the East Village and left a message.

A man with a vaguely European accent called me back a few hours later.

"I receive so many phone calls!" the voice on the other end of the line began. "But I ignored all of them. There are so many, I don't know what to do! People, they are crazy. But you . . . you have a very relaxing voice, on the message, so I call you back. Do you want to take a look at the room?"

While trying to discern if the apartment was a real two-bedroom, I learned that the man, Frank, was an Italian professor of French, living in his living room and renting out the bedroom for $700 a month.

Frank chattered on, saying that if I was his roommate, he would not hit on me. "Unless you want me to, and if you wanted me to, I would do whatever you say, because I love women!" After a few minutes I extricated myself from the conversation. He agreed with me that maybe it would not be an ideal situation, and we politely hung up.

Later that night, walking home from work at midnight, I got a call from an unfamiliar number. It was Frank. He immediately began talking. First he ran through his now-familiar "People are crazy, and I do not understand it" diatribe, and then we discussed his deteriorating marriage to some woman he'd left in China.

Listening to Frank, I realized that I had some things that I needed to get off my chest, too.

An hour and a half later, I found myself lying on my bed, telling him about Stefan. "I don't know, what do you think about that?" I asked after explaining the whole story.

"I do not know," he said sadly. "You seem like a nice girl. I don't know. But me, I am a terrible person. It's true. I left my wife in China and I had an affair with another woman."

"You're not a terrible person," I said. "You're just . . . I don't know. You made some mistakes."

"No," he said. "It is true. I am a bad person. But it's okay. You seem like a nice girl. And don't worry, I will find someone to rent the room."

It was the state of low-rent real estate in New York: We all needed a cheap place to live, but, apparently, we all needed someone to talk to even more.

I went to an "open house" for a basement room in Williamsburg renting for $800 a month. It was set up like a cocktail party. At least two dozen people were standing around chatting awkwardly, clutching red plastic cups of wine. I didn't know who the host was, so I wasn't sure whom I had to impress with my wit and conversation.

How humiliating: We were all expected to schmooze it up, and the winner got the privilege of paying $800 a month for a basement bedroom. I took some of the wine and talked with two girls.

"My boyfriend is a documentarian making a film about Haitian voodoo rituals!" one told me.

"Oh, my God," said the other. "*My* boyfriend made a documentary about Haitian voodoo rituals, too! Maybe your boyfriend has seen it!"

The other girl's eyes narrowed. "I don't think so. He doesn't watch other stuff because he doesn't want it to influence his work."

A tall, chubby brunette came over: the leaseholder of the house and arbiter of the precious room. "Want to see it?" she asked the three of us. We walked over to the room, just off the kitchen, and surveyed it silently. It was at basement—"garden"—level, with a tiny window, maybe twelve by twelve feet.

"It's nice," I finally said, and the other girls murmured in agreement.

The two girls who were dating the voodoo documentarians began chattering away at the hostess, edging me out of the circle, and I realized that they weren't going to give up. Out in the living room, the other guests milled around, craning their necks at us, trying to see what was going on.

The hostess and her little room were so much like the men who came into the peep show. They enjoyed having a bevy of people fighting for their attention, from which they could pick and choose, smug with their petty, temporary power. I tossed my plastic cup in the trash and left.

I eventually found a new place and moved out exactly four weeks later, which pleased Jesse. My room there was more than twice as big, only five blocks away, and $50 less a month. My new roommate, a Jewish guy a few years older than I was, seemed unobtrusive and friendly. I hired a pair of huge, stone-faced Uzbecks with a van to help me move.

Jesse and Chris were in the living room that afternoon, eating popcorn, glued to the TV. I led the larger of the two Uzbeks upstairs.

"Why you move, why you move?" he bellowed as soon as he got in the door. "You have bar downstairs. Is good!"

"That's a good question," I told him, giving Jesse a meaningful sidelong glance.

Jesse sighed with irritation and turned up the volume on the TV.

When the men were done loading my few possessions into their van, I popped my head into the window. "My new place is only a few blocks away," I said. "Can I ride over there with you?"

"No," he said. I sighed and walked over. They were already there when I arrived, waiting impatiently. I handed them $160 in cash in my little kitchen on the fourth floor, shut the door behind them, and lay on my bed.

Occasionally, I went on dates. Craigslist dating was big among a certain socially awkward type of Brookylyn hipster in 2007. Browsing the ads people put up in Greenpoint and Williamsburg was an amusing way to spend some time after work. They usually referenced riding bikes and watching movies on a laptop on the roof, and drinking malt liquor. Only a few years earlier, I'd half-jokingly made a pact with a friend back in Detroit that if either of us ever resorted to Internet dating, we would agree to shoot the other in the head. But Craigslist was okay, I reasoned, because it was lo-fi and sort of a slackerish way of meeting someone. It wasn't like joining a dating site and filling out a profile. It wasn't, like, *trying*.

I always said I'd met Liam when I was "out," because it made me seem like the type of person who actually went out. What really happened was that he'd sent me a message through MySpace, asking if I'd be up for a "social call," because he knew Ivan and had, apparently, seen one of the photos he'd taken of me.

A year earlier, I would never have slept with someone who admitted to having paid for sex, but when Liam told me, I just asked, "Where at?" Now, I assumed that everyone had, given the opportunity. I found this neither funny nor sad, just disappointing. I'd just read a statistic from a 1950s Kinsey report that said more than half of white American men had had sex with a prostitute, back when every major town had a red-light district.

"In Amsterdam," he continued. "Just once, you know?"

Liam was a hairdresser with a stocking fetish who had had spinal surgery in Bangkok the year before. (Why Bangkok? "It was cheaper. The hospitals there are like hotels.") His own dirty-blond hair was long, past his shoulders, meticulously coiffed and highlighted. He looked like a high-class fashion model in Diesel jeans. He was a good three inches shorter than me but made up for his height in arrogance. From what I could tell, an inheritance from his late father had made him a semi-wealthy slacker who no longer had to work. He'd let his hairdressing license lapse and, when he wasn't traveling, cut hair out of his East Village apartment for $80 and the chance to meet girls. He was thirty-seven, told girls he was thirty-three, and used to do hair in a strip club. I think that's why I liked him: Here was the one man who understood, sort of, what it was like to have my job.

"Let me see your haircut," he demanded in the corner of the bar where we met up one evening, where he'd ordered only green tea. The Paul Smith vest, the two-toned hair, the subtle eyeliner—none of that could cover up a thick Southern accent. His wasn't the musical, honeyed kind but an abrasive, white-trash rasp.

He examined my hair with his fingers thoroughly and with calm professionalism. He emitted a dangerous, sexual edge, and I felt a buzz as he gently played with my hair. I liked the feeling of being fussed over. "It's good," he conceded. "But I can do better."

He recruited most of his new clients in bars, bringing them back to his place for a martini-fueled haircut, sending them back onto the street at 3 AM or noon the next day. They were walking advertisements for his work—alt-pinup models and nightlife queens and professional dominatrixes. A good percentage of appointments in Liam's apartment-salon resulted in two different types of shags.

Not that I had a whole lot of leeway in terms of moral authority. I was the one who had been working in the peep shows. I was the one who had just suggested we leave the bar and watch porn. I didn't like porn and had no desire to watch it. I was just trying to show how cool and nonchalant I was.

"So let's go buy some," he said.

"If we go to Times Square, I can get us a good discount," I told him.

"You know," he said, "let's just go to 1st Avenue." The cab dropped us off at Blue Door Videos.

With Liam it was the first time I'd been able to disconnect sex from a relationship. That first week with him my world was reduced to a dingy, cluttered salon-apartment in the East Village and the inside of a porn store in Times Square, where I went at night to work. Neither place had any windows. Time ceased to exist in either one, like a casino. For sure I was gambling; I just wasn't sure with what currency yet.

The only way I knew that time was passing was because about every twenty-four hours there seemed to be a new newspaper. The days could be marked by Britney Spears' outbursts faithfully chronicled in the tabloids. One afternoon, for example, I was in line at the newsstand on 2nd Avenue (Britney, bald now, had attacked a paparazzo's car with an umbrella), and lotto fever was in the air.

"You gonna play?" asked the Arab boy behind the counter.

"Like being struck by fuckin' lighting," the guy in front of me mumbled.

"What?"

"I said, you gotta better chance of being struck by fuckin' lighting two times in a row," he repeated.

The boy's eyes widened. "Hey, man, you gotta be in it to win it," he said, full of that special brand of hope possessed by recent immigrants. When I thought about it, however, the lotto was truly democratic. I bought a ticket.

The only other thing that changed with the passing days was my stockings, bought on discount along 8th Avenue. For somebody with a true fetish, a sex worker is possibly the best person you can date. Liam had a specific type of stocking he liked—something about the way the nylon felt under his hand. One day, however, I decided to forgo them.

"Did you bring new ones?" he asked upon opening the door.

"I forgot," I said, waiting for his reaction. He paused for so long that I actually thought he wasn't going to let me inside. "All right," he said finally, looking disappointed and vaguely uneasy, wondering how he was going to deal with me without the protective barrier of nylon.

I started showing up at the peep show later and later, with an ever-changing array of sex bruises. It didn't matter. Nobody noticed; nobody cared. My proclivities were changing. I required more and more stimuli because I was going numb.

Meanwhile, the Playpen's high volume resulted in men just walking into the place and handing me money. It was my own personal slot machine—sometimes I'd be standing in front of my booth when I'd hear the creaking of my window going up, which meant a man had gone in without asking for a show first and just put the money in the machine. I'd turn around and dash into my booth, slamming the door behind me. Bills would already be on the floor, dropped through the money slot.

"Did you see this shit?" My coworker Lourdes motioned to a headline about a recent lotto winner in *The Post*, jabbing it repeatedly with her finger. "Guy's sixty fuckin' years old. I can't believe this shit. What's he gonna do with all the money?" She was probably the third person at work that day to point out how pissed they were that the lottery winner was old.

Out of the corner of my eye, I spotted a regular customer nicknamed Creepy lurking around a rack of videos, patrolling the aisles.

"What time does the shift end?" he asked me in his too-quiet voice, his darting eyes looking desperate behind his glasses. He was clutching an ever-present thick sheaf of papers under his arm, wearing the same beat-up brown leather jacket. I shrugged and examined my nails, feigning ignorance. He rolled his eyes at my act. "That last customer you had," he said, "that guy looked pretty weird."

"Yeah, well," I said. "I don't judge." I made a mental note: Look both ways when leaving work tonight. Perhaps even take a cab. Creepy, a white guy in his fifties, had a habit of stalking certain girls—he had stalked one so much that he terrified her into quitting. Almost nobody would give him a show anymore, but he still came in almost every day, begging for one.

"Mami," the other girls told me. "You gotta get some Mace to work up in here, you know? Or like a knife or something."

Exactly one week after I first met Liam, I counted the cash I had in my sock drawer after paying the rent. The bills just kept coming; I had hundreds of dollars left over. It had been so long since I had anything resembling a disposable income. I could buy all the stockings I wanted now: vintage stockings, Cuban heels, anything.

I headed into the city for the ten-to-three graveyard shift. We were only required to stay until 3 AM but usually stayed later, until four or five, to catch the bar crowd.

It was the weekend, and every hustler in New York was out and at the top of his game. On the train, no sooner had the doors shut when a man shouted "Showtime! Folks, he's only eight years old!" He hit PLAY on a beat-up boombox, and a small black boy stepped into the middle of the train car, jerking and shuffling his way through a hip-hop beat.

After work, around four, I went to the porn store two doors down to buy a new pair of stockings. I got an employee discount—same management as Playpen—but the Sri Lankan behind the counter (there were a ton of Sri Lankans working in the porn-store biz) gave me a better one. "I give these to you at cost," he said solemnly. "You save $4."

"Thank you," I said.

Stepping outside into the night, joining the crowd flowing down 8th Avenue toward the subway, I paused for a minute at the top of the stairs, wondering where I was really going. I had $400 in cash on me, $200 in each sock. It seemed like things could go on forever like this, if I let it.

"We accept her—one of us; we accept her—one of us!"

—*Freaks*, 1932

THE MOST POPULAR GIRL
IN TIMES SQUARE

I walked downstairs to my booth Tuesday night and saw that Ahmed had put me next to Katrina, the star of the Playpen's freak show. *Fuck.* I gritted my teeth and prepared to make no money.

She turned around. "Are you Shelly Morgenstein?" she demanded. A statuesque blond, Katrina was one of the few girls who read something besides the tabloids. I knew who she was talking about: Shelly Morgenstein was the sex columnist for one of the alt-weeklies.

"Noooo," I said nervously.

"She wrote something mentioning a Times Square peep show in her column last week," she said, staring me down.

"I'm not a sex columnist!" I squeaked.

"You told me you liked to write," she said accusingly. "Why else would she mention peep shows?"

"Ummm, I dunno."

Why had I told her a single thing about myself? Sometimes I'd loosen up and feel comfortable enough to tell someone something personal, and it would always come back to bite me in the ass.

"If I had my own column, do you think I'd be working here?" That silenced her for the moment.

Katrina, six feet tall, nearly six-four in heels, was the perfect Oedipal figure: a larger-than-life woman with massive breasts that could smother a man's face. They looked like watermelons, pale and oblong, protruding away from her body even without a bra, despite their heft. They were pale and oblong—tumescent—and protruded away from her body even without a bra, despite their heft.

The skin was stretched so thin around the implants that spidery blue veins pulsated just beneath the surface. They looked painful, like they were about to burst. Her nipples were a pale whitish pink, like a blind mole's eyes searching for light. They'd cost ten grand.

She was the Playpen's biggest star, the highest earner by far. There was just no contest. Every man wanted to see her. They lined up outside her booth for her, waiting while she gave shows to other guys. It created a vaguely homoerotic situation, probably the exact opposite of what they wanted, but they had no problem with seeing her after five or six or fifteen guys had jerked off to her that day. Of course this also made me feel ugly and unattractive, as I stood outside my booth, passed up every single time.

She used to work at the Empire peep show over on 33rd. We'd heard that it was an impenetrable mafia of blond Eastern European girls over there, so she made no money because she looked just like them—and she hadn't had her magical implants yet.

"I came over here, and I started making the real money," she told me. "It was like the stars and the heavens suddenly opened up." Katrina probably made $600 or $700 in a normal night, and she worked four six-hour shifts a week. Everyone else struggled, but making money was easy for her. She expected it, and it flowed right to her.

She wore her long hair in loose corkscrew curls. I always wondered how she tamed all that hair until one night after work when I saw her unclip two long extensions of fake hair from the sides of her temples.

Her cheekbones, nose, and tummy were also man-made. The nose job was fine, although the ski-jump look was long outdated. Her cheeks were overly sculpted and too high. The implants stretched the skin around her face, making her eyes look slightly catlike, veering into Jocelyn Wildenstein territory. Her belly looked like many of the older Playpen women's, with the telltale ripples of a sub-par tummy tuck.

We all knew what work she'd had done because Katrina was not shy about talking about her surgeries—she was proud of them.

"I don't care what anyone says," she once told me out of nowhere, looking at me through the mirror while putting on her makeup. "They're the best decisions I've ever made. Every day I look in the mirror and I feel good about myself. Every time I look in the mirror I like what I see and am happy. My boyfriend feels the same way, too. He's had seven surgeries."

I almost dropped my mascara wand at that last admission. I wanted to feel a little sympathy toward Katrina, but I couldn't. She had done all this to herself, turned herself into a freak, and it scared me. If Katrina's success said anything, it was that in order to be successful in the business, you had to give up looking like a normal woman.

I didn't know very much about her background other than the fact that she was from the South and had worked in a strip club in Georgia for a few years before coming to New York. She'd worked as a traditional stripper, a happy-ending "masseuse," a foot-fetish model, anything you could think of. "I've done every job in this business except prostitution," she once told me.

She shared an apartment in Hell's Kitchen with her younger brother. "He's an illustrator," she said. "I want to write a children's book someday. I'm going to write the words, and he can draw it."

"Does he know what you do?" I asked.

"Oh, hell, no. He thinks I'm a cocktail waitress. He'd completely flip out if he knew about this. My boyfriend knows, though. He doesn't care. He used to care, because he thought I was hanging out with hot guys or something. But I forgot my keys one night, and he came in here to drop them off. He saw all these guys, and he realized that they were, like, trolls."

Katrina remained a cipher, no matter how many pieces of information I gleaned about her.

A scruffy guy with a beard who looked like he'd been on a motorcycle for the last twenty years came in. I expected him to go to Katrina, but he locked eyes with me. He had longish hair tinged with the very beginnings of gray, and dark, feral eyes. He was wearing jeans and a denim jacket and was accompanied by a plain-looking white woman in her forties wearing a long, puffy winter coat.

Something clicked between us, some inexplicable chemisty. Suddenly, it was hard to look away.

I went into my booth, and he met me on the other side. Twenty dollars came through the slot—it figured he'd want the cheaper show. "Ten dollars in the machine," I said to him, through the wall, and I heard him ask the woman he came in with for some money, and then shut the door. I adjusted my violet wig and straightened my fishnets while waiting. When the window slid up, he was staring at me with that odd, intense gaze.

"Oh, man," he rasped, his entire body vibrating with manic energy. "Do you realize you hypnotize men every day with your eyes?"

"Actually, I don't," I said. "It's pretty slow."

"You're a writer, aren't you," he said.

"No."

"No, you are—I can see it in your eyes. You ever write stuff about this place?"

"Oh . . . no." Why was everyone accusing me of writing today? I hadn't published a single thing since I moved to New York.

"You should, man. You really should. Ya know?"

"What do *you* do?" I asked.

"Actor, comedian. Mostly comedian. Just recorded something for HBO. *Lucky Louie*. You ever seen it?"

"I don't have cable."

"You should come down and see me sometime. I'm doing a standup show this weekend."

"I had a show with this guy the other night," I said to Katrina the next time I worked with her. "It was so weird. The first thing he said was, 'You're a writer, aren't you?'"

She started laughing. "I know that guy," she said. "I've given shows to him. He said the exact same thing to me. 'You're a writer, aren't you?'"

"Wait . . . he did?"

"Yeah. And I mean, I've hung out with him. He's crazy. I mean, he's a cool guy, but . . ."

"Tell me about him!" I hated to admit it, but yet again, an obvious wolf had piqued my interest.

"Yeah, he came in here and I gave him a show and he gave me his number and said to call if I ever wanted to hang out. So I did. Because, you know, I love weirdos. I love freaks. I love walking around looking at people. That's why I'm in New York!

"Anyway, he lives in this hellhole at 38th and 10th, with the bathroom down the hall. His room is so weird. It's covered with these posters of guns, and truck magazines, and porn . . .

"Then I hung out with him and his manager one night, and they said they were making a documentary, and wanted to know if I'd make out with him for it. I had to get my boyfriend's permission and he said, 'Sure, I don't care.' I mean, it's acting, he understood."

"You made out with him?"

"Yeah, it was weird. But then I had to stop answering my phone. He's just too crazy. He started calling me in the middle of the night, like, 'I need you to come down here—I'm in the middle of a panic attack and I can't write . . . . .'"

It wasn't just Katrina or the comedian. I was one of the freaks, too.

Later that night, as we changed into our street clothes in the dressing room, I caught a glimpse of Katrina's bra. It was a thick, beige, matronly device. I wouldn't have been surprised if it had pulleys and suspension cables. She couldn't wear normal bras with her E-cups. She probably had to go to those places on Orchard Street where old Russian ladies sold industrial-strength girdles.

I pulled off my wig and placed it carefully in its plastic bag, wiped off my lipstick with the back of my hand, then scrubbed my hand with a Kleenex. Katrina carefully unclipped her long extensions, removed the fake eyelashes, and washed off her makeup. Her hair was dishwater blond without the extensions.

When she put on jeans, a sweater, and a winter hat, I saw that she looked years younger and completely ordinary. To everyone out on the street, she was just another cocktail waitress walking home from work. Nobody could tell she was secretly the most popular girl in Times Square.

THE FIFTH OF MAY

The usual Saturday-night Playpen crew was short a few girls, and I was happy for the chance to make some extra money. Raven wasn't there, despite being on the schedule.

"That means she went out last night," said Lourdes. We guessed that her New Year's experiment with sobriety had ended. She'd been going on and on about her resolution for months now and was getting a bit self-righteous.

"I was spending, like, $200 a week on drugs!" she kept marveling.

Around nine, Lourdes beckoned me over and then walked into her booth, swung open the door, slammed her suction-cup dildo against the window with one gesture, and sat down in her chair.

I ducked in as she shut the door, taking care not to bump into the putty-colored dildo. There was barely enough room for the two of us.

A customer had bought her a pint of rum and she held it toward me, still in a paper bag.

"Drink up, baby! It's Saturday night! *Woo!*" she yelled, slapping at the dildo for emphasis, sending it wobbling. "Don't get fucked up now, 'cause they'll blame me."

"Don't worry, I won't," I said, taking a drink. "I can handle it."

"That's right," she rasped, swigging from the bottle. "I can handle it, too."

I teetered back to my booth, a little unsteadily. The Playpen's edges were smoothed out now, the neon taken down a notch. I smiled toward Ahmed, the Saturday-night security/change man, who nodded back stoically. Everything was good. Everything was under control.

The rum had an invigorating effect on Lourdes as well. She promptly accosted a customer standing in front of the lineup by pumping her fists and stamping her feet, doing a little dance in a tight circle around him. Ahmed could only look on and laugh. It was impossible to control Lourdes; the best you could hope for was to contain, or neutralize, her.

After work, I walked through Times Square in an elevated mood. I had $380 in my wallet and a buzz, and it was only midnight.

The city was vibrating, the first warm weekend of the year. Street vendors were beginning to pack it in, but the tourists and the hustlers and street musicians were out in full effect. I walked through the crowds with a swagger, keeping an eye out for a cab. I was going to go downtown. I wasn't ready to go home.

I spotted Heidi ahead of me, cutting quickly through the crowds, head down. Her blond hair bobbed in a ponytail, and she was wearing a pink tracksuit. She must have just gotten off her shift at Gotham.

I made to say hello, but she looked so determined that I didn't want to startle her. I watched her disappear, cutting through the schools of tourists like a sleek silverfish, slipping into the night.

At 49th and 7th, a crowd of a hundred or so spilled out of the Playwright Tavern, filling up the sidewalk in front of the bar and across the street, all staring in rapt attention at some tiny point far in the distance.

It was the fight: De La Hoya versus Mayweather. The crowd erupted into cheers. I kept walking. Suddenly, the air was filled with red and white confetti, drifting down an empty part of 7th Avenue, swirling around like snow.

I was hoping to meet up with Liam at the bar. As I was crossing 46th Street, he called.

"You going to Luke and Leroy's?" he asked.

"*Yes,*" I purred, trying to sound coy.

Liam was kind of an asshole, I was discovering, which made me glad I didn't usually have to deal with him outside his apartment. We'd gone out to dinner once, and I found we had almost nothing to say to each other.

I hailed a cab and got in the back, where I changed into my black platform heels and put on lipstick. When I got out at Christopher Street, a man driving a car-service black Lincoln started hollering, "Hey, shorty!

"Hey, shorty, I'm serious! I just want to talk at you a minute! C'mere!" People were starting to stare.

"Get outta here," I snapped, walking more quickly. He drove alongside me for a block, calling out softly, as if to a stray cat, before giving up. I got in line outside the club, standing on one foot while putting Band-Aids on my heel where my shoes had been rubbing all night.

The girl at the door grabbed my wrist and turned it over, stamping something across it. WHORE, it read.

Liam arrived. "Who won the fight?" I asked, but he just shook his head, scanning the room. At the edge of the dance floor he reached up and yanked the cheap choker I was wearing off my neck. He put it in his vest pocket. "You can have it back tomorrow morning," he said.

On our way to the bar, I tripped over something large on the floor. "Is that a fucking duffel bag down there?" I asked.

"Either that, or it's Kevin Carpet," Liam said. I looked down; it was Kevin Carpet. Kevin was either a man with a serious fetish, or some sort of performance artist, or both. He could be found at any number of downtown bars and clubs, his entire body rolled up into a carpet underneath the bar, where people—girls, mostly—stood on him while getting a drink. He liked it when they jumped up and down on him in their high heels.

Back upstairs, out of the corner of my eye, I saw the familiar sight of someone holding a flash in one hand and a camera in the other. It was Ivan.

I smiled and put my hand on his arm. "It's me," I said. He looked confused for a second, and then he broke out in a big, goofy smile of recognition from down on high, six feet five inches above the ground:

"*How aaaare yooou?*" He snapped a photo. I was just another subject, another girl willing to take her clothes off in front of his camera. There were so many of us.

I got into a cab with Liam at three-thirty. At his place, we went up to the roof. The front side of the building didn't have a ledge, and I went to the part of the roof that sloped into infinity and lay down on it, my head just over the edge. Second Avenue lay five stories below. If the pedestrians below had looked up, they would have seen a tiny face hanging over the edge of a building, peering down at them. I didn't normally do things like this. I was too cautious to even move between cars on the subway. I realized that I was very drunk. I eased away from the edge of the rooftop.

Liam wanted to have sex on the roof, but I didn't, because I was too cold. He started yelling, and I realized that he was a mean drunk. I ran downstairs to the kitchen and then headed for the street, stumbling into a cab and pointing the driver over the bridge. Liam stood in the doorway, in his undershirt, hollering, "If you leave now, you'll never see me again! Get back here!"

"Leave me alone!" I yelled, as the cabbie witnessed yet another domestic dispute in silence.

At home, too shaken to fall asleep, I poured a little whiskey into a cup and added water. It was six o'clock in the morning. I sat down on the edge of the bed to drink. My wrist still had that stamp on it: WHORE.

THOROUGHBREDS DON'T CRY

"God don't want me to make money," announced a Jamaican girl to all assembled in the Playpen's dressing room. It was five-thirty on a Saturday night, the intersection of the day and night shifts, behind the blacked-out windows of the marquee above 8th Avenue. The windows were cracked, the blare of car horns and rumbling buses wafting in. I sat on one of the wooden benches and unpacked my things: wig, comb, clear plastic heels, lingerie, stockings, baby wipes, makeup, a bottle of water, a can of beer.

"People say, God will provide," she continued. "How? I go to work every day, I don't make no money? If God didn't want me to do this kind of work, then how come it's the only job I got? He must not care if I do it."

The dressing room was a place of soliloquies and speeches. Girls addressed everybody and nobody in particular.

"I know, right," said Susie, the white mom of three from Queens with frizzy highlighted hair. "And how come every time I go to church the sermon is about the whore? I went to church for the first time in a long time last week and the pastor's up there talking about Mary Magdalene. I'm sitting in the back going, oh, great."

"This guy came in here once, holding a Bible open," said Raven. "He comes up to me and points to a part and goes 'Here, read this.' So I do. It went: ' . . . *and the harlot* . . . ' Wooo! I was like, oh, *no*. Get that shit the *fuck* away from me."

"Know how this works, baby?" Joyce asked a customer, snapping her gum and grinning. A chubby, light-skinned black girl of about twenty-three, she was always grinning inanely and snapping her gum. She was wearing her usual uniform of black spandex chaps clipped onto her g-string and a bikini top. Her weave was down to her waist.

"Oh, yeah, I've been here a few times," said the man, an older, nondescript white guy. "In fact, I think I've even seen you before."

"Oh, no, I don't usually work this shift," she said. "Probably you've seen one of my sisters," she added casually. The man's jaw dropped.

"Your sisters?"

"Yeah, we all look alike."

"But . . . you all work here? How many of them are you?"

"Three. Three sisters," she said, completely oblivious to the fact that some might regard this as utterly, creepily weird. "We all look alike."

"Oh, my . . . okay," the man stammered. He couldn't take it and walked quickly away. Joyce continued to stare into the distance, grinning mindlessly, clueless to the fact that she had said something wrong.

But it was true. There were three sisters at the Playpen, like Chekhov. And they all did the same damn thing with their gum.

There was a ruckus as security wrestled a man to the floor, holding him in a headlock until the police arrived. He had pulled out a knife and was threatening other customers with it. They beat on him for good measure and the entertainment of the gathering crowd of customers.

I peeked around the corner for a look. He was on the ground, screaming: "Oh, Jesus, no! Oh, God, help me!" It was too much. I ran back to my booth.

"Now, he just got taught," remarked an older black man standing off to the side watching calmly, chewing on a toothpick. "That'll show him not to come in here threatenin' folks."

"That reminds me of the night someone pulled out a gun in here," said Joyce. "I ran straight upstairs when I saw that, and everyone else ran into their booths."

"I was the only one who didn't have a booth," said Susie. "I was running from one booth to the other, banging on the doors trying to get somebody to let me in!"

"Midnight was the only one who didn't do anything," said Joyce. "She just kept working. She just stood in front of her booth, going, 'What? What? What's he gonna do?'"

"It was a BB gun," someone finally said. "That's all it was."

Eric, one of my regulars, came in around nine. "Hello, Chelsea," he said cheerfully, handing me a large manila envelope. "I'll just give you some time to study this," he added over his shoulder as he walked away. I opened the package, wondering what I'd receive this time.

There were some playing cards; a script handwritten on several index cards in a large, childish lettering; a brand-new three-pack of granny-style white underwear (dated receipt attached, purchased from Duane Reade at 8:42 PM); a note; and a chocolate bar.

Eric was one of the few regular customers at the Playpen that I didn't hate. In his early fifties and chubby, with curly gray hair, he was rumored to be a public schoolteacher up in Westchester. He dressed sloppily, yet passably, in a baseball cap and jeans.

Eric was mostly interested in panties: panties and humiliation, with a peripheral interest in upskirt glimpses, pantsing, and accidental flashings. In short, he was good for about $150 in less than thirty minutes.

Eric was Lourdes's regular, but I first met him when she was upstairs on an ill-timed break. It was a break that would cost her hundreds of dollars over the next few months.

"Let me tell you what I like to do," he had said. "You can tell me if you're interested. I have several scripts written out, several, uh, scenes. We act them out. If you mess it up, or I don't like how you do it, we start over. We keep doing it until you get it right." He paused. "It's okay if you mess up. We just start over, that's all."

We acted out a short scene that first time. I kept my clothes on, and he gave me $20. Eric's games always began with his character thinking he was putting one over on me and always ended with him on his knees, pants around his ankles, masturbating and begging for me to tell him what a small penis he had. His penis was disturbingly, perhaps pathologically, small. Probably there was something wrong with it, which explained why he was here, working out his issues.

Eric visited me often over the next three months. He would cruise by my booth, present me with that night's package, and sail off, saying, "I'll give you a little while to study this." Afterward, he always asked when my shifts for the coming week were, and I would hear him taking notes after the window went down, his pencil scratching in his notebook.

Eventually, he composed scenes specifically for me, printed out on an old dot-matrix with my name at the top. He also saw other girls, Raven or maybe Lourdes, whom he also had created scenes for. The scripts were all tailored to our personalities. Lourdes's always involved yelling. And mine, well . . . I examined that night's yellow index card:

> I ask you: tell me about your School Days . . . Gym time . . . changing for Gym . . . were you "shy" or "embarrassed" about it OR did you look around a lot . . . what did you see? Describe The Bras/Panties/View . . . Colors. Styles . . . What was said . . . about underwear . . . Teasing? Funny Names?
>
> You ask ME: BOXERS OR Briefs (to me that's embarrassing so much). Then Comment (Truth) about my Underwear. Like It, HATE IT? Funny, silly, cool . . . WHAT?

"Wear the flowered schoolgirl panties," a separate note read. "I'll go wild!!!$$$"

The script involved strip poker. We each had a set of cards, the sequence planned out beforehand so that I eventually won the game. On the back of each of my cards, he had cut and pasted different lines of dialogue, along with soft-core upskirt photos printed off the Internet, meant to illustrate that he wanted me to flash the white cotton underwear under my skirt. It started out with me losing several hands and having to strip down to my bra and the granny panties he'd provided. But then his character got on a losing streak, right down to a ridiculous pair of pale pink polka-dot boxers he'd purchased for the occasion. I needed a drink.

After a few more weeks of receiving a brand-new pack of underwear on each visit, I finally told him that I'd kept everything he'd bought me upstairs in my locker: "You don't have to keep buying new ones if you don't want." I felt vaguely guilty about all the brand-new underwear I would never wear. It was nice that he always got me chocolate, though.

While cleaning out my locker several months later, Susie spotted the packages of brand-new underwear I was about to toss out. "You're not going to throw those away, are you?"

"That guy Eric bought them for me. I can't wear them; they're too big."

"I wear those kind all the time. Can I have them?"

"Sure."

"Awesome!" She stuffed them into her bag.

"You're pretty fun with this, you know?" Eric said one night after a show, after the window had gone down. We were talking to each other through the wall.

"Sure," I said. "I have fun, too."

"Do you mean that?" he asked, suddenly sounding very small and vulnerable on the other side of the wall.

"Of course." He couldn't see what I was doing: silently counting the money, folding it into my wallet, putting in back into my bag. "Of course I do."

Raven knew the customers so well that she could often spot a guy and whisper what he was into under her breath. "He likes white girls—smile at him," she might say. Or: "He always goes with Joyce. Forget about it." Or: "That's Katrina's regular." Or: "Cheap." Or: "He wants to be humiliated—you know, call him names or something. He wears lingerie under his clothes."

I got into the habit of asking her about an interested-looking guy whenever he strolled by the lineup. "What about him?" I asked quietly, pointing to a man who came in often but had never taken a show with me.

She didn't have an answer this time. She looked at him with pursed lips and arched her eyebrows grandly. She looked at me like I was dumb and gave a big shrug. "Whaddya think? He's a *trick!*" Just another customer, another sucker.

The Lipstick Man was another notable Playpen specimen. He wasn't *all there*, but few customers were. He was nondescript: white and middle aged, lumpy and dark-haired with glasses and business-casual clothes. His routine was walking slowly in front of the lineup of girls over and over.

I failed at hustling him for weeks until Raven tipped me off. The Lipstick Man didn't take shows, she told me. He liked lipstick. I watched as he walked over to Linda, stood in front of her, and nervously whispered, "I love your lipstick."

"Want a show?" she asked bluntly. He blinked, shambling off.

"Hey!" I called after him tentatively. "Do you . . . want to wear my lipstick?"

He turned around slowly, eyes lighting up: "Why, yes!" he said, surprised, as if this was the first time anyone had ever asked him this. He stood in front of me, and I motioned for him to give me $20. He handed it over without taking his eyes off me, and I gently applied my own lipstick to his thin lips, being careful not to touch him. I made a note not to use this tube on myself again.

"Thank you," he said, dazed, and wandered off to the video booths, clown-like with his bright red lips.

I put the twenty in my wallet, amazed at how easy it had been, but I also felt bad at what I'd done. Now he was wandering around looking like a freak in the middle of Times Square.

But still, he kept coming back for it. Some days the Lipstick Man wasn't so cooperative. I'd ask him if he wanted to wear my lipstick— or even keep the tube—and he'd just stand in front of me, assuming the position but becoming confused when I asked him to pay. He appeared to be almost in a fugue state.

One night he came to me three times for lipstick application. On the third, he asked for my number. He spoke so softly that I could barely hear him. I demurred, but as soon as I turned my back, rustling around in my booth, a folded piece of paper came flying in, landing softly on my chair. I turned around and saw the Lipstick Man scurrying away through the underbrush of the Playpen. "Diane," said the note (his female alter ego?) in shaky cursive, with two separate phone numbers—both 212 area codes—written on it. What was the second number, his *work* line?

At the end of the night, in the dressing room, I carefully asked Raven what this could possibly mean, what he could possibly want. A strangely beautiful peep-show thoroughbred, half Puerto Rican and half Trinidadian, she had taken a liking to me since I started at the Playpen. We both loved to surreptitiously drink vodka and read *The Times* and *The New York Observer* during our shifts. She liked Joe Conason's column. I was flattered by her attention—it was like the cool girl who kept flunking senior year suddenly wanting to hang out with a freshman.

She was also a transsexual prostitute who would never think of herself that way: a date here, a date there—the pleasure of her company wasn't *free*, that was all. Her real name was Tina, but who knew what her name was before that, what her parents named her.

"Oh, he probably wants you to take him out," she said, rolling her eyes. "He wants you to dress him *up* and put all this makeup on him, and go to, like, a fetish club, and tell him how *hot* he looks, and how everyone is *staring* at him . . . . It's really exhausting, but he has money, you know? He's cheap, but he has money." I wondered how she knew. "Anyway, if you do it, I would ask for at least $400, $500 if you can get it. I mean, for your time, you know? *Your time* is worth that much."

I could call this Lipstick Man, go to his apartment, put makeup on him, clothes, and take him out to a club, drinking and whispering encouraging words in his ear. He was so far gone that I'd barely have to worry about my safety. I could collect $400 or $500 from him, and nobody would ever find out. Everyone else here freelanced.

He wasn't my problem, of course, but I was complicit. I saw that something was wrong with him, and I still took his money.

"So *Chelsea*," Raven asked in her grand, magnanimous manner, shaking me out of my thoughts. She spoke in careful, educated diction, each word slow and enunciated. Her stutter may or may not have been from years of heavy drug use. "*Where* are you going after work?"

I recently learned her age: thirty-five. She'd been in the peeps for at least ten years.

"I don't have any plans," I said, sitting on one of the wooden benches, putting my street clothes on.

"I've told you about the Film Center Cafe? On 9th Avenue? They have a happy hour until 1 AM, $5 wells? Do you want to get a drink with me?"

"Sure." Raven's capacity for partying was legendary. "Just one drink, though, you know?"

"Yeah, I feel like just one, too," she conceded.

I waited as she admired herself in the mirror and slowly packed her bag. We both slipped on shades as we exited into the gritty neon glow of midnight Times Square.

"I can't believe I made only $100 tonight," she said, crossing 9th Avenue. "It's been so slow. But I mean, you gotta go out and *play*, while we're still young and hot, right?"

The Film Center Cafe was bathed in a blue glow, pleasantly empty. Televisions above either side of the bar played black-and-white movies and silent films with captions. Raven nodded to the pretty young Russian bartender, and we ordered chocolate martinis. We sat at the bar and talked about our tricks: Raven called them all tricks, whether they were peep-show customers or men she picked up in bars or met after work. It was sad to me: There was no difference between a trick and a man she wanted to be with anymore. Maybe there used to be, once, but that line had been erased. There was nothing more to be gained from them but money.

"That reminds me of the time," she said out of nowhere, "I met a customer from Playpen outside work a couple years ago. All he wanted to do was for me to meet him at a hotel. We did a bunch of coke and then he wanted to watch porn and masturbate. And I was on the bed on the other side of the room, and I masturbated too, and I got $800 out of him. I think I was in and out of there in forty-five minutes. I mean, I got paid to masturbate, you know?" *All he wanted. All I had to do.*

The TV above the bar was playing a Marx Brothers movie, *A Day at the Races.* Raven talked about Tokyo: "I went out there, ten years ago, to visit my boyfriend. I had yellow fever at the time, dating lots of Asian guys, but this one, I was in love, you know? I had to be with him all the time, or I was going to die. But then I got there, and I was staying in a hotel, because he lived with his parents. And I started to feel . . . trapped."

Onscreen, a group of kids entered the scene, singing and dancing. The Marx Brothers came out and danced with them.

"All God's children got rhythm!" the caption read.

"So I . . . started going out, you know? And got a job dancing. In a strip club. But after a week or so, I told the manager, you know, I'm staying in a hotel. It's a lot of money, you know? I think I'm going to leave. And he says"—she widened her eyes—"'*No, no, no! No, no, no, no!* You stay here! In apartment! No problem, you have place to stay, no problem!'

"I guess I was making them a lot of money. They let some dancers stay in apartments they owned. Because the Japanese strip clubs are associated with the, um, the . . . "

"Mafia?"

"Exactly. They have real estate, too. It was tiny, I mean, a studio, really small, but who cares? I'm living in Tokyo! In my own apartment! And my boyfriend, he got really upset, and he started to come by the club when I was working. So the manager . . . I guess he had a little talk with him. He explained that I was making a lot of money for the club, and if that he continued to, ah, interfere with that money, there would definitely be some . . . problems, you know?

"It kind of made me feel good. I mean, I'm a diva! Anyway, he never bothered me again. I stayed for three months and I came back with, um, $20,000. And you know what? I spent every last cent of it on designer clothes. I had Azzedine Alaia, all of it."

In my drunkenness, I decided that I wanted to go to Tokyo, too, to work in a strip club. I could live in Tokyo, in my own apartment.

"All God's children got swing!" read the TV screen.

"Or a hostess club!" Raven squealed in excitement. "Because you're so white! Girl, you *have* to . . . "

An older man took a seat at the barstool next to Raven. She turned toward him and smiled, holding his gaze a beat longer than necessary. Everyone was a potential trick, in one way or another. We devoured a plate of buffalo wings, my vegetarianism going out the window. I'd abstained from meat for eight years because I didn't like the way the animals were treated, but now it was wearing me down; it was just too hard to maintain. A lot of things were going out the window these days.

I stumbled downstairs to the bathroom and stared at myself in the mirror, running cold water over my hands and splashing it on my face. I was past the point of inebriation. Perhaps I'd been drugged? I'd heard of it happening before: older girls taking naïve new girls out after a shift, slipping something into their drink, and stealing the money they'd made that night. Ruby thought it had happened to her once, or maybe she had just blacked out.

No, I decided, just drunk. It was time to go home.

"Might not have no money!" read the caption on the Marx Brothers movie playing on repeat as I walked up the stairs and back into the bar.

"All right, mama," Raven said as I veered toward the subway. "You're going to the E train, right? Well, I'm going to go down the block to catch last call somewhere. I'll see you tomorrow!" She laughed. She was going, I knew, to try to pick up a trick around the bars near the Holland Tunnel before closing time. The key to hanging with Raven was not asking questions. Instead I waved, watching as she disappeared down 9th Avenue.

"All God's children got wings!"

HAVE YOU BEEN BAD?

The next afternoon, hung over, I walked into the back room of Gotham and saw a tiny piece of paper on top of the VCR. It looked as if it had been deliberately left there, so I went to pick it up. The small square was covered in neat block handwriting.

I sighed and sat down heavily in my chair, contemplating the note for a while, holding the tiny piece of paper between two fingers, wondering what it might say. I knew it was going to be a doozy, and I wanted to be prepared. I was the only one working that afternoon, so I had silence to think.

> MA'AM MY NAME IS TIM AND IM A 36 YR OLD BAD NAUGHTY BOY WHO LIKES TO ACT AND BE TREATED LIKE A BAD BOY. SO IF YOU KNOW HOW TO TREAT A BAD BOY PLEASE LET ME KNOW.
>
> 718 555 1212.
>
> THANKS,
>
> TIMMY

I thought about what would happen if I actually called the number. "Hello?" I'd say. "Timmy?"

"Who is this?"

"Have you been bad?"

"Who is this?" he would ask, scared now. And he would have a right to be. Why did I want to torture and harass this Timmy? But then again, why was everyone coming in here always seeking punishment?

"Have you, Timmy?" I would ask. "Timmy, listen to me . . . *have you been bad?*"

RENEE'S PANTY DRIVE

Renee was going to prison. He discussed his impending three-year sentence for gun possession with the same cheerful fatalism that the rest of the Playpen crew discussed their lives.

"Yo, I'm taking up a panty drive before I go in!" he shouted at the line of girls. "I'm collecting panties that I can hang up. I already got three pairs. But I also wanna get yours . . . and yours . . . and yours." The specified girls giggled. He didn't point at me, mercifully freeing me from the awkward situation of being expected to give him a pair of my underwear.

Renee apparently worked at the Playpen, although I had no idea what he did. That night, he was in an exuberant mood, sitting near the entrance to the video booths, leaning back on his stool while swigging from a forty of Olde English half-concealed in a paper bag, smoking a cigarette.

Nikki walked over and put her arm around him, pushing his head down and burying it between her giant, cartoonish breasts, which were smeared in baby oil to make them shine like orbs.

Nikki was a complete freakshow. She looked close to forty, maybe older—it was hard to tell under all the plastic surgery. I had no idea what motivated her. A big-boned, light-skinned black woman who stood over six feet tall, she possessed the most enormous pair of fake breasts I had ever seen, even bigger than Katrina's. They make her look like a linebacker or a drag queen.

I was fairly sure she was born a woman, but nobody was entirely positive. All her customers were the same: extremely short men, both black and white, all obvious Oedipal cases. They delighted in bringing her gifts every week, usually flowers and candy. At six o'clock she strutted back through the door to the dressing room carrying one or two giant bouquets of roses, as if she was the homecoming queen of Times Square.

She was also Midnight's cousin, and they often worked the Playpen's day shift together. They'd been in the industry for years and years, and when they were younger, they used to work together at Scores.

It was rumored that Renee had slept with quite a few of the live girls, although nobody would admit to it. He was about five foot five and wasn't handsome, but there was a certain *je ne sais quoi* beneath his clownish exterior.

At the end of that night's shift, Renee wandered into the dressing room. No male who worked at the Playpen could get away with this but him.

"Mimi, maaa-miiii," he warbled, holding his arms out toward her. Mimi did some shifts at the Playpen sometimes, too.

"Renee, get your ass of here," she said mildly.

"Come on, baby," Renee said. "I might be a little man, but . . . " He straddled the end of a bench and made humping motions. "I might be a little man, but . . . I'm a horny motherfucker." He collapsed onto the bench, laughing.

"C'mere, Renee," Mimi said suddenly. She grabbed him and pushed his face into her cleavage. Once again, he was at eye level with a pair of breasts. She grabbed his hair, pulled his face upward, and gave him a long, deep tongue kiss. She released him and then did it again. Soon, they were making out heavily.

"Tell your wife I said hi," she said, grabbing him by the hair and kissing him again.

Maybe she considered it his goodbye present, or maybe she was just crazy from the heat. A few weeks later, he was gone, upstate, serving his three years.

GET SOME

One night, a huge piece of the Playpen's ceiling crumbled and fell thirty feet to the floor, crashing next to the video booths. Somebody would have been killed for sure had it landed on a person or a booth. But it hadn't, so everybody resumed their activities.

A chubby, red-faced man came in around eleven, a tourist in a silly mood.

As I was going into my booth to give him a show, Raven ran over and stage-whispered, "He's high. He's *high*! Try to *get some*!" I couldn't tell that he was high. I was just a drinker, so drug behavior just wasn't on my radar. Plus, our customers didn't need drugs to act weird.

Also, I wasn't sure what she meant by getting some. Get a lot of money out of him? Well, yeah. Cokeheads were usually good for that.

When the show started, the man immediately pulled out a baggie of cocaine. Raven was right. He sniffed a bit and then actually lay down on the floor, head propped up against the door, watching my show, and was still lying there when the show ended. I left my booth without bidding him goodbye.

She accosted me as I exited my booth a few minutes later. "Well? Did you get any?"

"Yeah, I got $50. He took two shows."

"I mean *drugs*, girl!" She shook her head incredulously. "I told you to *get some*! We could've had coke right now!"

Not one to let an opportunity slip away, Raven glanced behind her and hustled the departing tourist into another show. He surrendered the cash happily, high and agreeable.

"It was only a $20 show," she reported five minutes later. "But hey, I got high, so what do I care!"

This was facilitated via the money slot. If nothing else, the slot, only long and wide enough to accommodate a couple of folded bills (in some cases it was just a small hole), was also useful in the carefree exchange of drugs. Anything that could be snorted, obviously. You could also slip a tightly rolled joint through there as well.

But I understood why Raven had wanted me to get some. Drugs took the graphic nature of the peep show down a couple notches. We all needed something to desaturate the Playpen, I thought, taking a break inside my booth, the door closed, sipping a beer. We all needed something.

"Chelsea, you're a pretty cool girl, right?" asked a young skinny guy a couple weeks later as he pulled out his wallet. I said I guessed that I was. He set his laptop down and pushed his glasses up on his nose. He looked like he should be at a hacker conference, not the Playpen.

"So, do you mind if I party while I'm watching your show?"

"You can do whatever you want while watching my show," I answered mechanically. He went into his side of the booth and locked the door. I could hear him feeding the $10 bill into the machine. The partition covering the window rolled up slowly. I took off my bra. He took out some tinfoil, rolled it into a large cone, and lit it, smoke filling up his side of the booth and obscuring him, while a sickly sweet smell seeped into my side.

He took a wet rag out of his pocket. I took off my underwear. He took out a lighter. Smoke started billowing out the corners of his booth. I began to worry about what I was inhaling. Still, I didn't say anything. What was I going to say? *"I meant you could snort coke but not smoke opium or heroin or whatever"*?

He wasn't watching me, too engrossed in his tinfoil, but I performed anyway. He gave me $50. It was the only money I made that night, so my laissez-fair attitude had been the right way to go, I told myself.

Not everyone agreed. We all had our boundaries. The following week Candy came running out of her booth looking for a spray can of Lysol.

"Some guy was smoking crack in there!" she exclaimed. "I told him he couldn't do that here and left! Damn!"

When I got home that night I realized I had left my keys in the apartment. "Fuck," I whispered. It was three-thirty in the morning. I turned around and trudged back onto the subway.

Both Raven and I kept our spare housekeys in our lockers in Times Square. "It makes sense, right?" she said. "'Cause it's always open." It always was.

Forty-five minutes later, I was at the Playpen. "Back already?" cracked one of the porters. "Yeah, I couldn't make my rent," I deadpanned and ran up the stairs to the dressing room and rummaged around the back of my locker for the paper bag with my keys inside.

I was presented with another chance to get some as I walked out the doors onto the glittery gum-wrapper-strewn 8th Avenue sidewalk. A tall black hustler fell into step beside me. Whispering into my ear, he said, "Get that *co*-caine, beautiful."

I walked quickly past him, into the Green Emporium deli to get a beer. A bride, her dark hair immaculately coiffed and her face made up and beautiful, was exiting the store in her long white dress, topped with a cream-colored jacked for the autumn chill. She stood out on the sidewalk with her groom, smoking, the train of her gown dragging on the dirty 8th Avenue sidewalk.

THE HAIRCUT

Liam opened the door to a grimy Bushwick apartment, where he had set up haircutting operations in the kitchen, being temporarily exiled from his salon-apartment in the East Village. A murky legal matter regarding his roommate, rent-stabilized status, and years of overcharging by said roommate led his lawyer to advise that while pursuing this matter in court, it would be best not to run an unlicensed hair salon out of the apartment in question.

"Come on in, I'm just finishing someone up," he said. He'd completely forgotten about the fight we'd had a few weeks earlier, and I conveniently put it out of my mind as well.

"I bet you are," I replied, sitting down on the couch and opening a flask of whiskey, wiping the sweat off my forehead. It was July and the apartment didn't have air-conditioning. A tail-less cat flashed by on its way toward the bedroom.

"Doesn't he have a tail?" I asked.

"Now, that's the kind of question you're only supposed to say to yourself," he drawled. "But no, for the record, *she* does not have a tail."

I turned to acknowledge the girl in the kitchen getting a cut, who was sitting there awkwardly.

"You look hot," I offered.

"Oh! Thank you!" she responded, sounding surprised.

Liam was the kind of guy whom women warned other women about. This was part of his appeal. Deep down he was racked with the same insecurities as the rest of us. He made up for these by sleeping with a lot of women; I made up for mine by working in a peep show. Neither tactic was working out particularly well.

I wondered why I was hanging out with such a sleazy guy. I was attracted to him, but that wasn't the reason. Womanizers made it easy for shy, insecure girls. I didn't have to do anything this way. There was no chance of rejection.

The Argentinean girl seemed the same way too—she was beautiful, but she didn't seem to know it. Instead, she stared in the mirror not at herself but at Liam, and carried herself uncertainly as she left.

I sat in the kitchen chair facing a mirror propped up against the refrigerator.

"Can you make it a little redder?" I asked. I never liked my hair the way it was. I always had to mess with it.

"Yeeee-ahh," he said thoughtfully. "We'll do a bit of that color I liked last time, but with more pop."

He painted the dye on my hair in a thick glop and set an egg timer for twenty minutes. While waiting, we sat in silence. Outside the bedroom, we did not have much to talk about.

"Now when the color starts to fade," he said, "just give me a call. I'll be back in town in about two weeks."

"I don't know if I will," I said petulantly. "You're so hard to pin down, and then there's all this *attitude* . . . "

"You know I *never* give you attitude," he said. After rinsing out the color, he cut my hair, roughly, grabbing chunks seemingly at random, chopping and slicing with a straight razor until I made a face.

"Come on," he said. "Work through the pain. So what's up? Still flashin' people in Times Square?"

"How's your *illegal hair salon* going?" I retorted. "You're like one of those back-room hair ladies in the Bronx."

"My salon is not ghetto," he bristled. "Anyway, how's it going?"

I thought for a moment. Yesterday, I had witnessed a pregnant dancer smoking a blunt in the dressing room. When another girl—a mother—chastised her in concern, she waved her away: "Naw, mami, it's cool; I still got 'til twelve weeks to quit this shit."

Raven, meanwhile, couldn't stop staring at the girl's breasts, swollen by pregnancy. "They're beautiful," she said quietly, with genuine reverence and awe. "Beautiful," she said again.

It was so frustrating, seeing the pregnant dancer. Didn't anyone else realize they couldn't do this job forever? That maybe no one really wanted to see them dance while pregnant? That we all had to figure out a way out?

"Every day I know less and less," I said finally.

After he finished cutting, Liam stood behind me with a comb, both of us facing the mirror. He smoothed down the stray hairs and gently arranged the pieces over my face. He put a hand on top of my head and left it there. We looked at each other in the mirror, silent again.

It took me until the next morning to realize that my hair was gone. Liam was careless with people and things, but I wondered if he'd done it on purpose, just to be sadistic.

Now I looked like a boy. I clutched at what was left, trying to pull pieces down to cover my face. How could he mess with my looks, of all things? Didn't he remember what I did for a *living*? I never called Liam again.

CALL ME A NIGGER

I was working alone at Gotham one night when a slight black man walked up to me and asked for a show.

He was utterly unremarkable, dressed in the uniform of business-casual, his age anywhere from late twenties to early forties.

"Will you," he mumbled, "spit on me and . . . call me names?"

"Sure," I said, although I didn't like it when guys asked me to call them names. It was hard to improvise and think of abusive things to say.

He went into his booth.

"Did you say you're having trouble putting the money through the machine?" I said loudly. "Here, let me show you." I opened his door, spit in his face, and quickly shut it. That was how you could get away with spitting on someone, which opened up a whole new revenue stream.

I went back in my side of the booth, where I could see him through the window.

He blinked, my saliva running down his face.

"You little bitch," I said.

"More," he said quietly, looking down at his feet.

"You're just a little bitch—that's why you come in here." He nodded vigorously.

"You fucking pussy," I said.

"Nigger," he whispered, barely audible.

"What?" I wasn't sure I'd heard him correctly, he said it so quietly.

"Call me a nigger," he repeated, looking me in the eye, pleading.

It was a plea but also, somehow, a challenge. Would I do it? Would the white girl do it? How many professionals before me had balked? It was so politically incorrect that you'd have a hard time even finding a paid sex worker to say it. I imagined how hard it must be to have this sort of impulse, wherever it came from.

I took half a second to decide what to do.

"Nigger," I hissed, the word feeling ugly and vicious, like a mouthful of salt. I was paranoid someone would hear me, even though we were the only ones in the back room.

"Nigger," I repeated, louder this time. The window snapped off.

I sat on my chair and put my clothes back on, stunned by what I had done. I opened the door a crack to see him out. He was waiting outside.

"Thank you," he whispered. I nodded, and he left.

He came back a few weeks later, this time following Heidi into her booth. She jumped up from her chair, blond ponytail bobbing. I knew the negotiation that was awaiting her inside.

"Oh *honey*, are you sure you want me to say that?" I heard her say a minute later.

I could envision his silent nod. Her voice dropped to a whisper.

IN STYLE

"Why don't you get an internship?" Luanne asked me while we were out at Clem's in Williamsburg one night. She was a curvy, curly-haired Texas girl who was going out with my friend Aaron, the longshoreman who'd let me stay at his house in Jersey City when I first moved to the city.

She had been working as a bartender but had just gotten a new job marketing things that didn't actually exist, like merchandise and tickets for concerts broadcast on Second Life.

"So the 50 Cent concert isn't actually real?" I asked. "It's just on the Internet?"

"It's *real*. It's just only on Second Life," she explained. Second Life was a video game, an entire virtual world. The 50 Cent concert she was promoting would exist only in the second dimension, but there was still, apparently, a way to monetize it. The Luannes of the world were so much better prepared for the future than I was.

"Seriously, you should get an internship. That's what all the girls I know do—bartend at night, intern during the day."

"I'm too *old*." I'd been out of college for years; the idea of an internship was embarrassing.

She gave me a look.

I thought about it. Actually, because of the money and flexible schedule of the Playpen, I was in the position to be able to afford to take an internship. I was already wasting my free time gulping both prescription and herbal anti-anxiety medications to stanch the creeping existential dread about the fact that I'd been working in a peep show for almost one year.

After a few weeks of résumé-sending, I had lined up two interviews, one at *InStyle Homes* magazine and one at *Ladies' Home Journal*.

"Nice dress," said Annelise, the editor who would become my boss, in her office in the Time & Life Building as I sat fidgeting in front of her in a green-and-blue plaid dress from Anthropologie. "Did you make it yourself?"

I stared down at my new dress, which had cost more than $200. Suddenly, I hated it. Annelise, I took note, was wearing a white eyelet shift dress by Cynthia Steffe.

"How clean do you keep your apartment?" she continued.

"Pretty clean," I said.

"I need you to be seriously organized," she said firmly.

Annelise was also from the Midwest, which was probably why she gave me a chance and hired me.

However, she found it amusing to pretend to forget my name, especially in front of other staffers.

"Shoshanna! Shelly! Shirley! Could you please come here?" she'd yell across the room at photo shoots. I sat at a desk in the corner of her small office, and she never had problems remembering it when it was just the two of us.

"Oh, Shosh," she said one afternoon in the middle of an daylong photo shoot. "You don't have to wear heels to shoots. You're going to be dying by the end of the day."

I shrugged. I was used to being on my feet in shoes much higher than the wedge espadrilles I was currently wearing. *You have no idea*, I wanted to tell her.

My other supervisor was an icy, WASPy blonde from the Upper East Side named Piper. She was only a year older than me, but she clearly hadn't spent her post-college years working in peep shows. Her office corkboard was punctuated with photos of vacations in Maine, and the head shot of a young male TV star she'd gone to prep school with.

I thought my re-entry into the working world would be jarring, like introducing a feral animal into a domestic environment. But it was fine, perhaps because I was so used to playing roles. The only thing that needed to change was my wardrobe, so I bought an armload of summer dresses from H&M one afternoon.

My days at the magazine were spent on my hands and knees in the home accessories closet. My job consisted of running a one-girl shipping-and-receiving operation for the products that the magazine shot: lamps, bedding, rugs, china, tableware, stationery, wedding tchotchkes, and pieces of furniture.

I often spent the afternoon at photo shoots, where Annelise might carelessly kick over a $500 lamp. Afterward, I'd stay in the studio alone and spend hours packing everything up—say, fifty delicate pendant lamps going back to different showrooms. Then I'd get on the phone with the PR girl and explain that we broke the lamp and that it was my fault.

Once a month, I sat down with a manila folder stuffed with receipts to do Annelise's expenses. This was my favorite part, because I got to peek into her life.

Let's see, I thought, sorting the expenses by date. *What has Annelise been up to lately?* There was the Paris trip for the Chris Cornell story, and lunch for the crew on each day of the three-day shoot. There was a $55 cab fare back to her LES apartment from JFK. A few ATM receipts. She had $1,200 in her bank account. That couldn't be right.

I kept adding up charges: a two-bottle-of-wine dinner at Bar Veloce while entertaining some marketing person. Receipts from London—another photo shoot—and then Art Basel in Miami. I couldn't figure out why she'd been there as far as it related to the magazine, but she'd shown me a video she took there: an installation of a life-size, taxidermied bear standing on its hind legs. The bear had hidden speakers in its head that played weird, tweeting techno music punctuated by *untz-untz-untz* thumps. For some reason, this was hilarious, and every so often, when she was in a good mood, she called me over to her desk to watch the video.

The magazine owed Annelise a few grand for all these expenses, which she'd paid out of her own pocket, which was why I had to get them sorted out ASAP. The apartment she'd just purchased with her boyfriend uptown required an unexpected $80 grand in renovations. She'd shown me the floor plan: It was a two-bedroom with a real dining room. On 208th Street.

"And now I'm starving," she said melodramatically, after getting off the phone—another renovation discussion about the goddamned Mexican contractors with her ever-patient boyfriend. "I barely have enough money to eat."

In fact, I knew exactly what she made, which was $105,000 a year. It wasn't that much, if you really thought about it using New York City standards—especially if you wanted to buy an apartment—but it was a vast improvement over the $10 an hour I was making.

"I think we need to watch the bear video again," I told her.

She cued it up, and our eyes glazed over as we watched the stuffed bear broadcasting techno music out of his furry head.

One afternoon, Piper came by the office I shared with Annelise holding a tray full of jewelry.

"Samples," she said. "Take one."

I picked up a long, single-strand pearl necklace off the silver tray, wondering if it had any resale value.

I wore it to work in the peeps. Gotham was only a few blocks west of the office, and I interned full time at the magazine while working there to make actual money. On Tuesday at six, I simply walked from the Time Inc. Building at 47th and 6th to the Gotham at 47th and 8th and worked until midnight. I worked at the Playpen on weekends; I could gross $500 to $600 working the Saturday and Sunday six-to-midnight shifts.

I was far from the only one of the peep show girls living a double life. It was part of the package. Some girls had entire relationships with a guy who didn't know. Many of them even had to hide it from their kids.

I usually told people I worked as a cocktail waitress at Latitude, the bar and grill at 783 8th Avenue, right next to Gotham. Since it was right next door, it didn't feel like that much of a lie.

I remembered the time I saw Zima in the dressing room, frantically rubbing glitter off her face.

"I gotta really make sure I get all my makeup off this time," she was saying. "My daughter, she notices. She goes, 'Mommy, you wasn't wearing all this makeup when you left the house this morning!' And what am I gonna say? That a fuckin' glitter bomb exploded on me? That I hijacked a glitter truck?"

The internship ended when the summer did, and the magazine folded soon after. Little had I known that I would help produce the last-ever issue of *InStyle Homes*. It was a bit of a relief that it was over. Going back and forth between a shelter magazine and a peep show was too dissonant, and the magazine wasn't hiring, anyway. Times Square, it seemed, wanted me back.

THE DELI

"I'm calling the deli," I told Ruby. "Want anything? Your usual?"

"Yeah," she said. "Two Heinekens, the big ones."

I scrolled through my phone to "Deli on Corner" and dialed.

"Bueno."

"Bueno!" I said cheerfully.

"Yes, bueno," he replied, sounding irritated. "What do you want?"

"Two Heinekens keg cans, a turkey sandwich with swiss on rye, a Sam Adams, and a diet ginger ale."

"And a large tea with five sugars!" shouted Mimi. "With a straw."

"Oh yeah, a large tea, five sugars, and a straw."

Click.

They always hung up without saying goodbye, but I knew we'd see one of the short Mexican deliverymen within half an hour, lugging plastic bags of food, plus a straw, so Mimi wouldn't smudge her lipstick.

The Green Emporium, on the corner of 48th and 8th Avenue, was the deli unfortunate enough to be the closest place to Gotham. It sold beer, had free delivery, and was open all night.

We caused the place an untold number of headaches, and delivery to 781 8th Avenue was periodically cut off. It was usually the day girls' fault. They'd argue over the bill with the delivery man, and they never tipped. The deli–peep-show relationship was always in a high state of tension.

Lourdes was the worst. She'd order from the deli, and when the guy arrived, she'd try to hustle him into shows. ("C'mon, don't," Zima told her. "Those guys make like seven bucks an hour. Don't do that to them.") It occasionally worked.

Between the shift changes and all the girls, we rarely tried to consolidate our orders, and a deliveryman was often summoned three or four times in a six-hour shift.

"So many problems," the Korean manager, Mr. Shin, quavered when Ruby called up ordering beer around midnight. "So many problems! No more 781! *No more delivery to 781!*"

"But it's me," Ruby pleaded. "I order every night. Three Sam Adams, remember me? I'm not those other girls. Those other girls, they work during the day, *they* are the problem."

He hung up on her, but obviously she had struck a note: a furtive-looking delivery man came ten minutes later, carrying beer.

The men of 8th Avenue—the deli-men and the hustlers and the porn-store employees—were, like us, an important part of Times Square's sub-economy. They were mostly recent immigrants, often illegal, and worked twelve-hour days, six or seven days a week. They shared rooms with other men, sleeping in shifts, and usually had an hour-plus commute from the Bronx or Queens.

At Gotham, there were Basil and Kumari, who spoke French and were from West Africa; Nemil, who had bullet wounds from war in Sri Lanka; Chinese Danny; Little John (tattooed, white, not to be confused with Big John); Chris (huge, white, and tattooed); T-Loc, another Sri Lankan; Ahmed, from Liberia; and Junebug, a felonious-looking fellow with an oozing open wound on his leg. There was Renee, and Gauge, who also had a burgeoning rap career.

Walking in one day, I overheard Chris telling a customer, "Depending on what you're looking for, we have some really high-end blowup dolls. This one goes for $275." Chris had a crush on me. He defended my honor when I needed to kick people out of the back room. I could tell he liked protecting all of us. He was also a part-time actor; he even had an IMDB entry. Several months later, he was arrested at the store. Apparently, he was addicted to crack and not only had been stealing from the register but also had multiple warrants out for his arrest in Illinois. He was shipped off to Rikers, and we never saw him again.

Upstairs in the dressing room, two girls and Basil were huddled around his cheap laptop. They were examining his digital snapshot to submit to an online dating site. The picture was taken inside the store— he worked seventy hours a week—and they were trying to figure out how to crop out the dildos and porn DVD covers lining the walls in the background. The scene had a touching family vibe. Basil once said that he never looked at the live girls "that way," because he thought of us as his sisters.

I was also partial to T-Jean. He had an accent I couldn't place; I only knew he was from one of the French-speaking nations in Africa. One night, about half a dozen men were clogging up the back room at Gotham, standing in front of the live girls staring, opening, and closing their mouths like guppies. They were all foreign, and they didn't understand that we were not prostitutes. One of them made a nasty remark while he was walking away. Suddenly, T-Jean swooped in.

"The sign says Live Girls, it doesn't say bitches or hos," he said sternly. "Gentlemen, respect yourselves. If your sister is in there stripping, doing whatever, it is because of situations. You have to respect. *We do not encourage or promote prostitution!*"

Ahmed, the weekday change man at the Playpen, was a recent Liberian immigrant. Besides handing out change, he was the casual supervisor of the live girls, breaking up catfights and yelling at staring customers. He had left his family behind to move to New York, where he was promptly hit by a bus, so he walked with a little bit of a limp and sometimes a cane. He couldn't eat sweets because they hurt his teeth, and he couldn't afford dental work. Still, he hoped to bring his wife and kids to New York some day.

Guys like Ahmed and so many of the other men of 8th Avenue really couldn't go home again. They wouldn't be allowed back in the States since they didn't have a green card. I guessed the money over here really was that much better; otherwise they wouldn't have put themselves through the hardship of being separated from their families in order to support them. But it meant that they wouldn't see them again until they were ready to go back home for good. One guy, a Sri Lankan who worked at the Playground and then the Playpen, hadn't been home in sixteen years.

A round, bald head poked through the plastic chains of the peepshow room.

"*What up, Hustla Man!*" Lourdes boomed. The rest of him lumbered in. Hustla Man was a middle-aged black guy, never without his oversized T-shirt-and-shorts ensemble. He took an empty seat and rested for a minute, panting.

Sitting down in an empty chair was taboo for visitors, but for Hustla Man, we made an exception.

"Hey, can you get a copy of that new PlayStation 2 game?" Lourdes asked. Hustler Man thought for a moment.

"I do know somebody who got that game," he said in his gravelly voice. "It's an old man, and he up in Harlem."

"Could you get it for me?"

"Well, I can check with the old man and see if he still got it. He up in Harlem. I'll check to see if he still got it."

Hustla walked the streets of the West Side every day, from Harlem on down, selling stuff, and buying stuff he could sell. He had a little bit of everything in his bag: cheap jewelry, knockoff perfume, CDs, the latest pirated DVDs, makeup, and discounted cigarettes that he bought in bulk down south and drove up here by the trunkful. He also took requests.

All I knew about his backstory was the condensed version he offered up once: "I'm from Brooklyn, but I had a lotta trouble in Brooklyn, even though I'm from there. I got jail time, I got *shot* three times, and I also had to shoot a nigga."

Hustla Man started pulling T-shirts, in light pink, baby blue, and white, out of his duffel bag. "I got those shirts you wanted to wear to the Hamptons," he said to Midnight.

"Oh, good," she said.

She held up four tiny-sized shirts. "Wait, what is this?" She held up an XXXXL white T-shirt, emblazoned with her modeling headshot.

I couldn't believe how gorgeous Midnight looked twenty years ago. The lighting and style were clearly from the '80s, but she resembled a young Whitney Houston. I also couldn't believe she had commissioned Hustla Man to print up a bunch of T-shirts with her old modeling photo on them.

"But you didn't even make them in the right sizes. I asked you for mediums—what is this?"

"Well, he done me dirty. I axed him for six shirts and he made seven, and he didn't do the size I wanted."

"I can't take these!"

"I'm saying, he done me dirty, I axed him for six, and he made—"

The debate went on for twenty minutes, and she never did pay him.

Our torturing of the Green deli wasn't for naught, however.

One day, there appeared a new deliveryman—a tall, handsome, 19-year-old Mexican with curly hair, fresh off the boat. His name was Carlos. Ruby was instantly in love. She pursued him until he was unable to resist. She stopped by his bodega when he was out back unloading boxes to offer him orange juice. She called the store and left flirty messages. She bought a "Teach Yourself Spanish" book to overcome their language barrier.

All of Ruby's exes were deli-men. Abdul had owned his deli, and she'd also had a fling with a young Mexican punk rocker who worked at a nearby convenience store.

As Ruby and Carlos's relationship grew, and he talked about taking her to visit his mother someday. This wasn't feasible, because he wasn't legal and they weren't married. But Carlos had a solution: They'd fly over together, and Ruby would fly home from Mexico the legal way. Carlos would enter the country again with a coyote, stuffed in the back of a trunk. It was nothing to worry about, he told her.

They never ended up visiting Mexico, but what struck me about his crazy plan was that it wasn't anything he thought twice about. In his world, and for so many others like him, that was just how things worked.

"I was still well under thirty. Like many young people, I'd assumed
the world—the physical reality of stores, restaurant locations, apartment
buildings, and movie theaters and the kind of people who lived in this or
that neighborhood—was far more stable than it was."

—Samuel R. Delany
in *Times Square Red, Times Square Blue*, 1998

693 8TH AVENUE'S
LAST STAND

The Playpen had been living on borrowed time for years. Two stories of decrepit old theater sitting on major air rights, 693 8th Avenue
was prime space. Rumors of its imminent closing had been around
long before I was there. But suddenly everyone heard it would close
at the end of May, then at the end of June, then July. A low, panicked
hum buzzed through the dressing room.

Peep-show girls were not regular strippers; they were a specific
breed. Many were too old and out-of-shape to work at a strip club.
All of us were accustomed to working behind glass; nobody wanted
to touch or be touched.

The electronics store on one side of the Playpen had closed up
shop, and on the other side, the Funny Store—a joke-and-gag supply
shop that had been in the area since 1957—put up a GOING OUT OF
BUSINESS sign. But the Playpen? It was almost impossible to imagine
it not existing.

I knew it was for real when the porter answering the phone
wouldn't put me on the schedule for the first week of August. "No,
last week, last week," he said. "Go to other place, other place work

now, okay?" They were supposedly putting in booths at one of the other porn stores Sammy owned, a block south.

The lot at 693 8th Avenue had been sold to a developer in 2003. Sitting in my booth reading *The New York Times*, I learned about plans from Tishman Speyer to turn it into a luxury condo or hotel.

I threw the paper against the wall. *Now what?*

And it wasn't just about forty or so peep-show girls being out of luck. At least a dozen porters would lose their jobs as well. Despite the twelve-hour, six-day-a-week shifts, it was a steady gig paying close to $600 a week—a lot of money to some, especially to those with a record, or who weren't citizens, or possessed only rudimentary English skills.

The guys who worked at the Playpen were lifers, especially in contrast to Gotham, where employees routinely quit by walking out the plate-glass door and into the night.

Sunday, July 29, 2007, 11 PM. The Playpen's last night of business occurred on the night of a full moon.

"All right, you guys," I said in the dressing room. "Let's really give it all we've got this one last time." Nobody laughed.

Downstairs, the store was already being dismantled around us. Big John's teenage sons were hauling up boxes from the basement, and the porters had all but cleared the shelves of videos. We stood in front of our booths, uneasy and unsure of ourselves. I felt more naked and exposed than usual.

"Last night," we said in a last-ditch attempt to get shows. "Last chance to see us! We're closing forever."

Many of the regular customers were so fully out of it that they hadn't realized the store was shutting down, even as it had been slowly emptied over the last two weeks, even though there was a GOING OUT OF BUSINESS sign on the door.

"For real?"

"Take a show!"

"Naw, that's okay."

It was amazing. Dozens of men had spent several days a week at the Playpen for years. Sometimes when I left the building at midnight, the same guys who were there at six o' clock were still wandering the aisles in a porn trance. And now they didn't care.

"Huh," several men said, shrugging and going about their way. Nobody expressed regret or remorse, or maybe even appreciation.

"We're *closing*," Raven explained slowly to a regular, an edge in her voice. The man had been coming around for years, but there was barely a flicker in his eyes.

We'd spent hours gleefully discussing what the hell these customers would do when the Playpen was gone. Where would they go? The Playpen was their entire social life. Now it was over. *They'd be sorry.*

But the customers were proving everybody wrong.

"You gonna visit me at the new place?" Susie asked another regular.

"I don't know, maybe," he said vacantly. "Sorry you're losing your job."

"I'll be fine," she snapped.

"Excuse me," a middle-aged white man asked me politely. "Do you have any shemales here?"

"No, just regular girls."

"Do you know where I can *find* any shemales?"

I shook my head wordlessly. He shuffled off.

"There's no shame in *his* game," remarked Susie, watching him walk away. "You know, they used to have shemales here. Or at Show World they did. They had their own stage. I guess it was a really good way to raise money for their surgeries—chicks with dicks. I mean, I can see how it would be the best of both worlds for some of these guys. It's like a chick, but with a dick, you know? Anyway, the sad thing was that after they had their surgery they were never really that popular again. It was their dicks that drew guys in."

She paused. "We danced on our own separate stage, and management didn't like us going in to see them, you know? But one day, I did. I was, like fuck it. We work together, we're doing the same thing. So I went in to watch them. They were all glaring at me. I guess they didn't like being stared at. I don't blame 'em." She shrugged.

Two German tourists wandered in.

"I am disappointed in New York," one said. Every European tourist said this in regard to our flesh trade when they learned that prostitution wasn't legal. "People told us it was supposed to be so wild! I don't see that."

He gazed up at the ceiling, pointing at the cameos of Greek goddesses. "I like those angels," he said. "This used to be a great place, no?"

I never trusted the men who approached from behind while I was at one of the side booths. They seemed to materialize out of nowhere, already talking and asking questions. This offender was a small black man, young, a little handsome, wearing a sweater and glasses, carrying a guitar on his back. It was the second time he had come to my booth to talk that night, but he hadn't quite gotten to the taking-a-show part. His speech sounded stilted and practiced. Talking to a stripper was much like giving a speech, or talking to yourself.

"One thing I'd suggest for you ladies," he was saying, "—after this place closes, or whatever—is some therapy. I would suggest that you all see a psychologist. Because the things you girls see every day . . . " he trailed off, distracted by my legs. "So how much is a show?" He was a bad person, I decided.

"Twenty-five dollars for me, ten for the booth. You have fifteen minutes left. Really. My shift is over in fifteen minutes."

He took the money out of his wallet, correct change and all, and held on to it, thumbing the bills thoughtfully. I fought the urge to snatch them out of his hands.

"Well, I gotta go down to the McDonald's so I can use the baf'-room . . . . Seriously, I have to use the bathroom, and I could not possibly enjoy the show you have to give if I don't relieve myself first, know what I'm sayin'? So, I'm sorry, I guess we don't have time. You know, I would have loved to see you—you're a beautiful woman. I wish you the best of luck in everything you do."

He refolded the money and put it away. He walked off slowly and then paused, turning halfway around. "Every day," he said solemnly. "Every day, do something that will further you toward your career, you know?"

"Yeah, you, too," I said drily, but he was too absorbed in his own narrative to hear the sarcasm.

It was midnight. They were running one last shift, the midnight-to-six graveyard, and then padlocking the doors—closing them and turning off the lights. I picked up my bag and left my red booth for the last time.

"I kinda just thought he'd *give* me the money," I said with irritation, recounting the story of my last customer to Raven upstairs in the dressing room. "You know?"

"I know, right? I mean, it's the last night, he spent ten minutes talking to you. . . . I mean, yeah. He should have just given it to you."

"He's an asshole," said Susie. "Tried to talk to me, I didn't let him."

"I'm sad. Just a little. It was a chapter in my life, you know?" Katrina said. "The Playpen saved my ass. It got me out of debt, and—" the next part was under her breath, "—bought me a new pair of titties."

The Playpen had saved my ass as well, although not in the same way or to the extent that it had saved Katrina's. It let me stay in New York and drop out for a while. I really was grateful to it for existing, for providing me with all the money I earned, and for the deception that making it was easy.

"I'm going to laugh so hard when all these guys have no place to go every day and stare," she continued. "Because the new place isn't set up like that. They won't be able to fuckin' stand in the aisles and hide or go around in circles for half an hour before taking a show anymore. They were in here doing that every day. Every single day."

Girls from other shifts came in to pack up their costumes, indiscriminately shoving heaps of bikinis and platform shoes into garbage bags. Lourdes and Kylie strolled in, fresh from an undoubtedly dead shift over at Gotham. "Ohhh, Playpen!" cried Lourdes. "I can't believe it!"

But longtime peep-show girls had been through this before: first with Show World closing around 1999, then the Playground in 2000.

Downstairs, Raven made the rounds, saying goodbye to all the porters with the haughty air of a grand dame doing her final curtain call. I hung back shyly and waved. I'd especially miss Lenox, the middle-aged, bearlike Trinidadian porter with a gray beard who handed out change during the week.

"Chelsea, after the neighborhood?" he'd asked when we'd first met.

"Yeah. Lenox, after Lenox Hill?"

Today, he called after me, "I'm gonna miss you. Do you like older men, sweetie? Come to papa!" He held his arms out wide and laughed until his belly shook.

"Do you ever wonder," asked one of the porters philosophically, mopping up the floor for the last time, "how many nut been busted up in here? Night after night . . . I mean, that's a lotta nut."

"Drink at the Film Center Cafe, mama?" Raven asked. We exited onto 8th Avenue at half past midnight. The air was humid, heavy with mist and steam.

"Well, I hate to be like this," she said, balanced on her stool in the blue glow of the bar, chocolate martini in hand. "But you missed it. You missed out on the really good money times here. Five years ago, six . . . it was almost $100 an hour. Two, three hundred? We thought that was a *bad* night. Now you're happy just to make two hundred! Back in the day . . . " she trailed off and shook her head suddenly, as if trying to dislodge a memory. "Back in the day . . . "

That night, I dreamt that someone came into the Playpen with a gun and a knife. He was firing shots, threatening to kill everybody. Raven and I ran, and she struggled with him, the fight somehow ending up in the basement. Like in a horror movie, she grabbed his knife and stabbed him in the head until he was dead. When he fell to the floor, I realized that there were twelve other dead bodies down there, other girls and porters he had killed.

My belt had fallen off in the struggle, and as I reached down, I saw that it was stained with blood. Suddenly, I was at Raven's place, a small white house, surrounded by trees and greenery and cats although, in reality, Raven lived in a studio in Fort Greene. I was trying to get home so I could make it to my internship the next morning, but it was already 8 AM. Susie was there, too, and my mother, for some reason. She wanted to drive us home. I was terrified that someone would mention work to her, that she'd find out what I'd been doing. "Don't tell her what we do," I hissed, but they didn't hear. I was trying to figure out how to hide my belt, still stained with blood.

A few months later, the Playpen was torn to the ground, leaving a gaping hole in its place. I walked by the site every day on my way to the new store. After a while, it became hard to imagine that the Playpen had ever been there at all.

ACT THREE

PDX

With the Playpen gone, I decided to take a working vacation. Ruby had talked about Portland often, the land of her youth and first experiences in the flesh industry.

"There are so many clubs," she told me, "that you can just pick a neighborhood and audition at a few of them in walking distance, and you can wear whatever you want and still make money—they have girls dancing in their glasses, short hair, even tattoos like mine aren't a problem." New York dancers had to hew more closely to the Playboy ideal.

Getting off the plane and walking sleepily through the carpeted airport, I took the light rail into the city, looking at the rolling green hills in the distance.

I spent the first day riding the bus around to different neighborhoods. Everyone chatted with each other on the bus, especially if they were sitting in the front section of seats that faced each other. They all said "thank you" to the driver when exiting. It was pleasant but bizarre. At nighttime, the buses turned on their interior overhead lights. They were pink and I thought of them as party lights.

I liked being alone in an unfamiliar city, like a girl in a noir movie. There were the warehouses of the Southeast side; there was weirdo gritty seediness of downtown and the quaint little houses on its outskirts. Smoking was allowed in bars, playing the lottery was practically an official pastime, and karaoke was unusually popular. I liked the city's working-class vibe, left over from its days as a scrappy port town.

Portland, Oregon also seemed like a great place to drink yourself into middle age. My view of it was a land of bars open at 11:30 AM, full of daytime drinkers and cigarette ash.

It had its own brand of seediness distinctly different from New York's. For example, riding the bus to the city's outskirts, on a depressed strip of commercial highway, every so often I saw a run-down wooden building with a hand-painted sign on it reading LINGERIE MODELING STUDIO.

Here was a setup I'd never even heard of before. I called Ruby.

"Oh, yeah, those," she said. "Jack shacks. Guys come in there and you do a show for them in a little room, but you're supposed to keep your underwear on. They can masturbate and stuff while they watch. It's like a peep show, but without the glass. But sometimes the girls there do extras. I never worked in one. I wouldn't recommend it."

Portland was a strip-bar mecca; there was a naked girl dancing on stage at dozens of dives at all times. They were listed on the signs outside the bars, right underneath the drink and chicken-wing specials: LIVE SHOWGIRLS, NUDE ENTERTAINERS. They didn't even get top billing over the chicken wings.

With the highest per-capita number of strip clubs in any city, the money was spread thin. It seemed as if every girl under thirty-five danced, or used to dance—there just wasn't the same stigma. The reason there were so many clubs was their state Constitution, with its extraordinarily strong free-speech clause. As a result, it was nearly impossible to keep the clubs out, and they'd grown like weeds.

I went down to a club on the Southeast side, Sassy's, before auditioning, so I'd know what to expect. I'd never danced onstage before, and I wanted to know what I was in for—if they used the pole, what kind of costumes they wore, if they really did wear glasses.

Sassy's was packed that Saturday night. A burly, tattooed doorman inspected my ID and removed a heavy chain doubling as a velvet rope to let me inside. There were two small stages surrounded by a tip rail that customers could sit in front of. The place was filled with guys of all ages—a few with girlfriends in tow—whooping it up and drinking beer.

The atmosphere wasn't depressing, like I was used to, but celebratory. AC/DC pounded out of the jukebox. A thin brunette with her long hair in a ponytail and a crocheted lavender bikini and black knee-high boots strode onstage and jumped onto the pole, spinning around to the floor. I sat down at the tip rail to watch. Immediately, the guy next to me put three $1 bills onto the rail. The men next to him did the same, so I pulled out a five. She flounced over to us, lay across the bar, took off her bikini top, and, with one motion, swept all the bills onto the floor of her stage. By the time she was done—naked and gorgeous, save for the knee-high boots—the stage was covered in maybe a hundred $1 bills.

She pranced offstage and immediately the next girl bounded out, a curvy, tattooed blond with bright-red streaks in her hair and black nail polish. I heard a familiar sinister marching beat, and I knew what song was coming.

Trent Reznor of Nine Inch Nails once bitterly joked that he should have named their *Downward Spiral* album "Music for Titty Bars," and it was true; the song "Closer" is one of the most popular song in strip clubs.

At first, it seems confusing as to why one would want to dance to such a brutal, nihilistic song—until you're the one onstage, naked and performing for dollars, everyone grasping for a piece. That's when the lyrics—"You can't have my absence of faith / you can't have my everything"—begin to make sense.

I watched the girl dance with complete disregard for the audience. She seemed to be exorcising something from deep inside her, and it felt almost too personal to be watching. "You bring me closer to God," the song screamed, and I thought there was an aspect of her performance that did bring one closer to God or something like it—she had lost herself in the moment, subsumed to something more powerful than herself.

Walking back to my shabby little guesthouse, I picked up the local industry magazine that listed all the clubs and sat down with a pen and paper to map out my auditions for the next day.

I went back to Sassy's first. I took a drink at the bar down the street to steel myself beforehand. I made a disparaging comment about playing the lottery during what I thought was innocuous bar patter and inadvertently offended the barmaid and the three other customers, all of whom played daily. Lotto was nothing to joke about here. I slunk out as soon as I finished my scotch.

Auditions at Sassy's were from noon to two. In the early afternoon, there was no scary doorman, no chain across the door, no rock music, and no people. The girls from the other night were gone. Instead, there were two bored-looking dancers performing to three customers who looked more interested in their beer. One was dancing to a slow, quiet Nancy Sinatra song, and the other was drinking at the bar. This, at least, killed my nervousness about dancing onstage for the first time.

"What songs do you want?" asked the bartender, a thirtysomething woman with dyed-black hair wearing a tight midriff shirt—she had to make tips, too. I asked for the Rolling Stones, "Gimme Shelter." I felt the desperation in the lyrics and the people nursing a draft in the middle of the afternoon slowly fading away. Onstage, I moved too quickly and stiffly, but catching a glimpse of myself in the mirror, I was surprised to see that I looked like everybody else. No one had to know if I felt awkward or nervous, unless I showed them.

There were no lap dances in Portland. In exchange for the all-nude entertainment, the Oregon Liquor Control Commission decided that there could be no touching between girls and customers, or even girls and each other. "Don't even shake another girl's hand if you're onstage," the Sassy's bartender warned me. Food had to be available in any establishment serving liquor, resulting in bar menus full of various items that could be fried.

Audition completed, I moved on to the Cabaret Lounge, a sprawling, decrepit lounge with blacked-over windows on West Burnside near a needle park and several missions. I worked there for two days, because the Sassy's dancer schedule was booked up until the next week.

One might have thought that the naked girls would be the Cabaret's main attraction. They were not; it was the video gambling. The zombie brigade lurched in around 3 PM, parking themselves in front of the lotto screen with a cigarette in one hand, beer balanced on one knee. They glanced at the stage only sporadically, occasionally finding the time to place a dollar or maybe a five, folded lengthwise, at the feet of the girl contorted fully nude on the floor or hanging upside-down on the pole.

Only a few of them seemed even remotely interested in the female scenery. It was as if they had picked a bar at random and ended up at one with strippers in it.

The girls there had a bitterly philosophical sense of humor about it all; scrawled on the dressing-room wall was a quote, "We are not human beings having a spiritual experience; we are spiritual beings having a human experience." The "showgirls," as we were quaintly called, sat in the basement dressing room, quietly reading paperbacks or doing homework between turns on stage.

"Chelsea, stand by for the second stage," crackled a voice over the intercom in the dressing room where I was still staring at the message on the wall. There was also a fist-size hole next to the quote, and a pair of panties nailed to the wall.

After making $60 that night, I decided that the next day's shift, would be my last time there. On my way out, the DJ inexplicably grabbed my arm and drew me toward him with a smile. He was sort of cute, if a little druggy-looking.

"Honey, what's your name?" he said.

"Chelsea," I said.

He grabbed me into a hug, holding me for longer than necessary, rubbing my back. I let myself stay in his arms for a moment before breaking away.

Mary's Club is the oldest strip joint in Portland, a tiny, seedy dive next to an SRO, and the best stage in town to make money. It opened at 11:30 in the morning; I auditioned at noon, ducking inside under the blinking neon sign—all nude revue!—and into the dark quiet.

Beat-up chairs were arranged to face the stage, making it resemble the waiting room at a DMV. A pale brown-haired girl in nothing but knee-high socks and black ballet shoes was dancing slowly, haughtily to Billie Holiday. She was mouthing the words, seemingly oblivious to the crowd, a sparse collection of old-timers and alcoholic regulars: *"Je ne peux pas travailler, je ne peux pas déjeuner . . . "*

She curtsied at the end of the song; the old men and two stoners in the front row respectfully placed bills on the stage. The room went silent because the jukebox needed feeding, and she walked slowly to the edge of the stage and cued up the next song. I was mesmerized. Now I knew why men came here: This scene was an oasis of calm where time stopped.

I picked "Ruby Tuesday" from the jukebox with my own change. Two young guys in the back came up to tip me, in addition to the old guy, the stoners, and a regular sitting at the bar who said his name was Steve.

Mary's was all booked up as well—a girl would be lucky to get one shift a week there. You had to work your way up. The club had a sorority of older dancers who had worked there part-time for years. They had their regular shifts, where they made four or six hundred bucks, and they had no intention of going anywhere. The protectionist scheduling policy was one of the reasons why dancers did so well. But many of them, I noticed, were well into their thirties.

Union Jacks was the punk-rock strip club where girls were heavily tattooed, pierced, and dreadlocked. I auditioned on a Saturday night and watched in awe as crowds gathered around a tattoo-covered warrior-princess with snaky blond tresses stalking the stage in only black combat boots, followed by a waifish redhead who twirled a Chinese paper umbrella, and a girl whose athletic routine was completely choreographed to her music.

They put me on the day shift—as a newcomer I had no seniority. Tuesday afternoon was nothing like the spectacle I had witnessed over the weekend.

In the basement dressing room, a handwritten sign warned that if anyone broke the mirrored wall behind the pole onstage again, accidentally or otherwise, they would have to pay $800 for a new one. The only other person down there was a cute lesbian who showed me her new genital piercing.

"It hurts so bad whenever I pee," she said. "Do you have any underwear I can borrow? I forgot to bring bottoms to wear." I handed her a pink pair with silver stripes. I didn't plan on wearing them again now, but I wanted to ingratiate myself.

I cultivated one regular in my three days at Union Jacks. Jeff was a nominally good-looking "consultant" in his thirties with a New York accent.

I first saw him gazing dreamily at me from the stage and sat down next to him afterward. He bought me a gin and tonic. My story for customers was that I had just moved to Portland a mere week before: "I just got tired of New York, I guess. It's so expensive!"

Eventually, I sold him a private dance. Although lap dancing didn't technically exist in Portland, at certain clubs "private dances" did. What that meant was we went behind a curtain, where the customer, Jeff, sat in a chair, and I danced fully nude in front of him, maintaining a six-inch distance at all times.

It was just a more private version of what men saw on the stage, and there was no worry of being expected to engage in extra activity—a camera was trained on us and beamed into the Russian mafia owner's home. He was known for enforcing the six-inch rule by chiming in over the loudspeaker during dances: "Hey, you keep it clean in there!" Big Brother was alive and apparently managing a strip club on East Burnside.

After Jeff and I exited the velvet-curtained area, a freckle-faced dancer with glasses and short brown hair rushed toward me. She was so cute, performing in just her knee-high argyle socks. I'd overheard her saying in the dressing room that she only bothered with dancing to keep in shape. It seemed that there were hundreds of girls in Portland dancing for fifty bucks a night.

"Did that guy Jeff do anything weird?" she demanded.

"Um, well, other than ask for my phone number and offer to take me out sometime, then no, just the usual," I said.

"Well, I had a dance with him the other week. He asked me if he could *bite my nipple!*" she replied indignantly. Her fury was endearing; I wondered how she would respond to the weirder requests at the Playpen. Portland's dancers were more innocent; they were exposed to so much less than the peep-show girls in Times Square.

The next day, Jeff came back to see me like he said he would. I was on stage, another slow afternoon. I'd worn my usual blond wig that day, but it made it hard to really dance without worrying about it slipping, so I'd removed it earlier. My own hair—short, dark brown, and mussed—better matched the atmosphere.

"You look so much better with your real hair," a couple girls said. They were right; I felt so much sexier. The wigs I'd been wearing were ridiculous.

Jeff sat down next to the stage, staring off into the distance. I realized that he didn't recognize me, so I crouched down with a smile: "Hey, it's me!"

He gaped.

" . . . Chelsea?" he asked, sounding horrified. "What . . . what did you do to your *hair?*"

"I cut it all off!" I laughed. I didn't feel like explaining that yesterday's hair was fake—hadn't it been obvious?

"I . . . I . . . " he looked around, shell-shocked. I sauntered back to the pole to let him calm down. When I turned around, he was already walking quickly out the door. Yesterday's love affair had been all about my hair.

After the lesbian girl and I made $60 each, three days in a row, I was forced to ask myself the question I'd been avoiding: What sort of people came into a strip bar to drink at three in the afternoon, often leaving without tipping, and why was I dancing for them?

But for a moment, that last evening at Union Jacks, none of it mattered. I was dancing to the ambient electronica of Portishead, a little buzzed, every move flowing into the next without thought. For four minutes, every slight was forgotten, and I was fully present, not just mentally but physically, feeling the grit of the stage under my heels, the beads of my long necklace hitting the floor, my muscles getting stronger from dancing every day, the good parts of my figure, the bad, all reflected in the mirrors behind the stage. I closed my eyes.

When I opened them at the end of the song, I saw that the bar—the men, the bartender, the other dancers—were riveted; they had all been watching. The music had stopped and the room was buzzing with silence. Slowly, they began to clap.

"In the end, junk is just another nine to five gig. The hours are just
more inclined towards the shadows."

—Jim Carroll

SFO

The day shifts in Portland felt like self-abuse, so on my third day
at Union Jacks, I decided not to go back. I felt like an idiot, taking my
clothes off in the middle of the afternoon for dollar bills that didn't
add up to anything.

"What am I doing here?" a tall brunette had asked her reflection in
the mirror in the dressing room on my last night.

"You're up on stage next, duh," said a blonde doing the splits on
the floor.

"No, I mean, what am I doing stripping? This is ridiculous."

It was ridiculous, my little idea of a working vacation. Running
around to strip clubs with a bag full of shoes and dresses and underwear and making $7 in stage tips was ridiculous. It was interesting to
learn about the regional differences in the stripping industry, I supposed, but I'd come to make money. This was, after all, my job.

So I went to San Francisco. Attempting a geographic cure was
common in the trade. You could show up in town with your costume
and Lucite heels and be working the next day. When times got tough,
strippers turned a glittery eye toward the Next Thing, a constant

variation of Fuck This Place, I'm Going to Go Where I Can Make Some Real Money. It could be Vegas, a new club, New Jersey. They were usually back within a month.

"Be with ya in just a second," said Max from the entrance to Roaring 20s, a small strip joint open at noon on San Francisco's red-light strip, North Broadway. He picked up the phone.

"Yeah, okay. Bachelor parties? What do we do for bachelor parties? Well, the bachelor and the best man are always free. Everybody else, $20. You can get a room, a private room, for $150 and $100 every hour after that. That doesn't include girls, though. Girls are extra."

Max was exactly how a strip-club proprietor should look: bearlike and rotund, with a long gray ponytail, and pointy beard. He wore suspenders. A few gold teeth glinted as he spoke into the phone.

"*And* we can get the bachelor on stage, have the girls jump up and down on him, have their way with him, whatever. Then we tell him to open his mouth and close his eyes because the girl wants to give him a big kiss. Then *we stick a dildo in his face!*" He roared with laughter.

"Hahaha, we snap a picture so you get something to blackmail him with, he gets a T-shirt, all that. That's sixty bucks to get the bachelor up on stage. So what time did you say you were coming? Friday? Friday night? Around eight? Yeah, sounds good. Awright, bye now."

A sad-looking young guy in his early twenties stepped out from behind the heavy maroon curtains shielding the club from the street, dressed in the requisite 1920s-style uniform of black pants, a red shirt, a top hat, and suspenders. He picked up a bouquet of balloons and glumly opened the door, heading out onto the blazing sidewalk to hustle customers.

"So ya wanna work," Max said, turning toward me and setting down the phone heavily. He drew back the curtains to the empty club and beckoned me inside.

The desperation inside Roaring 20s was palpable. It wasn't anything obvious; I could just smell it. This wasn't one of the fancier clubs on the strip, but I didn't feel like facing the scrutinizing physical inspections that the nicer places would perform. They would tell me to come back after I'd gotten a spray tan and a manicure.

Roaring 20s was a juice bar, which meant that the dancers were fully nude onstage but no alcohol was served. The "juice" was warm pop without ice served from the fountain behind the DJ booth.

Max led me through the velvet-curtained lap-dancing booths on the second floor to his dingy office. As I filled out some paperwork, I realized this place was owned by the Déjà Vu corporation, who owned most of the other clubs on this stretch of Broadway. They had a bad reputation among dancers for taking a large chunk of their earnings in the form of a "shift fee."

I snorted in disbelief when Max said the shift fee would be $140.

"Forty?" I asked, certain I had misheard him.

"One hundred forty," he said in a practiced tone that told me he had gotten this reaction many times before. Girls hired at these corporate-owned joints were just another source of income for the clubs themselves. It was a racket: One more dancer meant one more house fee, and if she hardly made anything above that, tough. Dancers hustled whatever scraps they could—or, more likely, they performed extras. They would slowly make adjustments to their personal boundaries, drinking more, lowering expectations. Max, in turn, would look away when he saw something going on in the dark corners of the club.

Max leaned across the desk to obliquely address this point. "The Champagne Lounge is fifty minutes," he said slowly. "You get two hundred. The rest goes to us. Try to sell the guy a bottle of champagne."

"Fifty minutes?" I asked.

"Fifty. Like a therapeutic hour," he explained.

I went downstairs to the dressing room and put on a new dress I'd purchased from a sex shop down the street. It was a short, silvery-blue flapper-style dress covered with fringe. A couple of girls wandered in sullenly, bitching about rides and kids, shoving arms and legs into thongs and dresses.

Max turned on the music, which boomed through the empty room, and we ran the shift.

Out on the floor, I sat in a booth against the wall and watched the other dancers while waiting for my turn onstage. They were workmanlike in their dancing, performing the same moves over and over during every stage set. A Latina dancer lowered her body parallel to the floor, hands behind her gripping the pole, waving her vagina in our faces. A pale, beautiful redhead lay on her back with her feet on the floor, grabbed her heels, raised her hips off the floor, and gyrated. Her face remained perfectly blank each time.

Customers trickled in but left quickly, as the place was dead, and the girls looked sullen and depressed. Guys paid $20 just to get in the door, so they didn't realize we also needed them to tip.

A middle-aged husband-wife tourist couple came in and poked each other while they watched me dance onstage, giggling. The lady put a few dollars next to me. Three young Mexicans wandered in and left after a couple of songs.

When there were no men at all, Max turned off the lights and the music, and we lay down on the couches to sleep. It was so boring, as dull as any office job where you were chained to a computer all day.

Max turned the music back on when the next customer came in, some bluesy-rock tunes. "You like that?" he asked me. "That's my band. I play guitar." I nodded my head in time with the beat to show him I liked it.

We all needed something else to believe in. If this was all there was, we'd go insane.

It dawned on me that I wasn't having new experiences as much as I was cataloging a travelogue of despair. New York, San Francisco, Portland: My view of them was all the same—just dressing rooms full of women struggling for dwindling pools of cash, indistinguishable days and nights, mitigated by various iterations of ennui and despair. We performed the same tasks every night, naked, and nobody seemed to care. We could go across the country and do more or less the same job in various strip clubs or peep shows, but it wasn't freedom. Nobody here was winning.

I was reminded of what else I had to look forward to if I continued a life on the outskirts when I received a phone call from my friend Ari, who was living in San Francisco now. I'd met him back in Detroit, through my boyfriend at the time, Drew. We'd spent countless hours in his Section 8 apartment in the Cass Corridor, getting stoned and watching cartoons while lounging on bucket seats torn from some dead automobile.

Ari was a gregarious, wickedly smart slacker, a Persian Jew from Russia who had scored a low-income apartment and was always letting Indian guys from the local university stay with him.

"They came to Detroit to get an education and get out of India," he used to say of his rotating cast of guests, "but then they found out that Detroit is worse than Calcutta!"

At this, Ram, one of the Indian guys staying with him who was Brahmin, spoke up to defend himself: "In my city, the people worship at a temple where the gods are named after my family!"

No one was really sure what Ari did for a living other than sell weed. Now he was living in San Francisco, doing much of the same but without the apartment.

"That's too bad," he said over the phone, when I told him I would be leaving in a few days. "Because I got a place lined up for three weeks and you could've stayed with me. Well, I mean, I'm homeless. But I'm about to have this place downtown, in Union Square—seriously! This gay European dude—I don't think he knows I'm not gay, but he likes me. I mean, he doesn't know me all that well, but he knows I'm homeless. Anyway, he's going to Burning Man and he said I could stay there the whole time. And I'm gonna need some help tearin' up the place."

Suddenly his voice seized up, and coughs and shudders shook the line. When he was able to speak again he sounded different.

"Shit, Sheila, I was staying in Oakland and I got a staph infection. It was eating up my leg. I still have a scar. And now I'm recovering from strep. They gave me antibiotics, and I've never taken those in my whole life until two months ago. And I got this weird rash that covers like a third of my body, from hanging around with all the other homeless people in the Tenderloin."

"Is there, um, a free clinic that you could go to?" I asked. Jesus Christ, Ari sounded grim.

"Yeah, like on a sliding scale, way better than the emergency room, and they have pamphlets there you would not believe. Like, they tell you how to shoot up the right way, they tell you—they tell you how to smoke crack the right way. Like, always use a clean pipe, and what kind of Brillo pad to buy. And then, the very last line of the pamphlet is about if you're going down on someone after having smoked crack, you should *try not to let them come in your mouth*. Ha! Wish I would've read that pamphlet before I let the last guy—haha, just kidding—" he was racked with coughs again. When he came back, his voice turned into a whine.

"Oh, shit. Oh, man. Anyway"—cough—"I'm probably gonna get my own place soon, in the Tenderloin, for real cheap. They got a program they use to hook up bums like me with apartments. So you should come back out here. Especially in the next three weeks. I'm gonna have that awesome apartment and bring a parade of freaks on through there—"

The phone cut out.

I couldn't keep going on like this or I was going to end up like Ari. When I got back to New York, I was going to have to quit. Definitely as soon as I got back. I would have to work more to save up some money first. But I'd quit after that. I just had to figure out what to do next.

It was only after experiencing a show as a customer that I began to have some understanding of its appeal.

San Francisco had a peep show called the Lusty Lady. The old theater, near the Broadway strip of nudie clubs, was dark and musty inside. The affable-looking young dudes sitting behind the counter handing out change did a double take when I came in, then quickly resumed their cool. Realizing that I was the only girl there for non-work purposes, I ambled through the dark, maroon lobby overly casually, pretending I knew what I was doing.

Once in the back room, I faced a line of dark closet-like booths and shut myself into one, fumbling for my coins. You paid in quarters, but a quarter only gave you thirty seconds of viewing. After I dropped in a couple, the curtain went up.

There it was: my first peep show from the other side. It was a girl vending machine, a mirrored fishbowl-like room full of girls, strolling and lolling around on hot-pink wall-to-wall carpet. They stalked their tiny space, zeroing in on open windows like lions on the plains hunting an antelope. There were four of them in there. A thick Asian girl with tattoos was facing a window on my left, lying on her back with her legs wide open, clacking her shiny black platforms together.

It wasn't sexual attraction that I felt, more like a longing to be one of them, to be the strange, painted, pretty creature everyone was looking at, to crawl in there with them and absorb their heated, rosy glow.

A sweet-looking white girl with brown curly hair and freckles sauntered over to me and smiled. She peered down at me. Female customers were an unusual sight.

"Hi," she said through the glass. I could barely hear her; it sounded like she was speaking from underwater.

"Hi," I said back. Seeing her was like looking at a version of myself.

She began to sway back and forth to the droning beat of the music playing faintly in the background. Suddenly she put her foot on a bar and opened her legs, giving me a long look at her vagina. I didn't know how to react—it was crude, but she probably didn't even think twice about it. Neither had I, until now. Was that how I looked? It had to be.

She straightened herself up and began swaying back and forth again in a style that was completely her own.

Another performer approached the window curiously. She was older than the first one but had a sprightly, mischievous grin, crimson-dyed hair, and a petite, bird-like figure. Her breasts were small with brown nipples, which she absentmindedly massaged with both hands while looking at me.

"You should come work here with us!" she shouted through the glass. "You're cute!"

"I already do!" I shouted back. "In New York!"

"What?" she said. "I can't hear you." She pointed at the speakers above her, blasting music. We were really just lip-reading.

"I work in a peep show in New York!" I yelled through the glass. I needed her to know for some reason.

She smiled and nodded, and I wasn't sure if she had heard me. We were losing contact. I wondered what they were like outside of here, how they spent their free time. I wanted to know all about their lives. The girls waved at me, and then the window went down.

I'd been a professional peep-show girl for over a year now, and for the first time, I had an inkling of what it was all about. The girls in the fishbowl had seemed to exist exclusively for me.

PERSONNEL CHANGES

When I returned to New York in September, everything had changed. A dark, urgent mood had overtaken 8th Avenue.

Back at Gotham, several of our favorite porters had vanished: Cumari and Nemil, a West African and a Sri Lankan, both of whom had been there since my first day.

"Immigration or something did a sweep," Ruby told me in an affectless tone. "And now a bunch of people are gone. Not just here, either, but up and down the avenue. You know, I always noticed, some of those guys got paychecks on Fridays, and some got envelopes of cash." Neither of them had papers.

"Oh, and Cumari wasn't his real name," she added. "Neither was Nemil." I felt betrayed until I remembered that Chelsea wasn't my real name, either.

Basil was also gone. He just walked out in the middle of a shift one night after an argument with a manager.

Everyone was knocked up. Girls were always getting pregnant, but a rash of pregnancies had broken out recently. Sapphire was huge now and had taken off to Florida. A couple other girls I didn't know well were pregnant too.

And then there was the new peep show. At 687 8th Avenue, about a block south from the late Playpen, it was a much smaller, three-story porn store referred to as Gotham 1. (The Gotham I'd been working at for the last year was known as Gotham 4 from then on, for reasons no one was clear on.) Big John and company added booths to the empty third floor to accommodate the Playpen girls.

A few weeks before the Playpen closed, management encouraged us to go over there and work, to try to build up a clientele or, as Big John put it, "get guys into the habit." I never went; I was in denial that my comfortable setup was about to change.

Ruby refused too, even as they threatened her with firing.

"I won't work that block," she spat out as we drank beers during a slow shift at G4. It was half a block from Abdul's deli, and Gotham 4 was a safe five blocks north. "I don't want to go to jail," she added. "If I see Jamal standing outside, smoking fuckin' cigarettes . . . . I'll do something bad, I swear I will."

But unless I wanted to scrounge and scrape for money again, Gotham 1 was my new home, and I didn't have much of a choice but to accept it. Unless I wanted to, say, quit. But in order to quit, I had to make some money.

When I went to work at the new place for the first time, all the chairs were occupied. I looked up to the balcony at the girls; three enormous pairs of fake breasts stared back at me, accompanied by three hard, unsmiling Spanish faces. Linda, the thirty-six-year-old schoolgirl, was there in her ever-present plaid skirt and belly-baring white oxford. Her breasts, stretched around a too-big set of implants, pulsed with blue veins. The other two were girls from the Playpen that I hadn't seen before because they worked days.

I trudged over to Gotham 4. The back room seemed even darker than usual, and the bright sunlight outside begged me not to shut myself up in the peep show on such a nice afternoon. It just seemed perverse.

I turned around, got on the subway, and went home. I walked over to Williamsburg and bought a novel, something by a young male Brooklyn writer who had been reviewed favorably by *The Times*, and sat in a café and read all day.

When I showed up the next week to follow through with my first day at G1, I saw immediately that there were going to be problems. The live girls were situated on the third floor in a long, narrow, dimly lit corridor lined with six booths.

The girls in the first three booths were the most visible and therefore at the best advantage for getting shows. The three other girls in the back could hardly be seen. Just looking at the corridor made me itchy again. We rotated booths every half hour as at the Playpen, but it still sucked. Cramped into a hallway-size space, we couldn't escape the choking cleaning fumes, or each other.

There wasn't a dressing room, so we had to change inside our booths, with no mirrors. There were only a few lockers, already claimed by the suck-ups and kiss-asses. The rest of us had to drag our shit over from Gotham 4 or from home. This made things complicated, because some girls needed to hide their dancing gear from husbands, boyfriends, or kids.

Ahmed had gotten to keep his job and was posted on a stool in the corner, giving out change and watching over us. The day-shift porter was Freddy, a kindly old man who spoke more Spanish than English.

Behind them, two steps up, were rows of bookcases, lined with ancient, abandoned pop-culture throwaway books from the '70s and '80s, stocked to satisfy the 60/40 rule—one of Giuliani's brilliant ideas, which required adult businesses to dedicate 60 percent of their floor space to "non-adult" material. So G1 had piled up some overstock on the third floor and called it a day. Behind the forest of books were the same microwave and stained folding table from the Playpen.

On the opposite end of the peep-show corridor was the office. It was mostly full of boxes of shoes—Ellies, a reliable stripper-shoe brand—and bottles of Rush, which had to be refrigerated. It also held the schedule, which we were no longer allowed to personally touch. We couldn't sign up for shifts ourselves anymore; instead, we had to call Big John, a weekly adventure. It seemed like he just wanted to have more control over us.

This conversation increasingly took place in the lobby of the journalism building at Columbia University, where I had started an unpaid internship at the *Columbia Journalism Review*—answering phones and checking facts, mostly. I was preparing, as everyone always threatened, to get the hell out of Times Square.

Big John always answered the phone sounding as if I had called him in the middle of a knock-down, drag-out argument.

"*Hello?*" he bellowed.

"Um, yeah, it's Chelsea. I want to be put on for Tuesday and Saturday, six to midnight."

"Chelsea! I'm shit of this shit from you! You're either working too many shifts or too few! I don't have six to twelve for you, okay? I'm not going to take it anymore."

Slam. I'd wait a couple minutes and call him back.

"Then put me on graveyard," I said when he answered.

"Chelsea, I'm not going to put up with this—"

"I said to *put me on the graveyard!*" I screamed back, and hung up the phone.

Vito made himself right at home in the new space, holing up in the office many nights, watching the game. The window, overlooking 8th Avenue, was partially blocked by the big neon GOTHAM CITY sign. The blinds were often drawn, but it didn't matter: The pink-and-blue neon sign shone through the blinds twenty-four hours a day, like a buzzing chemical sun.

Although Vito and Sammy and Big John had expressed high hopes for the new place, predicting that girls might even draw more business there than at the Playpen, it wasn't happening.

Girls who had coasted by working three nights a week were suddenly fighting to work five. Joyce, the gum-snapping sister, actually made plans to get breast implants in a desperate bid to increase her income. Everyone else was canceling cable.

The ex-Playpen crowd, cooped up in our dark hallway—already bitchy, competitive, and prone to drama—was tense to a breaking point.

The boredom made Raven loopier than usual—in one night, she threw up after taking some OxyContin bought off a customer ("I have no idea why it made me do that!"), made orgasmic moaning sounds into the mike, and rubbed herself against the door of her booth, shrieking, "Wanna see my *chooooooch?*"

She wrote out a script to follow on the microphone, which she had somebody translate into Spanish: "*Choca caliente eeeen tuuuu carrrra! Hot pussy all up in your face, guys, ohhhh, papi..!*"

The next night, I watched her laugh as she reenacted a bizarre scene with a customer, all sincere and overdramatic:

"I started telling him, 'I love you, baby. I love you so much," she said, covering a snicker from escaping before she got to the punch line.

"He started crying," she said, pantomiming masturbating and crying at the same time, laughing through her impression.

"*What?*" I asked in disbelief. It was beyond taboo to fuck with a customer by telling him you *loved* him, of all things. She must have gotten really burned out while I was away. "Did he . . . did he *come?*"

Raven thought for a minute. "Yeah," she snorted, laughing some more. "Yeah, he came."

Some of the Playpen's weirdo regulars followed us over to Gotham 1, but the new guys were a mystery. The new peep show was four storefronts closer to the Port Authority, and there was no doubt that this contributed to the stranger raft of customers.

"No touchin'? Aw, fuck that," a middle-aged black man, barechested underneath a dirty winter parka mumbled, walking away. "I got seven years backed up in me—the least I wanna do is touch." I could only imagine he had just gotten out of prison.

That was almost quaint compared to the Stroller Incident. One dead Saturday night, we were all hanging around, watching the full-color TV monitor that showed the first floor. It showed us how many customers were downstairs so we could get on the mike and entice them to climb three flights to see some live, nude, tired girls.

The monitor showed a man pushing a stroller around while looking through the porn videos.

"Hey, does anybody else see what I'm seeing?" I asked.

"What the fuck?" Lourdes yelled. "This guy has a *baby* in here! Look!"

"Oh, my God." We were all gathered around the TV now, watching him push the stroller through the store. A woman came into view beside him.

"Oh, look, he's with his wife or whoever."

"Well, that don't make it any better."

Suddenly the man took his jacket off and threw it over the baby in the stroller. So it couldn't see the pornographic video covers or the wall of dildos and vibrators?

"Oh, noooo, he didn't!" we shrieked.

"Somebody get on the mike and tell him to get the fuck outta here!" Vito came upstairs.

"Vito, look! There's a guy with a *baby* in here!" He peered at the monitor. It was too much for even him.

"Goddamn it," Vito said. "Fucking assholes. These fucking guys. Goddamn."

He got on the office phone and called down to the front desk: "Get those assholes out of here."

The couple and their baby left before anyone could shame them into it.

A nondescript, middle-aged white guy came in a few hours later.

He motioned toward me and then Elizabeth, a short, curvy Spanish girl with bleached-blond hair.

"He's really cheap," Elizabeth whispered.

On cue, he handed us each a $20 bill, bestowing them as if they were hundreds. I crowded in to her booth.

"He's going to ask you to spank me," she told me, just before the window went up.

Sure enough, as soon as the lights went on, the man sat down and said, "Now I want you to bend her over your knee and spank her like the bad daughter she is."

I closed my eyes for a second as a wave of dizziness hit me, then composed myself.

I sat down and raised my hand. For just a second, it shook while hovering over Elizabeth's plump bottom.

HEIDI'S LAST DAY

Heidi was coming to the end of her peep-show days. She was hugely, heavily pregnant. She sat on her chair in flat jelly sandals, belly in front of her like a big rubber ball.

I never understood why women insisted on working pregnant. It just seemed taboo. But some guys—not weird fetishists, either—some guys just didn't care.

"You know how some women don't lose the weight after they have the baby?" Camry said, watching Heidi wobble up the stairs to the dressing room. "I think Heidi gonna be like that. That weight gonna stick to her." She smiled affectionately; she didn't say it to be mean.

Many women bounced back to work after their baby, sometimes even got plastic surgery. But Heidi's days as Gotham's top earner were probably over, even though she kept saying she would come back.

"How long you gonna keep working?" asked Camry.

"Here? Until it's uncomfortable for me physically. At the hair salon, up until the very end."

"You shouldn't work around those chemicals, mami, with the hair dye and stuff. You bought a baby book yet? So you know what to expect?"

"No, not really."

This was surprising. Heidi was one of the most responsible, functional girls here. At seven and a half months, I thought she would have started to prepare.

One day, working alongside me and Ruby, she was rejected for being pregnant for the first time. The guy didn't realize she was pregnant when she was sitting down, because she was wearing a flowing gown. But when she stood up, he backed away, stammering an excuse.

She tried to talk him into it anyway. "You don't understand. I don't take the robe completely off," she told him. "So you don't see . . . that. You see here"—she gestured to her breasts—"and down here." She gestured to below her waist. He wasn't convinced and backed away.

It was so bizarre to me. Some guys were fine with masturbating to a visibly pregnant stripper. Others were not, which seemed more normal. I knew that the girls kept working because they needed the money, but I still couldn't wrap my mind around it.

Heidi was used to making most of the shows in any shift, but this time, Ruby made all the money.

"I think I'm done," Heidi said, laughing about all the men passing her up. "I think this might be it."

THE JOB INTERVIEW

I was sitting across a desk from a tall, tough-looking guy with a shaved head in the basement of a bar in Brooklyn. Reggaeton thumped through the ceiling. The lighting was dim and fluorescent. I stared at the chipped linoleum floor while waiting for him to finish scrutinizing my ID.

"Eric," he said, outstretching his hand. "Mac-Clear, you say?" he asked, squinting at my driver's license. "You Irish got a problem with the drinking. Us Norwegians, though, we ain't much better. So you know Ruby, huh?"

"Yeah. We're friends and I worked with her at another place."

He nodded. "Guys like Ruby," he said somberly. "She's pretty quiet, but guys like her."

Someone pounded on the door, and a bleached-blond Latina girl burst in, tottering on heels and tugging her short dress down with one hand. She handed Eric a thick pile of one-dollar bills, and he ran them through a dollar-counting machine that rifled through the bills in seconds. He glanced at the machine's reading and handed the girl $240 in twenties.

"Eric, call me a cab?" she asked, folding the bills into a thick wad and stuffing it into her purse.

He got on the phone: "Yeah, I need a pickup at Pumps," he told the dispatcher. "*Pumps*," he repeated in irritation. "You know, the bar? Well, you should know. We order about a hundred, hundred-fifty cabs a week from you guys. 1089 Grand Street."

"Metroline," he told her. She nodded and left.

"Stand against the wall," he motioned to me and snapped my headshot with a digital camera. "Like that one?" he asked, turning the viewfinder toward me. He put the camera into the computer and made a printout from a small white box, then pinned my photo to the wall and wrote CHELSEA underneath.

"Photo printer," he said. "Pretty cool, huh. You ever see one?"

"No . . . " I dutifully admired the shiny white box.

"Listen, Chelsea, get your outfit on, do whatever you gotta do to yourself, and then meet me back upstairs so you can audition."

I went into the dressing room where some black and Spanish girls were changing, mostly older. Some glared, and others simply ignored me. I put on my bluish-silver fringed dress that I'd worn in San Francisco, some fishnets, my black heels, an auburn bobbed wig. I caught one girl rolling her eyes at my getup and practically heard her thoughts: *That skinny white girl thinks she's gonna work here, no way, she got no booty . . . .*

Upstairs, a hip-hop song was going, "*Uh-uh, oh-kay, what's up, shut up . . .* " Eric gave me a quick once-over, but there was no leer in his eye. Ruby was right, I thought: Eric was a good guy. He was one of us.

"All right," he said. "You don't gotta go up on stage. I'm not gonna put you through that. You free tomorrow?"

"Yeah." I needed a break from the peep shows, again. The desperate atmosphere at G1 was so different from the party atmosphere of the Playpen, and I thought maybe I could make more money here.

"Okay then. We open at four."

Once again, I was hired.

Ruby had been working at Pumps because she was just as tired of the peeps. It was a topless dive in Bushwick, near the BQE, where girls danced on a narrow, carpeted stage behind the bar, one twenty-minute set every hour. There were three poles. For tips, we navigated around the bartenders to let the patrons slip money into our garters or bra straps.

You could also make a little money by doing the occasional lap dance, which was totally cool because we were required to keep our clothes on and the guys weren't allowed to touch. The outer-borough stripping industry was totally different. It barely existed in Brooklyn, with only two or three clubs, although Queens had a cluster of downscale strip joints near the 59th Street Bridge. It was mostly local girls working at these places, with a local, usually working-class clientele. The biggest difference was race: The clubs outside Manhattan hired black and Latina girls, while it was well known that the upscale clubs in the city avoided hiring minorities unless they were Russian, Eastern European, or otherwise light-skinned.

The next afternoon, Eric bought me a gin and tonic while I sat at the bar with three other dancers and watched a white woman in her forties spin gracefully around the pole to an empty room.

Loca, a big, curvy Puerto Rican girl with long curly hair, dark lipliner, and drawn-on eyebrows, grabbed my arm and pulled me outside. I didn't smoke but went along anyway. Hanging on a hook near the door were black satin robes for us to wear when we went outside to smoke in full view of the passing traffic. THERE GOES THE NEIGH-BORHOOD, it read in hot pink script across the back.

I stood outside the club with her and another older white woman, Gypsy.

Gypsy looked ancient under the halogen streetlights. Her lips were painted a garish purple, her skin beginning to wrinkle. She looked like a washed-up '80s punk rocker, but I liked her.

"Loca said you're cool, that you're like us," she said, peering at me. "But I haven't got the chance to talk to you yet."

"Eric was worried that you wouldn't get along with people here 'cause you're not from out here," Loca drawled. "But you're like us. You're a *bitch!*"

I wasn't a bitch, I was just quiet, and so people projected whatever they wanted onto me. That was my job: to be an empty canvas.

Loca's arms were scarred from elbow to wrist with scarred-over razor marks, and she rummaged around in her purse, first removing a vial of cocaine and sniffing a bump off her pinkie nail, then extracting a pill bottle. "Prozac," she said, rattling it at me. "Want some?"

"Oh, no, I'm cool."

"That customer you was talking to at the bar, owns that store down on Grand?" Gypsy continued, referring to a young Hispanic guy with an accent so thick I could only understand maybe a third of what he said.

"Yeah, that one. He says he's gonna find me a loft apartment in this neighborhood. I play drums, man, and it's hard to do stuff late at night, fuckin' neighbors. But in a loft, man, you can do whatever the fuck you want."

Twelve hours and four gin and tonics, a shot of Jager, a shot of Hennessey, a Heineken, and a glass of whiskey later, Eric called me a cab, just as he had done with the girl the night before.

"Be sure to ask what company they're from," he told me. "You can't just be getting into any car that stops in front of this place. Tonight I'm using New Eastern."

I waited in front of the bar under the awning, and soon a van pulled up. "What company?" I asked suspiciously.

"New Eastern," said the man in a West African accent, and I crawled in. It had the middle seats taken out and I collapsed onto the bench seat in the back. I had $287 in ones stuffed in my purse. I hadn't bothered to have Eric run them through the bill-counter and exchange them for twenties, because I was too tired, and $287 for twelve hours at Pumps was bullshit. Two or three times that amount wouldn't be enough. It would never be enough.

This was not what I had imagined when I moved to the city. The exhausted 4 AM cab rides from strange, desolate parts of Brooklyn, all the nameless, faceless men, *the heaviness*. It was the heaviness that got to me.

I realized that things never changed in this world. I could hop from city to city and from club to club, but there was no geographic cure, and no upward trajectory or arc or hope for the future. There was simply the grind, and the money. There would be $500 nights and $50 nights.

But all of them would end with me getting into the back of this car near the BQE at 4 AM, asking the driver, "What company?" And eventually I'd be too old to do it anymore, or maybe I was already.

> "I exist down here now, if you won't be offended by me putting it that
> way . . . I'm standard-issue . . . Every creature has its habitat, and I'm
> in mine right now. If I think I'm above it, I'm only kidding
> myself, and I've stopped kidding myself."

> —Tom Wolfe, *The Bonfire of the Vanities*

THE TURKEY'S NEST

Luanne and I strolled into the Turkey's Nest one night in early
October, midway through a night of drinking. It was an old-line
dive on the border of Williamsburg occasionally infiltrated by hipsters but mostly populated by old men and Hasids watching sports.
She walked in and immediately took over the room. Everybody
would know her by name by the time she left. She was working as a
publicist now.

I spotted Scott, who'd alternately slept on our couch and flirted
with me when I lived at Jesse's apartment, in the back of the bar. He
was leaning over the pool table, wearing tight jeans, cowboy boots
(another Southerner), and a mustache instead of his usual beard.
Looking up from his cue, he saw me looking at him and sauntered
over and gave me a hug. I felt a pleasant jolt.

"What you been up to?" he said with a grin, motioning for the
bartender.

"Nothing," I said, trying to make it sound sexy. I just existed, floating through life and bars and subway stations.

I leaned back against the bar. He leaned back in his chair and drank his whiskey. Meeting his eyes, I did the same. An hour later, we were making out in front of the bar.

Luanne had already left, having conned a cab ride out of some bald-headed friend of Scott's. She'd convinced him that it would be cheaper if they shared a cab. I knew that she'd end up getting the driver to go to her place first and stick the guy with the entire bill.

"Let's get out of here, sweetheart," Scott said, pinching me on the cheek. He held my hand while walking back to Greenpoint, down Bedford, and across the park, him wheeling his bike with his free hand.

"You're so hot," he said as we kissed and groped on the deserted corner of Manhattan and Norman.

"Call me later, okay?" I said, easing out of his grasp. I liked Scott, and I wanted to see him again, and if I went home with him now, he would never call. Standing there, he looked as confused as he did the time I took the beer from him and went straight to my room.

It didn't matter; he still never called. For a few weeks afterward, toward the end of a long night dancing behind the bar at Pumps, I sometimes saw his face in the crowd, but whenever I got a little closer to accept the dollar bill, it blurred and morphed into someone else.

But otherwise, things were turning around. I got a part-time job writing posts for Gawker, a media blog that fancied itself in the tradition of *Spy* magazine by way of Fleet Street gossip-mongering. They paid me $12 an hour to work two or so days a week. My first assignments were arbitrary and vague: I spent one afternoon wandering around the courthouse downtown and another at the public library going through old issues of British tabloid *Private Eye*. I wrote posts about a sparsely attended picket line at *The Wall Street Journal* and fly-on-the-wall accounts from parties I hadn't been invited to.

I also wrote about what I knew, without saying how I knew it.

My editor must have been scratching his head after I filed the following slice-of-life dispatch about Pumps while conveniently forgetting to mention why or how I was there in the first place:

"Stripper" is the styling-of-choice for so many non-stripping ladies these days. So what's the difference between an actual pole-dancer and,

say, classily "branding" yourself as a young, sex-positive lass? (Heck, even the housewives of New Jersey have stripper-pole workout sessions in their own homes.) Can anybody tell the difference between a strip club and the basement of Happy Ending on Tuesday nights anymore? This weekend, I went deep into Brooklyn to a neighborhood strip bar to find out if it felt just like the playgrounds of Manhattan.

"You're, like, a reporter, huh?" asked the owner. "You met Joey, the big guy sittin' at the bar? Yeah, he works for The Daily News. In here all the time."

Alcoholic regulars lined the bar in front of the stage. A lone Hasid in a backwards baseball cap sat in the back. He said his name was Haim and he's a student of the Torah.

"Are you married? My wife would kill me if she knew I was here," he said. "She's very conservative!" He sounded afraid.

In the ladies' restroom, which was single-occupancy, a dancer pounded on the door. "Let me in, I'm insane!" she said. "I'll slit my wrists, I'm known for it!"

Her stage name was the Spanish word for "crazy," and she asked if she could ask a question. "I don't want to offend you," she said. "I just want to know if you sniff." Actually, I didn't. She pulled a baggie of cocaine out of her purse and scooped up a bump with the long, square nail on her pinkie.

Moving on to the next drug, extracting a giant pill bottle from her purse, "What about Prozac?" she asked, rattling the bottle. "'Cause I can get you some.

"I just got outta the psych ward," she continued. "And since I'm insane? They can't lock me up if I do anything bad again. They'll just send me to Bellevue. Did I tell you what I did? I stabbed this girl. I stabbed her in the stomach and cut her uterus out. I carved it out with a knife."

She paused. "It's because she threw a plate of spaghetti at me, and the plate, it had tomato sauce on it and shit," she said.

Living the weirdness was a whole different thing from writing about it, especially when confronted with Loca in the bathroom, her eyes boring into mine as she told me how she cut that girl. She cut a girl? In the uterus? I was positive she was making that one up. But why? And who would admit that they willingly went back to that sort of place after hearing that twisted bathroom-stall confession?

I thought I was so clever, writing about my double life, but it was really just bravado. It was my life, not a series of anecdotes to be told as jokes.

And I wasn't really an outsider, like I'd pretended to be when I wrote the above. I belonged there. Oh, I belonged: I had three wigs in my closet, worked in a strip club on the weekends, bought Xanaxes off of Gypsy. I fit right in. That's what I was learning from New York: You could fit in anywhere if you hung around long enough.

Every so often, I was reminded of just how entangled I was with this world I saw myself as not really being a a part of. As I was leaving a party in Williamsburg at 2:30 in the morning one night, a middle-aged man fell in step beside me. He was cross-dressed as a woman: long, skewed black wig, short black skirt and boots, smeared pink lipstick. He looked familiar.

"Nice night out," he said.

"Yes," I agreed.

"Wish it was warmer," he added. A pause.

"God bless you guys," he said suddenly.

I glanced at him, confused.

"The kinds of insults you girls take from people . . . it's just amazing."

With that, he crossed the street and disappeared into the night.

Suddenly, I remembered how I knew him: I'd seen him several times at Gotham, wandering around the store late at night, always alone. I'd been his live girl.

THE HANGING HEART

When fall arrived, I started getting headaches. They were like clock-work: there when I woke up in the morning, subsided during the after-noon, and started in again at 7 PM. I could feel them coming on when my vision started to blur. Light—sunlight, car headlights, computer screens, overhead lights—became painfully bright. My evenings were reduced to lying in the fetal position in my darkened bedroom.

If you subscribed to the idea that repressed emotions could mani-fest themselves as physical pain, the cause for my migraines was obvi-ous. All signs pointed to what had happened with my dad at the end of the summer. And maybe—just maybe—some of it had to with my guilt over stripping.

One afternoon when I'd still been working at *In Style*, my mother kept calling my cell phone. I couldn't talk on my personal phone during work hours, but she kept calling and calling. I waited until Annelise was out of the office to call her back.

Dad was in the hospital again, she told me. It was serious this time. "He's septic," she said, her voice shaking. "I asked the doctors if I should have my daughters come in from out of state . . . and they said I should."

I hung up, numb, but blocked it out for a product run-through with Annelise and Piper. After, when I was asked to take back the products—the wedding plates and napkins and bookends—to the accessories closet, I burst into tears. I was mortified. Crying at a women's magazine was the ultimate sign of weakness.

But Annelise just ushered me into our office and shut the door. "Tell me what happened," she said. I told her.

"Listen," she said, and I heard a note of compassion in her voice for the first time. "Listen," she repeated gently. "You need to go home. You need to do it right now. Get on the phone with United. They have discounted flights for people whose family members are in the hospital."

I didn't respond.

"Go home," she repeated slowly. "Sheila. Do you hear me?"

I nodded, wiping away tears. Mascara was all over my face, and I fumbled around in my purse for a tissue.

"Call the airline," she repeated. "Go home and call right now, okay? Don't worry about the magazine."

I nodded again, gathered my things, and left. At home, I curled up on my bed with my phone. The man on the end of the line was very nice about it and gave me a discount. I was on a plane the next morning, grateful to Annelise. I'm not sure how quickly I would have acted otherwise; in the state I was in, I could have lost an entire day just staring at the wall, trying to process it.

Picking me up from the airport, my mother told me what happened: She had found him unconscious in bed, and he was medivaced to the university hospital in Ann Arbor. He had an infection that had gone septic and was in intensive care. The first few days, he was unresponsive. Lying immobile on the bed, he looked like a big bear shot down by a tranquilizer dart.

"His body needs the energy to fight the infection," the nurse explained. He looked like he was just asleep.

My mom, sister, and I took turns keeping vigil next to his bed. I watched the fluctuating numbers on the beeping heart and oxygen monitors. His heart rate was too high at 119 beats per minute. His oxygen was dipping below 90, so they hooked him up to a tank.

The university hospital was an hour and a half away from our town, so we stayed at the mini-hotel for relatives inside the hospital. Our room had only two beds, so I had to share one with my mom, while my sister got the other. There were three of us in the room, and there was no privacy.

My sister gave me a Valium to take the edge off, but it didn't do anything. I wandered downstairs into the hospital lobby, and called my ex-boyfriend, Drew, from a pay phone.

He was sympathetic. His parents had been having health problems, too. "Listen," he said. "I think my mom had a stroke, but we don't know for sure because she refused to go to the hospital. You want to know what she did to me last week? She was driving away, and we were having an argument, and she tried to *run me over with her car.*"

After six weeks in intensive care, Dad recovered. He was too weak to walk at first, so he went to a facility to get stronger before going home. He was going to have to go on dialysis in a few years, but he wasn't going to die.

And so, back in New York, the blinding headaches began.

I had four jobs at the time: Besides working part-time at Gawker, I was still doing the unpaid internship at the *Columbia Journalism Review* two days a week. To make money, I worked one night a week at Pumps, and two days at the peep show.

Since I had no health insurance, I decided to find an acupuncturist as a last resort. Kevin's office was half a block from the Gawker office.

The waiting room was empty when I walked in. Water trickled down one of the white walls over a glass pane and into a small pool.

After fifteen minutes of listening to the clock tick, a tall, thin, Ethan Hawke look-alike with artful facial scruff and light brown hair stepped out and called my name. I looked up and realized that I should've gone downtown and found a nice old Chinese acupuncturist, because this one was too attractive, and it was going to be a problem.

"Come on back," he said with a trace of a New York accent, smiling. His jeans, the expensive kind that were supposed to look distressed, hung too low on his thin frame, and he wore an oversized sweater.

He shuffled over to the kitchen to get a glass of water, presenting it to me. I followed him back to one of the white-walled treatment rooms.

Inside, he sat down gently in a wooden folding chair and gestured for me to sit in the one across from him. I explained the headaches.

"Let's try a little feng shui," he began. "Tell me how your apartment is laid out."

"Um . . . I don't have a living room, so it's just my bedroom," I said. This was ridiculous, but my head was killing me so much that I was willing to throw money at anyone and anything that might make it stop.

"Is there anything under your bed?"

"Just some luggage. A bag."

He leaned forward, his interest piqued. "And what's *in* the bag?" Was he for real?

"Just some sweaters."

He sat back, having hit a dead end.

"My dad's been sick," I said tentatively.

He nodded. "Emotional blockages can cause headaches," he said.

"I'm going to leave the room while you get changed," he said. "Take off everything except your underwear and bra, okay? You can leave that on."

I nodded, but I was confused. I'd gotten acupuncture before, back in Detroit, and they'd always given me a gown. I folded my clothes up carefully on the chair and lay down, self-conscious about my soft belly and the pink underwear that didn't match my bra. I didn't like being half-naked in an unfamiliar place, where someone else was in charge.

After sticking needles all over my face, from my temples to between my eyes to the top of my head, he put a few in my feet and then sat down at the head of the table. Gently, he took my head and held it in his big hands, rocking it slowly back and forth.

"Cranial-sacral therapy," he said. He starting talking quietly, murmuring things to me. I don't remember what he said, but by the end of the hour I had tears streaming down my face, silently slipping off my face and onto his hands.

"That was good," he said quietly as I placed $80 in cash on the table. "Come see me later this week."

That night, I was scheduled to work at Pumps. Around eight o'clock in the evening I was in the bathroom putting rouge on my nipples, getting ready to get on the bus, when I had an epiphany: I didn't want to go back to work at the club. I felt cleansed after that weird acupuncture session, and I didn't want to ruin it by jumping right back into the fray of Pumps.

I called Eric.

"I just . . . can't do this anymore," I told him. I didn't know what else to say. "I can't come to work."

"Don't worry about it," Eric replied, sounding almost as if he had been waiting for this moment all along. "Don't worry about it. Don't feel bad. It's not for everyone. Listen, you tried it, it didn't work out . . . . Listen, Chelsea: If you ever want to come back sometime, we'll always be glad to have you. And you're always welcome to come down as a customer."

It took two months of treatment for the migraines to subside, never to appear again. I was dancing less, too, showing up at Gotham only once a week or so. Afterward, however, I kept going to see Kevin.

I began to realize that my reliance on him was becoming more than therapeutic upkeep and that my attraction was textbook transference. This sort of thing happened all the time, it happened to *me* all the time, with my customers, but it couldn't possibly be happening to me personally. Could it? I knew better. How pathetic could I be?

One evening, I was his last appointment of the night. When I placed the money on the table, he didn't get up. Instead, he remained seated, and we stayed, in his office above Spring Street, for half an hour, talking about nothing in particular. Everyone else in the office had gone home.

Outside, a bum on the street below began bellowing.

"That's my next patient," Kevin deadpanned. I dissolved into giggles.

"I make him come late so he won't bother the rest of my patients!" he added, looking pleased that I found him so hilarious.

Kevin's job, I liked to think, was very similar to mine. So many people must want more from him, I thought. I could feel his distance, sometimes, sense the ways that he walled parts of himself off.

He was so finely tuned in reading people's energy that I was worried he could tell what I was thinking about him. I was afraid that he could sense it, just as I could always sense it when men in the peep show were falling for me, and I'd have to move further and further away from them in my mind.

Because I wasn't entirely sure that he *couldn't* read my thoughts, I developed an image that I meditated on during acupuncture. It sort of looked like Jeff Koons's "Hanging Heart"—a large-scale sculpture-installation that Sotheby's had recently auctioned off. ("It's a beautiful, candy-colored heart," said a friend of mine who worked there as an art mover, "yet it's made of steel and not really meant to be suspended, and you know that if it falls it'll kill you.")

I imagined a huge, translucent, membranous heart, like a big red heart-shaped balloon, hanging in a white room. A girl with white skin and long black hair sat in the middle of it, perched above the viewers. I meditated on being inside the membrane, on view, looking down at Kevin, who regarded me from below. If I was an artist, I would build the installation and switch the live models every three hours.

Kevin came back in the room to take the needles out, startling me out of my reverie.

"That Joni Mitchell song 'Chelsea Morning' just came on my iPod the minute I walked out of my office," he remarked. I wondered why he'd said that. He didn't know that Chelsea was my stage name, or that she even existed at all; he knew nothing about that other part of my life, that other headache.

A few afternoons later, sitting at my desk at Gawker—really just an IKEA table perched in a Soho storefront—I saw somebody approach the window. It was Kevin, and he rapped on the glass and smiled. Even at my legit job, I spent my time behind a plate-glass window, on display to passers-by.

I waved and blushed, watching him lope eastward down the cobblestone streets.

I decided that the encounter meant something, and, with my laptop already in front of me, I sent him an e-mail. After waiting a week, he sent one back, something about how he didn't discount my feelings but also that transference was not uncommon in a clinical setting, and no, he didn't think getting coffee sometime would be a good idea.

His smooth, brutal response was humiliating, but I also had to admit that he was a professional. It was exactly what I would have said to a lovelorn customer.

THE ANGEL OF TIMES SQUARE

Christmastime again, and an angel was haunting Times Square. A bum who won the lottery had been going between all three peep shows, bestowing thousands of dollars on the live girls. Allegedly, he gave Joyce around $2,000 one night. One slow Sunday evening, Lourdes told me about the night he gave her $1,200.

"It was in late November," she said. "I'll never forget it. He came in and kept asking me questions, like, 'So if I want to see a show for half an hour . . . ' and I'm all, 'Then you put about $50 into the machine and you need to give me $150.' And he's all, 'Can you get me change?' and gives me $100. And I get it for him, and come back, and he's all, 'Can you get me change again?' and hands me another hundred.

"At this point I was about to be like, 'Listen, you gonna take a show or not?' 'Cause he's asked me all these questions and I haven't even been paid yet. But as I'm getting change the second time, Nikki looks at me and whispers, 'Go!' so I guess she knew something.

"So he puts $50 into the machine and gives me $150.

"It was like I was on a game show. He kept asking me questions, and when I answered, he was like, 'That's correct.' I mean, you could tell he was smart, you know? Like, he was a bum, but you could tell he was smart.

"Then he asked, 'Do you think you're going to get punished for this? Are you religious?'

"I said, 'Yeah, I am, but no, I don't think I'm going to get punished for this. No, I don't. After all, Mary Magdalene was a whore.'

"And he was all, 'Yeah! I like you! You've read that *Da Vinci Code* shit!'

"After a while he was like, 'What if I give you . . . $700?'

"And I'm like, 'Uh, sure! If you want to give me $700 you can do that.' And he put it through the slot. Seven $100 bills.

"Alicia had her ear to the door, she was listening to all this. She said I was in there less than half an hour. Twenty-eight minutes. She timed it.

"Then he told me that he was sick. He said something happened to him in '92 and he was sick. And he put his head down, and he starts crying. He was crying, and he wouldn't stop. I was like, 'Sweetie, talk to me, tell me what's going on.'

"He was like, 'No, no, I can't tell you. I can't tell you.' He kept feeding tens into the machine but his head was down, 'cause he was just crying, I kept telling him to tell me what was wrong, but he wouldn't.

"He asked me, 'Do you know what the Holy Trinity means?' And I said, 'Yeah, it means three.'

"He put $300 through the slot, got up, and left."

"Just for the record, I would like it known by anybody who cares that I don't think life is a perpetual dive . . . . We're all stuck on this often miserable earth where life is essentially tragic, but there are glints of beauty and bedrock joy that come shining through from time to precious time to remind anybody who cares to see that there is something higher and larger than ourselves. And I am not talking about your putrefying gods, I am talking about a sense of wonder about life itself and the feeling that there is some redemptive factor you must at least *search* for until you drop dead of natural causes."

—Lester Bangs, *Gig*, 1978

THE FULL MOON

I stopped working at G1 for good after Christmas. I didn't quit, exactly, just stopped going with the intention of eventually going back. I was tired of the bitchy girls, of Big John screaming at me over the phone, of the claustrophobic hallway reeking of bleach. I decided I only wanted to work at Gotham 4 with Ruby from then on.

My last night at G1 was on the night of a full moon. This event always turned customers weird, guaranteeing a spooky night full of guys shoving sundry objects into various orifices, or maybe smoking crack or crying.

It was just me and Mimi working, and the evening was quickly shaping up to be an event. Two different customers picked me for a show, put $10 into the machine, and then refused to pay the rest, forcing me to leave the booth. Another man came in and did the same thing to Mimi.

'Oh, Lawd, it's going to be one of those nights," moaned Mimi, as the third guy in a row who appeared to be a deaf-mute walked away.

It happened every month without fail.

"Nights like this in the business, it's going to be bad," said Ahmed.

"Those guys saying they won't pay, that's a bad sign. You can't fight it, just tell them to go away, don't argue with them. It's gonna be a bad night. I know this business. I seen this before."

"Oh, shut up, Ahmed," grumbled Mimi. "What the hell you talking about? You know I'm the only one who even tries to understand you through your damn accent."

Two foreigners wandered in, asking for sex. I stalked to the break area and sat down in a huff. While I was gone, new men filed in and stood around shifting their feet.

"Chelsea, Chelsea, come here! There are men!" Ahmed called, desperate. I stomped to the edge of the stairs. There were two guys standing there, waiting to look over the merchandise. An Indian man took a look at my bony chest and curled his lips in distaste. A British man looked me up and down and said, "I'll wait."

"Get out!" I snapped.

Mimi emerged from her booth. "What the fuck is going on?" she asked mildly.

"It's like the Twilight Zone in here tonight," I muttered.

The British man came back up the stairs to check out Mimi, having already rejected me. But my anger must have piqued his interest, and he sidled up to me. "How much is your show again?"

"Forty dollars," I spat, prepared to tell him I didn't *want* to give him a show, when Mimi broke in.

"You should take a show with her, boo," she said sweetly, trying to salvage my night. "She gives a really great show."

"Yeah?" he asked, looking me up and down. "Well, she's gorgeous."

He went into the booth, and I pointed to the money slot. He ignored it.

"I'll give you the money after the show," he said.

"You'll give it to me now," I replied through gritted teeth, and he reached into his back pocket and fumbled the money out of his wallet.

Half an hour later, two dapper young men came in, jabbering away in what I thought was German but turned out to be Dutch. One man was blond, the other Asian. One wore a long wool coat in black, the other in brown. They both had Burberry scarves and expensive shoes.

I could already tell they were going to be a problem.

"It's a show," I told them, before they could even say anything. "You only watch."

"In Amsterdam, where we are from," said the blond man, "we don't watch. We do! Money can buy you half an hour with a girl to do . . . whatever!"

I scowled at him in warning.

"We are very disappointed in New York," his friend added, oblivious.

"In New York, it is more about the mind," I intoned. I knew I was being absurd, but I didn't care. "It's about appreciating eroticism."

"Of course, but—" the Asian man interjected.

"Appreciating the *sight* of a woman," I continued. "That said, you may do whatever you like as you watch her show. But here . . . it is more about the mind . . . which sometimes, as I'm sure you know, can be more powerful than the body."

The blond guy guffawed. An animated conversation in Dutch ensued. The Asian man would take a show with Mimi. The blond man stood and stared at me dumbly while his friend followed her into the booth obediently.

"Come on in," I said, gesturing toward my booth. "Don't let him have all the fun."

"No, that's okay."

I didn't blame him for not wanting to spend time with the snide stripper who'd just given a lecture about appreciating eroticism.

Meanwhile, I heard the well-heeled Asian man raising his voice from inside his booth.

"You mean I don't get anything for $10?" he was yelling. "You are cheating me!"

"Babe, I told you three times, it's ten for the machine, but then you tip the girl for the show, the kind of show you want," Mimi was saying plaintively. "I told you."

"No, you didn't!"

I listened as he spent the entire time her window was up arguing over paying her while she stood there clothed, trying to explain. He stormed out of the booth.

"She cheated me," he started in with Ahmed.

Ahmed raised his hand for him to stop. "Go downstairs, man," he told the Dutch man. "Just go downstairs." Cursing under his breath, the Burberry-clad tourist from Amsterdam left in a huff.

I left at midnight with a shameful $90. I didn't have a locker at the 43rd Street store, so I had to store my stuff at the 48th Street site. Walking up 8th Avenue toward Gotham in the rain, I burst into tears, vibrating with anger.

Just then, as I was crossing 44th, a giant SUV with Jersey plates barreled around the corner, running a red, almost hitting me. They barely slowed as I flipped them off, so I punched the hood of their car for emphasis. I could see the men inside, big dudes with gold necklaces, open and close their mouths in silent fury.

At Gotham I ran upstairs to the dressing room.

"Oh!" cried one of the porters, a young African immigrant, jumping up when I opened the door. He relaxed when he saw it was me. He and Kylie were in there packing a giant bong.

"Heeeeyy, mami," she mumbled through the haze. Her money was scattered all over the counter, disorganized, mixed in with her makeup. She was carefully picking stems and seeds out of a bud.

"You know," I said, "I just might need a hit of that."

We sat there, smoking and exhaling in silence. Sniffling back tears and smoking pot on the second floor of a porn store, it seemed as good a time as any to take a good, hard look at myself. The night has demonstrated that I was letting them—the Dutch guys, the men, Times Square—get to me. It simply wouldn't do. I couldn't go on like this; I couldn't allow myself to be viewed and picked over like a piece of merchandise anymore. I'd thought I could stay on my side of the booth, aloof and unaffected by the work. I couldn't. No one could.

"It's just mystifying to me that places like this still exist. Everyone should experience living like this just to know what's still possible in society . . . . This, for me, this is a break from reality. No one knows I'm here."

—Max R, in *Flophouse: Life on the Bowery*

HOW TO DISAPPEAR

In Times Square, people really could disappear. I knew about half of the girls' real first names but none of their last names. No one shared that information freely. It was considered pushy to press for personal details.

When Raven stopped coming in there was nothing for us to go on as far as finding out what happened to her. Many girls lived a decade behind the times; most didn't have computers or regular Internet access. Jocelyn, her best friend and a former old-school peep-show gal, had been dispatched to get in touch with her, but she hadn't been returning her calls. She didn't have a cell phone, and her landline had been disconnected.

The last time I worked with Raven was right before Christmas. I made only $140 in a double shift. I had to face that no matter how much I worked, there wasn't any money to be made here anymore.

Raven was fine then. The usual: getting sick off OxyContin she bought from a customer, making orgasmic moaning sounds into the mike.

In April, I heard that she'd been exhibiting signs of illness. She'd mostly stopped showing up to work, but when she was there her hair had started falling out and she looked skeletal. Nobody could explain why.

"The last shift I worked with her, she spent the entire time, like, huddled on her chair, wrapped in a blanket, clenching her fists and rocking back and forth," said Ruby. "She was really quiet, and she had sores all over her body."

Nobody had seen her since.

"I think she's dying," said Ruby. "I think she might have AIDS."

I thought about it. I couldn't imagine what was wrong with her that would make her so sick. I'd thought Raven was invincible, but I had always wondered what she would do when she got too old to work in the business.

Even considering how little we really knew about each other, it was considered uncool to just disappear. The week when I suddenly had to go out of town to see my father in the hospital, I'd checked my voicemail to find two messages from Ruby.

"Sheila!" she had said, practically sputtering. "What's up? I mean, *what's up*, what's up? We haven't heard from you, Sia missed a couple of her shifts, nobody can find Gina again, she disappeared and left her baby with her mother, and Kylie's scared to come to work because of her stalker . . . what's up?!"

The right thing to do was to give a heads-up before going AWOL so no one worried. Although Raven often disappeared for a week or two at a time without explanation, she always came back.

I thought about what else I knew about her. I knew her first name was Tina. I knew her phone number—disconnected. I knew she lived in a studio in Fort Greene, and that her rent was $800. I knew she had a brother—or was it a sister?—in New Jersey. But I never found out what happened to Raven. Maybe she was fine; maybe we were all wrong. We never found out either way.

I thought of a conversation I'd had with Jerry, the Ghanian porter with the temper, just a few weeks after I'd started working in the peeps eighteen months before.

"I only here for so long, man," he had said to me, mopping the floor. We were the only two working that night. "One day you'll come in and I'll be gone. You will run into me some day. You'll see me again, and I'll be a big man then.

"You'll say, 'Hey, do I know you? I know you from somewhere.' I'll say, 'No, I don't think so.' You'll be like, 'No, remember me? From that place? I'm Chelsea.'

"'Okay, Chelsea,' I'll say. 'Nice to meet you.'

"You'll say, 'No, Jerry, I know you from somewhere.'" He continued the conversation with himself.

"'No, I don't think so . . .'" He put the mop away, pushed the bucket aside, and headed down the stairs, still fantasizing. "'I don't think so . . .'"

The next week, he was gone.

In the end, I disappeared, too. That was how you did it.

I didn't clean out my locker. Live girls quit by abandoning their things, not taking them with them. The point was to not own wigs and stripper shoes and sparkly dresses anymore.

The lock would be cut off my locker after three or four months, and my things would be thrown out.

The only person I kept in touch with was Ruby. The rest of the girls would notice I was gone for good eventually. They would assume I'd found something better, and they'd be happy for me. And I had found something—I was going to be working for Gawker full-time. I was going to be working in SoHo from now on, not Times Square, not 8th Avenue, not in the back of a porn store.

Ruby reported back for the first few months after I left that men were still coming in to the peep show asking for me. Such requests became fewer and farther between, until they stopped, and the guys, the ones who'd paid my rent over and over, forgot that a pale brunette named Chelsea had ever been there at all.

"After such knowledge, what forgiveness."
—T. S. Eliot

PULP LOVE

It had been about eight months since I quit the peep show. I was working full-time at Gawker, and I still couldn't believe I had gotten lucky enough to be paid to write.

Working as a professional blogger made me virtually connected to thousands of people every day via my laptop, but it was also alienating. People commented on my posts in real time, but I was either working from home in front of my screen in my underwear, or working in an office surrounded by other people sitting in front of their screens, all of us wearing earphones, listening to our separate music. I was happy about the way things were going and how much my life had changed, but I was still floating, disconnected through cocktail parties and restless dreams and faceless Internet commentators.

One day my editor commissioned a gossip item on the author of an alt-weekly article who had chronicled his long struggle to kick heroin.

"When I was shooting up every day for seven years," went the first paragraph, "the last thing I wanted was a girlfriend in addition to my all-consuming vice." It was good stuff. It had everything: sex, drugs, self-hatred, and rock and roll.

I dutifully aggregated the article with a brief aside, poking fun at the author—a guy named Matt whose bio listed him as a "writer and bartender"—by advising to enjoy his "fifteen minutes of microfame."

A couple hours later, Matt sent me an e-mail saying he had no problem with my post; he thought it was funny.

I congratulated him on his sense of humor, but I had more items to write. My fingers burned up the keyboard every day, and the shooting pains in my elbows and wrists sent me back to getting needles stuck in them to reverse the effects of repetitive motion. I had a nice old Chinese acupuncturist on Grand Street now. I also had health insurance and, for the first time, a shrink, who had an outpost in Greenpoint. After some trial and error, he prescribed me Cymbalta and Lamictal—and antidepressant and a mood stabilizer—that worked in tandem to keep me away from the void. The void was becoming a distant memory.

On a Monday night two weeks later, I was sitting in a fluorescent-lit classroom at the New School for my first day of a writing class, when Matt walked in. I recognized him from an old photo I'd found on the Internet, but he was better looking in real life. He resembled one of the handsome delinquents in a John Hughes movie, with a leather jacket, jeans hanging too low on his hips, and black hair styled almost in a pompadour. The ends were sticking up, making him also look a bit like a bear cub. He eased himself into a chair, ten minutes late.

I found myself staring at him, perversely focusing on the crooks of his arms for evidence. Here was someone who could understand, I thought. Both of us knew about the care and maintenance of a double life, how days could become years.

I probably wouldn't have introduced myself had I not written about him. It wasn't that I didn't want to, but I was just too reserved. Stripping hadn't cured that.

"Sorry I mocked you on the Internet," I told him after class.

He just smiled and hoisted his messenger bag onto his shoulder. I could tell he was good at putting people at ease—bartenders often were. Up close, I noticed that his hair wasn't all black; it was struck through with wisps of white around his face, although he was only a few years older than I was. They didn't take anything away from his looks; in fact, they gave him an air of gravitas.

"I'm covering an event for the paper," he said. "You want to come?"

Outside, it was raining lightly. He hailed a cab and we got out at 30th Street, at the club Rebel. Inside, drag queens and the almost-famous posed for photographers in front of a step-and-repeat. A band was playing, and the cast of MTV's "Real World Brooklyn" was there, being followed around by a film crew.

Matt placed a hand on my back and pressed a bill into my hand. "I have to go get some quotes. Will you get me a vodka grapefruit?"

"Sure." Were recovering heroin addicts allowed to drink? Maybe they were.

I followed when he went out to smoke with his editor, Adam, and some others. I only smoked when I wanted to seem cool, so I bummed one and inhaled ostentatiously, four of us standing around some scaffolding to keep out of the drizzling rain.

"Ladies, keep it moving," intoned the bouncer at a gaggle of girls clogging the sidewalk. I was looking at the ground, noticing how all of our shoes also formed a circle—my pink Converse lined up with Matt's nearly-identical black pair—when he reached over and nudged my foot with his. I looked up at him, surprised. He laughed, and I looked down again, blushing.

Matt, Adam, and I walked toward the end of the block to hail cabs home.

"Where do you live?" I asked Matt.

"Midtown," he sighed, as if beleaguered by such a convenient address. He got his taxi first: "See you in class."

"Okay," I said, already looking forward to it. I stared into the steam coming out of the manholes as his cab drove off. But . . . heroin? *Needles?* I didn't know what to think, but I also felt like I wasn't in the position to judge, and anyway, it was too late. I could feel something happening already. The numbness of the last eighteen months was beginning to thaw.

"I'll tell you about being a junkie if you tell me about being a stripper," Matt whispered to me in bed.

"Okay," I whispered back.

"Turn off the lights."

It was five days later. He'd walked me home from a party. We'd been at the "soft opening" of a new bar-restaurant on the Greenpoint-Williamsburg border. Although it wasn't open to the general public, it was already a hotspot because Heath Ledger had been an investor. It was ghoulish: A dead movie star could pack unopened restaurants. The space had been purposely distressed, its authenticity meticulously crafted into the worn-looking wood and artificially rusted mirrors.

Matt showed up in a black dress shirt and a fedora, doing his roving-reporter routine, weaving among the patrons with his notepad. On most men I'd find a fedora silly, but on him it seemed to work. At the end of the night, he placed his hat on my head and offered to walk me home. On the way, he grabbed my hand on the street, pulled me toward him, and kissed me.

At my apartment, he teased me about my little room, calling it a "rabbit warren," and drunkenly tried to fix my bike, parked next to my bed. Then he asked that question.

The next morning, I reached for his watch to see what time it was, turning its face toward me.

A long, raised red line ran above his wrist, with a matching track on his other arm. The inside of his elbows were scarred.

"See my track marks?" he said, suddenly self-conscious. "They haven't gone away yet. I don't think they're ever going to."

"It's okay," I said, tracing the scarred-over tracks with my finger. "It's good that they're there. Like a reminder." His watch was heavy and silver, hanging loosely around his wrist. "Nice watch."

"Thanks. I managed to hold on to it. I used to pawn it all the time."

I couldn't stop asking about his track marks. It fascinated me, that some mistakes could leave you marked. My questions didn't seem to bother him; if anything, he seemed flattered that someone might be curious.

"What do you do when you go to the doctor?" I asked. "What do you say?"

"He knows."

"And he didn't make you stop?"

"Well, no one can *make* you stop."

"What about when you get blood drawn? Do the nurses ask?"

"Yeah, sometimes. I just usually say, 'Misadventure.'"

Misadventure. It was a too-easy way to put it, but it worked well enough for the moment. I would learn the rest eventually.

"Do you want to go to a very special doughnut shop?" I asked him. "It's called Peter Pan."

The next night, he invited me to his apartment to watch a movie and eat Chinese food, a very New York City second date.

I'd never been to Tudor City, on the far east side of 41st Street, near the U.N. The huge old buildings were beautiful. His apartment on the sixteenth floor had leaded-glass casement windows overlooking the quiet hum of the FDR Drive. It was also the location, I noted, of the scene in *Taxi Driver* where Martin Scorsese makes a cameo as the crazed passenger watching his wife's silhouette in the window of another man's apartment, telling Travis Bickle, "I'm going to kill her with a .44 Magnum pistol."

It was a masculine apartment, with an old leather couch and a stuffed black bear as a footstool. The walls were lined with bookshelves, and more books were piled on the windowsills and in big stacks on the floor.

He'd mostly bartended during his decade-long relationship with drugs.

He'd grown up in the East Village. Matt was a sensitive child, and when he visited his dad in his Soho loft before he got remarried, his father and his friends attempted to toughen the boy up by pretending to toss him out the window.

We watched *Farewell, My Lovely*. Matt loved noir movies, especially '50s noir films as they related to Freud, who was, he taught me, a major influence on mid-century cinema. Given my recent foray into psychotherapy, this appealed to me. Like a character in a Woody Allen movie, Matt had been seeing a shrink for about fifteen years. "Well, you don't really get the hang of it until after about the first five," he joked.

He'd never quite gotten over the New York of his childhood, a city that was magical and wide-open and that no longer existed. In a way he was stuck in another time, and the old movies were as close as he could get to going back. A giant pharmacy and a bank had plopped themselves across from his old apartment on Bleecker Street. Highrises were shooting up in Astor Place, an old copping spot.

"I moved up here to get away from the dealers," he said of Tudor City, "but there aren't even dealers downtown anymore."

He had started snorting heroin when he was twenty after getting kicked out of a Catholic college upstate for drinking and fighting. This reminded me of my dad, who had also flunked out of Catholic college not once, but twice, until he went to Vietnam, came back, got hip to the program, and became an attorney. But while my father never abused anything stronger than Kools, Matt started using needles with a girl he met in the Hazelden rehab in Minnesota, after he ran away and hitchhiked back to New York. He'd been clean for about a year now.

"Is it hard?" I asked. He thought for a moment.

"No," he said. "It's not hard. But I have a lot of nightmares."

We saw each other nearly every day for the next two weeks, sitting next to each other in class on Mondays and walking around the city holding hands afterward.

"I shot up in that bathroom once," he occasionally said when passing certain establishments.

I learned about Matt's other scars, memorizing their stories until I knew their origins better than he did. There was a thin white line under his lip, from nodding out in a stairwell and hitting a radiator face-first. There was a more sizable chunk out of his eyebrow from falling down and hitting his head against the kitchen countertop at his mother's house after taking too much Xanax in an attempt to kick. And then there was a gash just below his right lip, near his chin, origin undetermined, probably from a teenage scrap.

I spent more and more nights at his place, lying in bed, reading Mark Jacobson essays, old pulp novels, anything from his piles of books, while he worked on his nightlife column in the next room.

In the morning, I walked down East 42nd Street to Grand Central, the buildings rising up on either side of me like a valley. Sometimes I'd forgotten to plan and bring a change of clothes for work and bought something cheap from Ann Taylor or Strawberry on the way. I was glad some clothing stores were open at 8 AM, selling business casual careerwear for busy gals on the go who needed to make it look as if she'd been home since the day before. It didn't bother me. I'd never realized how important it was to know that you had somewhere to be.

I started waking up in a cold sweat in the middle of the night. "What's wrong, hon?" Matt would whisper.

"I had that dream again." I'd been having recurring nightmares that I was an addict. They were so graphic. This last time, I'd been stumbling through a party in a big warehouse, a needle dangling from my hand. "Why am I having them?"

"I don't know. Maybe you're just addicted to me."

Matt had nightmares, too, often waking up in the middle of the night in a panic, hyperventilating. I would rub his back until he calmed down. One night, he was in such a state that I instinctively grabbed his head and held it tightly against my chest. He sat up and whispered, "I love you."

And he did love me—not the alter-ego I'd created in Times Square, but the silly, shy, awkward girl I had gone to such extreme lengths to hide.

One Friday night, I was waiting for him at his apartment. I'd taken one of his Xanax to sleep, and it was starting to set in when Matt burst through the door angrily.

"I've done something I shouldn't have," he announced. He'd been covering a party on the West Side for the paper, and I could tell he'd been drinking. I propped myself up on one elbow, feeling woozy.

"You did drugs," I said warily.

He looked confused. "No. I went over to Times Square. I visited your old work."

"Did you tell everybody hi for me?" I knew I was going to be in trouble for being flippant, but I didn't know what else to say.

"It was empty. I went up to the third floor and there were just . . . booths. They looked like little cages."

"Really? It's empty? There must have been a bust." I was mulling over what could have happened when Matt exploded.

"*I don't want my fucking girlfriend working in a little cage!*" he yelled.

"Will you stop *fucking cursing*?" I shrieked back.

He sat down on the edge of the bed and put his head in his hands. "I can't believe you worked there," he said. "I can't imagine you doing that."

"At least I wasn't shooting things into my *arms*."

He didn't listen. "I just picture you with a very blank look on your face, looking empty . . . "

That sounded about right. We both knew how it felt, the dulling escape into unreality. We both knew about the void.

Matt didn't hate the peep show because he wanted to control me; he hated it because he saw it had been bad for me. He saw that I was too clumsy and sensitive to be in the world he had just seen, and he knew that I would always end up hurt.

We went on a walk through McCarren Park the next afternoon. Sitting on a bench, Matt leaned back and closed his eyes. I put my hand against the side of his face and studied the white peppering his hair. He leaned against me, his leather jacket creaking, and put his head on my shoulder. I suddenly felt a fierce urge to protect him. It felt like it was coming from somwhere deep inside me, a part of myself I hadn't accessed before, like finding an extra room in my house that I never knew I had.

I burrowed my face into his neck and breathed in. I could already imagine us old together, sitting like this on this same park bench. I had that familiar floating feeling and I closed my eyes, drifting into my own reverie. I was looking down on the city below, floating above the park. It wasn't always a bad feeling, I realized. You just had to be connected to something.

I wanted to reach into his chest and grab onto his heart with my fist, holding and feeling it squirm and pulse with life, flopping around like a fish refusing to die, fighting to keep beating no matter what. At the same time I had another sensation—a stirring, rustling thing.

It felt like something was growing, or at least taking root.

END NOTES

Ruby lives with Carlos, whom she met at the peep show while delivering our beer. She no longer works in the business. They have a baby.

After Lou's arrest, his club was shut down, and he was barred from practicing law, his day job.

There is a class-action lawsuit pending against Déjà Vu-owned clubs for charging exorbitant stage fees.

As of this printing, there are two live-girl peep shows left in Manhattan.

"When this place is ready for redevelopment, neither the dirty bookstores nor the porno movies will keep it from its final improvement."

—real estate developer Harold Warsawer,
to *The New York Times*, 1970

"In order to bring about this redevelopment, the city has instituted not only a violent reconfiguration of its own landscape, but also a legal and moral revamping of its own discursive structure, changing laws about sex, health, and zoning . . . willing, even anxious, to exploit everything from homophobia and AIDS to family values and fear of drugs."

—Samuel R. Delany,
Times Square Red, Times Square Blue, 1998

SOME PERSPECTIVE:
A HISTORY OF THE PEEPS

The Captain remembered the old days.

"You ever get a pain right here, on the left side of your chest?" he asked, hobbling into the peep show with his cane one night when I was working alone.

"I get all sorts of pains," I told him. He didn't seem to hear me.

"Oh, well," he said. "Maybe it's my time to go. Maybe I'll finally take a show with you, and it'll knock me right out. *Sayonara!* One foot in the grave, the other in the, well . . . " He looked around, trying to discern exactly what he meant.

"Eighty percent of this business is personality," he said after a pause. "It's personality, it's talking. It doesn't matter what you look like."

I'd nicknamed the man—a stately, older African American with an old-fashioned conked hairstyle—the Captain because had been coming around to the 8th Avenue peeps in the wee hours of the morning for years, just to chat. I got the feeling that he was lonely and spent his evenings wandering the Square, the captain of our underworld.

"The first peep show?" he said. "Let me tell you about the first peep show. I was around, you know. It was on 42nd and 8th, but closer to

6th Avenue . . . . And it was like this bar, and this little Chinese girl was working there . . ." he trailed off.

"And then the touching came in, and they even had—and you're not going to believe this—but they had the live sex shows. A couple would be on the stage, and they would actually, well, perform intercourse."

He trailed off again. "I saw it all," he said, and turned around, shuffling slowly out into the night.

What the Butler Saw

Blame Thomas Edison for the modern peep show. He invented the Kinetoscope, a motion-picture device designed for a single viewer. First publicly demonstrated in 1891, it was a simple wooden box containing sheets of filmstrips that scrolled quickly enough to simulate motion.

By 1895, the Kinetoscope was losing out to a newer, cheaper peep-show device, the Mutoscope, which worked more like a flipbook. Like its predecessor, the Mutoscope showed clips of boxing matches and vaudeville acts, as well as girlie scenes considered scandalous at the time. "What the Butler Saw" was a popular attraction, aping a butler's-eye view through a keyhole and showing a woman partially disrobing.

Times Square didn't invent voyeurism, nor was it the first place to look at a naked lady in New York. The brothel-windows in the Bowery entertainment district and Five Points slums provided the earliest-recorded organized peeping, where in the street-facing windows, "girls in varying stages of undress paraded to lure street trade."[1] But the Square took voyeurism to a large-scale level suitable for mass consumption, and its history is defined by the various crackdowns on the resulting vice.

Nearly every decade since the area around 42nd Street between Broadway and 8th Avenue became a public square in 1904, business interests and politicians have declared war on the general seediness that has always been a part of the entertainment district, augmented by the sheer number of people passing through its major transit hubs.

By the time I got there, in the mid-aughts, there wasn't much left—in fact, the first words out of half of the guys who walked into our little back room at Gotham were, "I didn't know these places still existed!" But the live girls were in fact part of a long and colorful history.

In the '30s, Mayor La Guardia was so concerned with the "amoral" burlesque houses that he banned them. By the '40s, the "riffraff"—prostitutes, street peddlers, pickpockets, panhandlers—had become the new scapegoat. *The New York Times* reported that 42nd Street was "infested with out-of-town hoodlums and gangsters who sally out to molest pedestrians from parked cars."

Something For a Nickel

In the '50s, the first zoning laws were proposed to clean up the "midway" feel of Times Square, which was lined with open-air booths, arcade shooting galleries, freak shows and game rooms with skeeball and pinball. The carnival environment created a god-awful racket, complained its critics.

The lawyer representing the arcade owners argued the merit of the amusement centers; they were "the only places in the world a person can get something for a nickel."[2]

The "arcade ban" was approved in 1953. It wouldn't shut down the existing places, but would phase them out, preventing new establishments from replacing the old.

However, the rezoning did not create the type of improvement in the way that city officials had hoped. In 1961, Kitty Hanson, gal reporter for *The Daily News*, wrote a series of gonzo-style articles based on her solo walks through the Square. It was "a place where a man can lose himself for a couple of hours—or a couple of days," she reported.

Young Kitty took in an 8:30 AM movie in a grind house, filled with sleepers, salesmen between appointments, and pervs. She visited a Fascination gambling parlor, went to Hubert's Museum to watch the flea circus, and came to the conclusion that "any woman who wanders along [in Times Square] like this is asking for any remarks that come her way."

That same year, twenty-two were arrested in a smut raid on bookstores, and "truckloads" of films, photos, and "indecent literature" were carted away, wrote the *Herald Tribune*.

Times Square was "trying to shake off . . . a 40-year slide into honky-tonkism," said *The Daily News*. Operation New Broom, a drive to clean up Times Square and the Village, was launched in 1966. But if city official's thought it was bad then, they would have shuddered to think of what was to come.

In 1966 and 1967, two court rulings had a profound effect on Times Square. In 1966, the Supreme Court restricted the definition of "obscenity" to only that which was "utterly without redeeming social value." That phrase provided leeway for pornographers, and many films were made under the conceit of sex education.

In September of 1967, prostitution was decriminalized by New York State—it was no longer a misdemeanor nor a crime, but an "offense." The maximum sentence dropped from a year to fifteen days. This had the unintentional effect of blowing Times Square wide-open for prostitution, with girls and would-be pimps flowing in from around the country to work.[3]

By 1968, Times Square was being referred to as an outdoor "sex supermarket."[4] At night, 8th Avenue "harbored more than a thousand hookers."[5] (The Sunday News put the number at six hundred.)

Billy Graham visited in 1969 and expressed his horror to the entirety of Madison Square Garden later that night, arguing that porn existed not because the laws were lax but because "the hearts of the people are violent." Earlier that day, he had walked the streets of Times Square in disguise, wearing dark sunglasses and a hat. When he took off his shades to peer into the eyes of the people, he said, "I found vacant stares and emptiness—they seemed to be searching for something."

The media, police, and politicians stopped assigning the denizens of the Square any sort of humanity. They were referred to in the papers as "whores," "mincing perverts," "a walking freak show," and "human detritus." It was Sodom and Gomorrah, Slime Square, the "Cesspool of the World."

"The dregs of the entire country drain into our sump," a plainclothes police officer told The Times in 1969.

Novelist Earl Shorn published an essay about the area in the Sunday New York Times in 1971 that referenced "whores" no fewer than four times. Yet the piece ended on a jubilant note: Looking out at the roiling night, a bum exalted, "This is living. We're alive!"

The King of Peeps

The peep show as I would come to know it was born in 1966, the creation of a bearded hustler named Marty Hodas, from Brownsville, Brooklyn. In coming years, he'd be called the "King of Peeps," but it all started with thirteen old jerry-rigged wooden film machines, $7,000 in borrowed cash, and a dream of making a fortune in quarters.[7]

With a flourishing jukebox route in Long Island, Hodas had an idea of how to capitalize further on the pay-for-play idea. Making a film peep booth was easy—they worked "the same as any other vending machine or jukebox," he later explained to the *Post*.

And so he cobbled together the coin-operated peep show—not the live-girl variety, but booths that showed clips of dirty movies for 25¢ a pop. (He later incorporated live girls into his enterprise.)

He nailed together with plywood the single-occupancy booths, which resembled "make-do cattle pens."[8] The viewing matter consisted of 8mm loops, demure by today's standards, often depicting one person because two might violate obscenity laws.

A *New York Times* reporter who watched an early peep of Hodas's in 1969 discerned "nude girls gyrating," as well as "two nudes . . . entwined with only the upper parts of torsos visible." ("As long as there's no auto-eroticism or sexual contact, it's all right," Hodas told the reporter.) It cost 25¢ for one to two minutes of viewing, although later it was eventually shortened to about thirty seconds, after he realized customers would gladly pay up.

Hodas formed over a dozen shell companies and branched out. Not only did he show the movies on his peep-show machines, but he also started producing, manufacturing, and distributing them via his companies like Dynamite Films, East Coast Cinematics, and Adult Films Inc. Soon he had machines not only in New York City but also in Philadelphia, Baltimore, and Atlanta.[9] They were housed "in dark back rooms of porn bookstores, which reeked of urine and old orgasms, shown by nickelodeon or projected in curtained-off booths."[10]

The mob quickly moved in. They couldn't let Hodas, an unconnected indie, make all the money from this new cash-and-carry business opportunity. Everyone wanted a piece of the action. As early as 1970, the State Commission of Investigation reported that three peep-show machine companies were duking it out for control of the industry. One was Hodas's. The two others were both mob-funded.

In 1971, a boss in the Tramunti crime family "threw out all Hodas's machines from his store onto the street and replaced them with his own," from competing peep biz Motion Picture Vending, reported *The Daily News*. That same year, Hodas said he was down to a hundred and thirty machines from three hundred, and the legal fees were eating him up.

In the beginning, splitting up the profits between himself and the store operators was simple: Hodas simply weighed the quarters on a scale and divided them up—half for the store operators and half for himself.[7] But now he was trapped in the maze of a never-ending cat-and-mouse with the City, which went after him for every possible violation, real or imagined. ("Here, look at these," he complained to *The Daily News*. "The fire department asked me for proof that my curtains are not flammable, so I send them a sample. Is that good enough? No, now they want an affidavit from the curtain company stating how long they'll stay that way."[11])

And then there was the mob. In 1974, Hodas's Long Island house mysteriously caught fire, with his wife and children inside (they were rescued uninjured).[12]

Soon after, his son disappeared one day after nursery school—picked up by two men who told the boy they knew his father and took him out for ice cream. A call was placed to Hodas's office in the meantime. ("Marty, where's your son?" a man's voice asked.) The mobsters returned the boy home safely with a note that read, "We just want to let you know we've been thinking very seriously about you."[13]

Hodas was also convicted of tax evasion in 1976. He had the chutzpah to argue in court that the weekly payoffs he made from 1968 through 1971 to the Colombo crime family, totaling $175,000, were a cost of doing business, and that he shouldn't have to pay taxes on extortion fees. The court was not convinced, and he served a one-year sentence in a Florida prison.[14] A year later, in typical contradictory Hodas fashion, he outright denied mob influence in the porno industry. "Nobody on the street is paying off anyone," he declared.

In 1984, after pleading guilty to an obscenity charge after a sting caught him shipping porn VHS cassettes across state lines and to Canada, Hodas got out of the business. Peep shows made Hodas a rich man, but had he known what was in store for him—from the constant legal hassles to the mob threats to the year in jail to the brief kidnapping of his son—he might have decided it was not worth it. He was a broken man at the end of it all.

"I wish I'd never heard of it," he said to *The Times* in 1972. The business has "shown me nothing but misery," he said in a different interview.

Live! Nude! Girls!

The original live-girl peep show, in fact, was not quite exactly as the addled Captain remembered, but it was close. Gail Sheehy wrote about witnessing one of the first live girlie shows while on assignment for *New York* magazine.

The joint was called Peepalive, located at 109 West 42nd Street. The year was 1972. "We served them with a summons yesterday, you won't believe it. It's the most degenerate we've ever seen," the accompanying policeman warned her.

The sign on the second-floor landing read:

PEEPALIVE—NEW YORK'S ONLY

LIVE PEEP SHOW!

25¢

"Inside, Srg. Patrick quickly shepherded me into one of the twenty black-curtained booths arranged in a circle. Red light on. Performance in progress.

"I bent to peer through a window the size of a mail slot and there it was—my first peep—a silver-booted black nude spread across a revolving turntable, on her back, chewing gum. Indeed, had it not been for the gum she would surely have been asleep."[15]

The porn stores and massage parlors lining the streets were able to flourish because their off-the-books cash allowed them to pay two to three times market rent, accept month-to-month leases, and serve as "a lucrative source of short-term income pending demolition," according to *The Times*. They were allowed to stand because developers were playing a "waiting game" on the area, which would someday—but not yet—be ripe for redevelopment.[16] These vice-holes were just placeholders for what would eventually come, already the stage was being set for gentrification.

Times Square was truly living up to its Slime Square moniker, between the live sex shows, nearly a thousand peep machines, and a graphic new breed of pornography.[17] Grind-house theaters were filled with cruisers giving anonymous blowjobs. Matt recalled walking through the Square with his grandfather as a child in the early '80s and seeing a giant movie poster advertising PLEASE DADDY RAPE ME.

Mayor Lindsay launched an anti-smut campaign in the summer of 1972, vowing to use the "full range of legal powers" to regulate everything from peeps to prostitution hotels to massage parlors to dirty bookstores. Interestingly, many of the prostitution-oriented hotels were owned by the Durst family, whose business was in redevelopment.

Around 1 PM on a hot August afternoon, three Times Square theaters—the Paree, the San Francisco, and the World Theater—were raided as part of the anti-obscenity campaign.

The matinee crowd was rousted from the theater and emerged blinking in the afternoon sunlight, covering their faces with newspapers. A crowd gathered to watch the police take down the signs.

At the World Theater, which was showing the mob-financed porno *Deep Throat*, they arrested the manager and cashier. At the San Francisco Theater, another arrested cashier named Eugene Brogan protested the bust. "We're doing a service by keeping men away from women and children," he told *The New York Times* as he was led away by police. "You don't have to be a Peeping Tom no more."

Guys like Brogan were just small fish caught in the net. As a ticket seller, he was neither producing nor distributing any of the allegedly obscene material.

In a demonstration of the adult industry's cockroach-like staying power, all three theaters were back in business the very next day. Theater owners had painted and erected new marquees overnight.

There was at least one voice of conciliation within the police department: John Guideo, Inspector of the Public Morals Division. He suggested that porn be legalized, because there was no way to control it, as the Times Square economy had repeatedly demonstrated. At the very least, legalization would "knock out all the profits of organized crime," he told the *Sunday News* in 1971.

Licensing was another ploy aimed at shutting down the peeps, but that ruling was overturned in 1972 when a State Supreme Court ruling stated that peep shows did not, in fact, need a license to operate, and requiring one was unconstitutional because it infringed upon free speech.

With the heat off, activities in Times Square ramped up. By mid-1978, store owners, boosted by the fact that there hadn't been a major bust in a while, figured, "What the hell—we'll take the windows out." The glass partitions were removed from many of the live-girl peeps, boasted to passersby with signs advertising OPEN WINDOWS. The peep show took on an entire new level of interaction—customers could now touch the girls, and they could touch back.

An open-and-shut game began with the City that wouldn't end until 2000, when all of the windows went back in for good. Over at Lee's Baby Doll Revue in 1979, management was "forced to put glass back in the partitions after a year of frivolous open-window encounters between patrons and dancers." At Show World, a customer could request "tit, twat, hind end, have a leg hoisted into his boot, a boot in his face. Starving octopus hands grabbed over girls' bodies."[18] Richard Basciano, owner of Show World, put the windows back up in all of his stores in 1980. Things were getting "carried away," he said, referring to the adult petting zoo it had become.

A Deterrent to Rape

The late '70s and '80s belonged to Richard Basciano. His Show World opened in 1974, and he was a pioneer in the sex-store evolution. Nicknamed the "McDonald's of Sex," Show World was known for its clean and well-lit design—a first in the business.

His stores, as well as his insistence that he was a businessman and not just a smut purveyor, were a precursor to the eventual mainstreaming of porn. After all, Basciano made too much money from pornography for his customers to be solely weirdos and pervs.

"The porno shops on West 42nd Street weren't there because the middle class had fled," *The New York Times* wrote in 1986. "They were there because the middle class was there."

Basciano was a shameless opportunist and pure capitalist. His stores were a "deterrent to rape," he insisted in 1982.

Show World had a circus theme. There was a carousel horse for the girls to ride (topless, of course) as well as live-girl peeps. The Big Top Lounge upstairs had a stage and a pole. They booked thirty-two "booth babies" a shift.

"Imagine, hustling against thirty-two girls every night," recalled Lourdes of her time working there in the mid-'90s. "But there was enough money to go around. Some girls bought houses. Everything was right there: drugs, booze, your girlfriends. You didn't need to go out. I did drugs, partied . . . I had a few years of really good times."

Basciano, a former boxer, got his start in the '60s selling girlie mags. His partners were two known mobsters, Sam Rappaport and Robert "DeeBee" DiBernardo. (Basciano professed ignorance about their mob ties.)

DeeBee's operation was in distribution and manufacturing—of books, movies, magazines, and "paraphernalia." He had the honor of being profiled as one of Times Square's "Sultans of Smut" in a long-running *Daily News* column. His Star Distributors was one of the biggest national distributors-manufacturers of dirty books, films, and magazines. (Among their clients was Al Goldstein's *Screw* magazine.)

After Marty Hodas got out of the biz in the wake of his federal obscenity bust in 1984, he sold some of his properties to Basciano, who owned the Show World building at 42nd and 8th, Show Palace (across the street from Show World), and Show Follies at 49th and 7th. Basciano would eventually own more than a dozen properties in Times Square.

In 1986, Dee Bee was killed on the order of John Gotti, who saw him as a potential rival. With DeeBee and his business out of the picture, no one else in the mob had the same knowledge of the porn biz. Thus, they allowed non-mobsters to move into the business—mostly

Sri Lankans and Israelis. With the advent of home video, the mob no longer had the distribution power they did with film with Dee Bee's Star Distribution, which had created a vertical supply structure—the theaters and peep shows they owned showed the films they created and distributed.

Basciano's lawyer, famed First Amendment defender Herald Price Fahringer, wrote a letter to *Crain's New York Business* in 1989 explaining that Show World had "voluntarily discontinued its live sex shows," which entailed male-female duos performing intercourse on stage. Fahringer noted on a separate occasion that Basciano had a "remarkable reputation for compliance," which was true. Basciano likely saw Hodas as a cautionary tale.

Another perspective on Show World came from Sly, who worked there as a booth-mopper in the mid-'80s, when he was just fifteen.

By the time I met him, Sly was a successful jazz saxophonist. When he wasn't touring Europe with his group, he worked security at the nightclub where I was doing coat-check for extra cash.

"Man, some of the things I saw," he said in his deep voice, leaning over my coat-check counter as if he needed support for the weight of his memories. "I could write a book. I had a moustache, so I was able to get hired because I looked like I was sixteen."

He referred to each of the outrageous Show World anecdotes as "episodes."

"There was this girl we called Rina the Butt, because she had such an amazing ass. Oh, man, it was *glorious.* Every time she walked by, every man turned around to look at her, especially us brothers. I even dated her for a little while.

"I also knew this girl named Pinky . . . Spanish girl, whatta body. But she was sixteen years old, and also a prostitute sometimes. A john murdered her, poked her eyes out, and stuffed her in the trunk of his car." Working girls were targets for loose cannons. Serial killer Joel Rifkin killed 17 women between 1989 and 1993, many of them prostitutes.

The incident that chased him from Times Square for good happened one dawn on a desolate 8th Avenue as he was leaving after his shift at Show World.

"This guy walked out of some building, stood in the middle of the sidewalk, put a gun to his head, and POW!—blew his brains out. Right in front of me. No one else on the street. You know, I was at a point in my life where I could go either way. I could keep playing the sax and go the legit route . . . or I could go to the other side and live a life of crime. I was teetering on the edge." That was Sly's final Show World episode, and he quit soon after.

The Beginning of the End

In 1994, Marty Hodas made a reappearance on the Avenue by investing in the trifecta of the original Playpen, Peep-O-Rama, and Playground peep shows.[20] Unfortunately for him, Republican Rudy Giuliani had just been elected mayor. Both a moralizer and someone with great interest in the redevelopment of Times Square, he was about to go on the anti-porn drive to end them all.

Times Square's filth was holding up redevelopment, where the big bucks could be made. Giuliani declared that he wanted to push the adult businesses "into the ocean, where they belong." The only way to do it would be through zoning. Giuliani's Adult Use law passed in 1995 and took effect in 1999.

The ordinance banned adult-oriented businesses within five hundred feet of a day-care center, school, or church, as well as residential areas. Nearly every area smut hut was now at risk. Show World was less than five hundred feet from the Church of the Holy Cross, which had been bemoaning the filth and honky-tonk of the Square for decades. By 1996, five porn stores on 42nd Street had closed.

However, a loophole called 60/40 provision allowed adult-oriented businesses to keep on grinding, so long as 60 percent of their floor space was devoted to non-adult usage or stock.

Clubs and porn stores busied themselves with complying with 60/40. Strip clubs added restaurants. The Harmony Theater added flimsy walls dividing the nude girls from the bar area. X-rated stores stocked up on non-pornographic VHS cassettes, like exercise tapes and instructional guides. Show World even lost its carousel during renovations to comply with 60/40.

Basciano fought back via funding the Coalition for Free Expression, a ragtag group of sex-store owners who wanted to sue the City and block the zoning change, citing their First Amendment rights. But Basciano's buildings were on prime space, so he could profit from gentrification as well as sleaze. Either way it would turn out in his favor. Between 1992 and 1995, he sold at least four sites to the 42nd Street Redevelopment Project, earning a reported $12 million to $14 million.

Around four o'clock in the afternoon on March 12, 1998, fifty agents from the INS, police, and State Department stormed the Playpen and the Playground, acting on a tip that there were Czech girls working there with phony papers. The women had been trafficked from the Czech Republic and installed in the peeps by their handlers, who expected them to hand over at least $100 a day.

Twenty-nine people were arrested in the raid. Girls were still talking about it eight years later when I got there; it had become folklore. A few whom I worked with at the Playpen and Gotham were present at the time, or had at least been in the business when it happened.

"Those were some workin' bitches," remembered Lourdes of the Czech girls. They did double shifts like it was nothing. Man, the cops had the TV cameras outside, just waiting. They wouldn't even let them change."

Four months later, the 60/40 rules were reconsidered by the Supreme Court after the Coalition for Free Expression sued the City over free speech. And so, in the summer of 1998, everybody on the Avenue—from strippers to store owners to cashiers to bouncers—shifted their feet nervously as they awaited their fate. Every adult-oriented business played it safe in the meantime. Show World closed temporarily, and plexiglass shields went back up at the Playground. The touching wasn't legal—the law banning contact was ten years old at that point—it had just been ignored.

In August, New York State Supreme Court Justice Stephen Crane concluded that 60/40 was a "ruse" as well as a "bad interpretation of zoning codes."[21] Game over.

Strip bars turned into "lingerie bars." Billy's Topless in Chelsea became Billy's Stopless. The Harmony Theater, a downtown strip club/gropefest, was shut down. There was no more touching at the Playpen, a live girl told a *Times* reporter performing due diligence.

Customers migrated to the strip clubs of Queens for their adult-oriented needs. In Sunset Park, Brooklyn, three clubs and four porn stores popped up, to the dismay of the locals.

Show World closed down for the final time in 1999, and Basciano began leasing out parts of the site. While the neutered remains of the famous sleaze pit still existed on the first floor, the place was "going legit," according to the *Daily News*. It aimed to go back to Times Square's roots as a family-friendly entertainment center and had plans to turn itself into a full-fledged entertainment complex with "family fare and stage plays."

Basciano rented the second floor to a group who used it to show short (non-porn) films. They paid rent to Show World and split the admission. Theater groups rented the rest of the space.

Today, what's left of Show World is up for lease or sale. There's still a porn store on the ground floor as well as a theater complex and the Laugh Factory comedy club.

The L-shaped parcel includes a twelve-story tower of apartments and offices.

Basciano still lives in an apartment above Show World and has an office on the fifth floor, as well as his own gym. Eighty-three years old now, he works out every day. In 2008, he gave his first interview in thirty years to *The Daily News*.

Although he made $14 million on the condemnation of his buildings, he told *The News* he still hated Giuliani, calling him his "nemesis," noting that the money he made off the buildings he sold was "less than market value."

The windows at Peep-O-Rama slid down for the last time in July 2002, the last of the 42nd Street peeps to close. But 'Rama wasn't shut by the Adult Use law—it was because Durst Organization wanted to build an office tower there. Times had changed—the Durst family was known for owning many of Times Square's prostitution hotels in the '60s and '70s.

One of the workers defended his business to *The Daily News* as he was closing up shop for the final time. "I have very good customers," he protested. "Decent customers! People need sex. Everybody!"

In the summer of 2006, I was one of the last live nude girls in Times Square. There were maybe less than fifty of us left. The Playpen was closed and demolished the next summer, leaving just Empire Erotica and Gotham 4. They're the last vestiges of this bizarre industry—for better or for worse, the only places left in New York where you can still see a naked girl behind glass. Be sure to smile and wave.

NOTES FOR HISTORY CHAPTER

[1] Edwin G. Burrows and Mike Wallace, *Gotham: A History of New York City to 1898* (Oxford University Press, 2000).

[2] "Times Sq. Called 'Blight' As Rezoning Is Argued," *The New York Times*, November 1953.

[3] Gail Sheehy, *Hustling* (Dell, 1971), 100.

[4] "The Sex Supermarket," *Sunday News*, by George Nobbe, September 1968.

[5] Josh Alan Friedman, *Tales of Times Square* (Delacorte Press, 1986), 128, 143.

[6] Gail Sheehy, *Hustling* (Dell, 1971), 23.

[7] "That 42nd Street Porno? Well, Meet the King," *New York Daily News*, by William Sherman, December 11, 1972.

[8] Gail Sheehy, *Hustling* (Dell, 1971), 17.

[9] "The King Harvests Lush Pornfield," *New York Daily News*, by William Sherman, December 12, 1972.

[11] "Knights in Blue Crumbling the Porno King's Castle," *New York Daily News*, by William Sherman, December 14, 1972.

[12] "Porno King's Wife Rescued in Fire at L.I. House," *New York Daily News*, December 21, 1974.

[13] "Peep Show King Eyes New Times," *New York Daily News*, by Dave Saltonstall, November 12, 1995.

[14] "Peep Show King Has Lust for High Life," *New York Daily News*, April 13, 1977.

[15] Gail Sheehy, *Hustling* (Dell, 1971), 131.

[16] "Builders Play a Waiting Game on Times Square," *The New York Times*, by William Robbins, March 1968.

[17] Josh Alan Friedman, *Tales of Times Square* (Delacorte Press, 1986), 78.

[18] Ibid, 79.

[19] Ibid, 81.

[20] *New York Daily News*, by Robert Gearty, May 13, 1994.

ACKNOWLEDGMENTS

Thanks to my agent, Holly Bemiss of the Susan Rabiner Literary Agency, as well as to my editor, Denise Oswald, who provided much-needed insight and was responsible for acquiring this book for Soft Skull Press, as well as Anne Horowitz. Also thanks to Counterpoint editor Julie Pinkerton, Laura Mazer, and everyone else at Counterpoint.

Matt Harvey, for listening. Other great listeners: Ian Spiegelman, Dan Hobbs, Parvez Sharma, Carly Sommerstein, Ethan Ryan, and Dr. Don Kerson.

Jim Naureckas, for giving me the idea to write it all down.

Sue Shapiro, writing teacher and connector, and the members of the 23rd Street Salon.

Chris Erikson, for help with research materials.

Ben Hamper, a fellow Michigander, whose book *Rivethead* was the model and inspiration for this one.

My mom, dad, and sister, of course.

And thanks to the live girls and the men who watched them. Times Square would never be the same without you.

Printed in the United States
by Baker & Taylor Publisher Services